COLLEC

SHORTER P

1946 – 19

HAYDEN CARRUTH

COLLECTED SHORTER POEMS

1946 – 1991

COPPER CANYON PRESS

Grateful acknowledgment is made to the publishers and editors of the following publications, in which the poems in the final section of this book first appeared: *Pulpsmith, The Iowa Review, Ploughshares, Kentucky Poetry Review, West Branch, Home Planet News, The American Poetry Review, Exile, The Southern Review, The Seneca Review, The Quarterly,* and *The Beloit Poetry Journal.* "Homage to John Lily" and "Mix the Ingredients" were published in *Northwest Review.* "The Bearer" was published in *Poetry.* "Pa McCabe" originally appeared in *New Letters* (51:2, Winter 1984/85) and is reprinted with the permission of *New Letters* and the Curators of the University of Missouri-Kansas City. "Æolian," "Gods," and "Opusthirteen" were published in *The Hudson Review.* "August" and "Fourth" were published in *Grand Street.* "Silence" was published in *The Atlantic.*
In addition, grateful acknowledgment is made to James Laughlin and New Directions Publishing Corporation for permission to reprint poems from *From Snow and Rock, from Chaos* (Copyright © 1965, 1966, 1968, 1969, 1970, 1971, 1972, 1973 by Hayden Carruth), *Asphalt Georgics* (Copyright © 1983, 1984, 1985 by Hayden Carruth), and *Tell Me Again How the White Heron Rises and Flies Across the Nacreous River at Twilight Toward the Distant Islands* (Copyright © 1984, 1985, 1986, 1989 by Hayden Carruth); to Marilyn Kitchell and Salt-Works Press for permission to reprint poems from *The Oldest Killed Lake in North America;* and to Bernard Taylor of The Press of Appletree Alley for permission to reprint poems from *Sonnets.*

The publication of this book was supported by grants from the National Endowment for the Arts and the Lannan Foundation.

Copper Canyon Press is in residence with Centrum at Fort Worden State Park.

Library of Congress Cataloging-in-Publication-Data
Carruth, Hayden, 1921–
[Poems. Selections]
Collected shorter poems, 1946–1991 / Hayden Carruth.
p.   cm.
ISBN 1-55659-048-2 (cloth) : $23.00 – ISBN 1-55659-049-0 (paper) : $12.00
I. Title.
PS3505.A77594A6   1992
811'.54–dc20   92-3389

For my children

MARTHA WARD
and
DAVID CARRUTH

Note

The poems in my life have sprung from contrary occasions and have taken inconsistent forms. Some were written very quickly, some very slowly; some in pain, some in pleasure; some deliberately and others by way of discovery. One hopes this doesn't mean merely a fragmented personality and that a thread of connection may be found among them. But who knows? The present book comprises about two-thirds of my previously published shorter poems and perhaps one-fifth or less of all the poems I've written. A few poems I should have liked to include are lost.

At times I think this collection is everything of its kind I wish to save. At other times I think it is simply all I dare to offer. It doesn't matter. It is enough.

Of course I'm indebted to many writers who have helped and influenced me over fifty years, too many to call by name. But I shall mention ten who have also been my close friends. Four from the past: Henry Rago, J. V. Cunningham, Raymond Carver, and George Dennison. Six from the present: Denise Levertov, Wendell Berry, David Budbill, Adrienne Rich, Carolyn Kizer, and Galway Kinnell. I am especially grateful to the poet Joe-Anne McLaughlin Carruth, my wife, for her sensitive advice and assistance in the preparation of this book.

To the reader: you are the one who has been continuously in my mind and heart for more than sixty years.

H. C.

25 August 1991

TABLE OF CONTENTS

I. From *The Crow and the Heart* (1959)

II. From *The Norfolk Poems of Hayden Carruth* (1962)

III. From *Nothing for Tigers* (1965)

IV. From *The Clay Hill Anthology* (1970)

V. From *From Snow and Rock, from Chaos* (1973)

V I. From *Dark World* (1974)

V I I. From *The Bloomingdale Papers* (1975 [written 1953])

V I I I. From *Brothers, I Loved You All* (1978)

IX. From *If You Call This Cry a Song* (1983)

X. From *Asphalt Georgics* (1985)

XI. From *The Oldest Killed Lake in North America* (1985)

X I I. From *Sonnets* (1989)

X I I I. From *Tell Me Again How the White Heron Rises and Flies Across the Nacreous River at Twilight Toward the Distant Islands* (1989)

XIV. New Poems (1986-1991)

« I »

from

THE CROW AND
THE HEART
[1959]

❯ The Wreck of the Circus Train

Couplings buckled, cracked, collapsed,
And all reared, wheels and steel
Pawing and leaping above the plain,

And fell down totally, a crash
Deep in the rising surf of dust,
As temples into their cellars crash.

Dust flattened across the silence
That follows the end of anything,
Drifted into cracks of wreckage.

But motion remained, a girder
Found gravity and shifted, a wheel
Turned lazily, turning, turning,

And life remained, at work to
Detain spirit: three lions, one
Male with wide masculine mane,

Two female, short, strong, emerged
And looked quickly over the ruin,
Turned and moved toward the hills.

❯ The Snow

I

This is the white king's palace: snowflakes flounce
On every draught, dally in secret aisles,

Bow and depart, an instant clap of fury,
And winds, o sparrow, shake your chandelier

That leaps and branches toward the reeling walls.
Huddle yourself, small brother, fear our host,

The hostile one who'll blizzard through the room
And catch us fast inside a bursting cloud.

The drowsy freeze creeps on us, and the dance
Proceeds in silence; all these many motes

Array the dark with folding tapestries,
O birdlet, wearying our eyes. One sees,

One nearly can observe, almost believe,
The servants hurrying behind the snow.

I I

The sparkling meadows rise to farther hills,
Luring a snowcaped fancy to the rim

Where sun's profluent aureate flood descends
And gilds the frozen billows. Through the glow

The crystal trees branch up to spear the beams,
Letting the sun's blood fall and jewel the air.

This is the wintertime's most rare event,
Diamonded and candied like a dream,

The countryman's white vision of the earth
As every loveliness, unlabored, turned

By the softest sleep of midnight from a myth
That murmurs always in the formal elms –

Beyond the mind's belief. Sparrow, unharmed,
Alone make harmless movements in the trees.

I I I

Chicago, city of all discoveries,
Bold fact and bold belief, canst rear our hope

By subtle starts, by sudden vista'd towers,
Or quick perspectives to an arching bridge?

Build us our knowledge, rivet fast our fear,
Light us with glitter through the sleepless night.

But smoky morning twines among the streets;
The night's inevitable rust has tinged

The snow where sooty sparrows starve and freeze.
Quickly the old akimbo forms show through,

Scarcely acknowledging their new decay.
Gray houses and black lawns shed winter's blood,

Our sludge of seasons, spring-mire, summer-rot.
This is no city, sparrow, for your kind.

❯ *The Fact of the Matter*

> *Such is the account of this extraordinary bird. It has, no doubt, a mixture*
> *of fable; but that the phoenix, from time to time, appears in Egypt,*
> *seems to be a fact sufficiently ascertained.* — TACITUS

Fortunate land, that Egypt, where
    From time to time the phoenix comes
    And wheels among the temple domes,
A golden circle in the air,

Trailing no doubt a whiff of spice,
    A sweet Arabian perfume
    That southern gentlemen presume
Is fragrance steeped in paradise.

A visitant aloof and lone,
    The phoenix comes on swooping wings;
    The wind against his feathers sings
A song that stays when he is gone.

Indeed, the phoenix always flies
    Homeward to Araby; and few
    Have followed where the phoenix flew
Or heard his own true voice uprise.

Some say beyond the first-fired sun
    The phoenix builds his funeral nest
    Of leaf of clove the spiciest
And nutmeg root and cinnamon,

And there among the pungent flames
    His brilliances of red and gold
    Entwine to make a manifold
Ascension, while his voice proclaims

Glories of reaspiring breath,
    The sweetest, most melodious dirge
    That ever sung against the surge
Of heart's blood beating unto death.

Do the Egyptians know their home
    Blest in faith and blest in fact?
    Could some heroic prayer attract
The splendid phoenix here to Rome?

Accede no glories to the earth
    Nor powers to the pounding sea.
    The phoenix sings! Mortality
Lies in the ashes of his birth.

His golden plumage will appear
    Upon the low Egyptian sky,
    A fact that they shall certify
Who were most cautious and austere.

O eastward travelers, on your way
    Be watchful, cull the Arabian sands,
    Bring us from undiscovered lands
The facts, lest Roman faith decay.

Cappadocian Song

What shall a poor girl do
Now men are gone warring?
I dreamt the long night through
But cannot at morning.

The barley stalk breaks in the field,
The little mice play on the road.

Have you heard of a mad king?
Cambyses slew his brother,
Darius heard a bee sing,
Xerxes flogged the river.

Thousands have gone away,
Mine, my sister's.
Now the old crones say
They're over the waters.

Does hunger fill my eye?
Dust fills the meadow.
We were born at the end of time
In the moon's shadow.

The barley stalk breaks in the field,
The little mice play on the road.

On a Certain Engagement South of Seoul

A long time, many years, we've had these wars.
When they were opened, one can scarcely say.
We were high school students, no more than sophomores,

When Italy broke her peace on a dark day,
And that was not the beginning. The following years
Grew crowded with destruction and dismay.

When I was nineteen, once the surprising tears
Stood in my eyes and stung me, for I saw
A soldier in a newsreel clutch his ears

To hold his face together. Those that paw
The public's bones to eat the public's heart
Said far too much, of course. The sight, so raw

And unbelievable, of people blown apart
Was enough to change us without that bark and whine.
We grew disconsolate. Each had his chart

To mark on the kitchen wall the battle-line,
But many were out of date. The radio
Droned through the years, a faithful anodyne.

Yet the news of this slight encounter somewhere below
Seoul stirs my remembrance: we were a few,
Sprawled on the stiff grass of a small plateau,

Afraid. No one was dead. But we were new –
We did not know that probably none would die.
Slowly, then, all vision went askew.

My clothing was outlandish; earth and sky
Were metallic and horrible. We were unreal,
Strange bodies and alien minds; we could not cry

For even our eyes seemed to be made of steel;
Nor could we look at one another, for each
Was a sign of fear, and we could not conceal

Our hatred for our friends. There was no speech.
We sat alone, all of us, trying to wake
Some memory of the selves beyond our reach.

That place was conquered. The nations undertake
Another campaign now, in another land,
A stranger land perhaps. And we forsake

The miseries there that we can't understand
Just as we always have. Yet still my glimpse
Of a scene on the distant field can make my hand

Tremble again. How quiet we are. One limps,
One cannot walk at all, or one is all right,
But one has this experience that crimps

Forgetfulness, especially at night.
Is this a bond? Does this make us brothers?
Or does it bring our hatred back? I might

Have known, but now I do not know. Others
May know. I know when I walk out-of-doors
I have a sorrow not wholly mine, but another's.

> ## Sparrows

Spring comes and autumn goes,
Likewise in the town of sparrows.

Under the eaves and in the ivy
They wage dispute of polity.

If someone speaks, someone demurs;
They are indomitable bickerers.

One can easily imagine them
Asquabble in the copses when brave William

Led his band by, or even once
In the dust near Hannibal's elephants.

Maybe in the primeval firs
They went at it: what's his, what's hers?

Apparently they do not welcome
Finality in sparrowdom.

Summer's Early End at Hudson's Bay

The old sandpiper contemplates his age
As one only can, in ignorant unease,
And the scene imparts a mood of sad alarm.
The steady winds bend the thin grass,
And sunlight also streams thinly, distantly.
The first ice gleams on the water,
Embracing the rocks and reeds with brittle strength.
The flock is nervous; like clockwork toys the shapes
Mill and bob, a confusion of white and gray;
A hundred dances of anxiety
And fluttering movements begin and flare
And subside. The old one too turns on his rock,
Round and round with ceremonial steps,
His eyes wary for the others. And this old land
That had been so alien once
And then so familiar is alien again,
A point of coldness.
The imperfect young are fledged or dead,
Scarcely remembered now.
Upon the evidences of the scene
Mount tremors, warnings, subtle arguments
That urge his shivering nerves and awkward wings;
The other land is an impulse he must keep.
Into the uncertain air, on painful wings,
The aging migrant labors,
Dull to the image of the other land
And to the storms that prowl the long seas of Brazil.

The Buddhist Painter Prepares to Paint

First he must go where
Not even the birds will brave his solitude,
Alone to the sunburnt plain to try his mood
In silence. Prayer

Will help him to begin
Perhaps, or tell him if after all tomorrow
May not be better. But, alas, his sorrow
    Is genuine,

    The requisite of art.
He kneels, eyes bent in humble palms. To see
In perfect light is difficult; one must be
    Blind from the start.

    And then the sevenfold
Office, the chanting of the hundred names,
The offering of flowers, none the sun shames,
    But marigold

    Of his imagination,
Jasmine of the pure mind, ghostly for the ghost
Of Buddha; he speaks the uttermost
    Foliation,

    He whispers, he merely thinks,
Thinking the perfect flower of the universe.
And the primal vastness comes to intersperse
    His thoughts, he sinks

    Through the four phases
Of infinity to the abyss, crying, "Die,
O world. Sunburnt grasses, fade." The sky
    Turns on its huge axis

    Under him; all is lost,
Fingers, heartbeat, the singing brain, gone,
Or glittering there in that resplendent one
    Who shimmers, posed

    In the wide abyss.
The holy impassivity of his goddess dances

Without motion. The painter sighs. Expanses
    Of unknown bliss

    Widen through death, through birth,
Acheless, moving the goddess, the one, the all,
Who dances in the void of the painter's soul.
    But something of earth

    Something of his old dolor,
Calls back the painter now from the reflected
Essence to the form of the goddess projected
    In line and color.

    His sadness is like the itch
That gives his fingers back: among the many
Loves that preceded his pure ceremony
    There is one which

    Denies the formless, paints
Something that might be the goddess dancing, dressed
In green flesh with four arms and three heads, lest
    The loveless saints

    Alone find rapture. Why
Must the painter paint? For love of forms so trite?
Or is it that love of minds and hearts finds sight
    Within his eye?

    The painter's love is his
Great penalty, because to fashion even
This sham goddess, he must deny the heaven
    Where the goddess is.

❯ *Lines Written in an Asylum*

Lost sweetheart, how our memories creep
Like chidden hounds, and come to reap
All fawningly their servient due,

Their tax of pity and of rue,
So that my hope of sanity
Like sternness dies and falls from me.
The day I build with plotted hours
To stand apart is mine, not ours.
Its joyless business is my cure;
Stern and alone, I may endure.
But memory though it slumber wakes,
And deep in the mind its havoc makes.
A distant baying reels and swells
And floods the night, and so dispels
My hardness; hours dissolve and fall;
My loss is double: you, then all.
Dearest, are you so unaware?
For here, in mine, your senses share
These broken hours and tumbled days
That are no longer mine. Your ways,
The body's blossoms, breast and eye,
The soft songs of your hands, the shy
And quick amusement of your smile –
My constant losses, these beguile
All my new bravery away.
If you have gone, why do you stay?
If here, then why have we no ease?
Loss is a blindness that still sees,
A handless love that touches still.
Loss is a ravage of the will.
And the incontinence of loss,
Mad loneliness, turns all to dross,
Love to a raging discontent
And self to a shabby tenement.
The mind is hapless, torn by dreams
Where all becoming only seems
A false, impossible return
To a world I labor to unlearn.

> Anxious View of a Tree

Out in the soundless
World that the window
Encloses – the pane
Sinks through your eyes,
The frame seizes
Your shoulders – out
In the soundless
World of the rain,

The tree, but the ground
Flees, and the tree,
The lawn bending
Moves like a sea,
The tree, the bright
Yellow bench
Turns in the glistening
Rain, the tree,
The tree fills
Your echoing sight.

> Reflexive

Of all disquiets sorrow is most serene.
Its intervals of soft humility
Are lenient; they intrude on our obscene
Debasements and our fury like a plea
For wisdom – guilt is always shared. The fears
Fall, if for just an hour, all away,
And the old, essential person reappears.
Sorrow can shape us better than dismay.

You have forgiven me, old friends and lovers,
I think you have forgiven me at last,

As you put by the banished fugitive.
And if I'm sorry who was once aghast
For all the hurts I've done you, I forgive,
I too, the self this sorrow still recovers.

❯ *The Fat Lady*

> *Hink! Mink! The old witch stinks,*
> *The fat begins to fry!*
> *Nobody's home but Jumping Joan,*
> *Jumping Joan and I.*
> — OLD RHYME

"A lovely house it was. We all thought so,
Anyway after we got used to it. All
That redwood and that queer roof – modern, you know.
And the window! Enormous, like a wall – "
Which burst like spindrift inward when the flames
Were most intense, showering the dear creature
With foamy glass and giving the fervent neighbors,
Who stood like choristers on the lawn,
An even better view.

        "She'd call us dirty names,
All of us, but we didn't mind. She was mad.
Why, right at the end she laughed out fit to bust.
And sometimes she'd just lean back and yawn
Like an old mare and go to sleep.
She said it took a might of resting – and eating –
To keep the life in such a heap.
Four hundred fifty pounds! That's three of me,
And she no higher than a pasture gate.
We told her she ought never be alone;
We told her, but she always knew it all,
With her fancy books and that funny mechanical doll –
All gone now. It's kind of sad."

Saddest because she cackled at the end,
Mad and mortal in a ring of fire,
And still, O Lord, house to the girlish lust
For heroes who could never part the flames.
Saddest because I think of that old lust,
Her flesh that flowered like any other, slowly,
Assembling hues and textures through the seasons,
A trick of eye and lip, the shoulder's lift
Above the proud young breast; her moment came,
The moment of perfect form, growth's triumph, life
Verging . . . oh, verging on all conjectured joys,
Expectancy, consent. Only a season,
An April, a poise, three stepping-stones where laughter
Weaves quietly beneath the willow trees –
For her not even this. Like rain her shock
Pelted upon her ceaselessly, and growth
Went on and on, the moment lost in dread,
Horror of the flesh, mounting, mounting,
Flesh whose rolls and waves encompassed her,
Crushed her, sank on her tender heart, like heat
That swarms and lies on equatorial towns.
And speech became a gasp, all beauty gone,
As fat fish gasp in puddles when the tide
Falls fast down the beach.

                              "You would have thought
They'd make these fancy houses fireproof
At least. Hell, she burned like tinder,
Everything, walls and roof,
Except the tiles and that glass ball.
You'll find them somewhere there among the cinders."

Burning, burning, she faced the centuries,
A metabolic mound that time alone,
The way of flames and ashes, could reduce.
To move was torture, why then should she move?
Her moment fled, or rather smothered. She
Attuned her mind to practical affairs.

She was a monster. All right, let them pay;
And twice a day she had them hoist her up
Against the gaze that washed her like a sea,
While she stared back like rock, a promontory
Eating chocolates. The barker cried his creed,
"You won't believe it, she's impossible,"
And she dreamed hexes on that facelike sea.
From stand to stand she rode the baggage car.
Yet more than once she did not sleep alone;
Temptation hung like smoke among the smells
Of gin and elephants, as black-nailed hands
Flickered and passed the bottle round and round.
She was astonished when her lovers came,
Stealthy and drunk, dared to that mammoth bed.
In the skittery dawn they fled like mice. Not one
Was ever seen again.

     "What can you do
With such a crazy dame?
She sat there every day.
She knew, she knew."

Between the joys of staring down the sea
("My audience, the brutes – all of them")
She cultivated a cold mind and ate,
Ate everything in sight, her barker said.
She took a mechanical turn, and bought a toy,
A doll on the end of a string, whose antics soothed
Her massive immobility. She jerked
The string with one fat finger while she read
Tracts of the star-gazers – interpretations,
Systems, prophecies. "Nonsense," she said,
And dropped the books about her on the floor.
And yet she bought a lovely crystal ball.
Mostly she ate, a rhythmic munch and crunch,
And felt the love flow from her jaws like blood.

Round and huge and decked with tarnished beads
That fell like chains from her neck's greased machine,

She sat, a queen, a tawdry giantess,
Fruitful, unloved, obscene, the essential mother
Who bore through pain's interminable years
Without a yell and cursed us all and gave
Her life to be the image of our love,
Her utmost curse; we wander in our love,
Disconsolate and cowardly and free,
Kicking the rusty coins above her grave.

"That crystal ball's what finally done her in."

She'd no more quit her triumph than her pain,
And when she tired of baggage cars, she built
A house around a window and a chair,
A window large enough to frame the brutes,
A chair . . . well, large enough for her. And still
They came to stare, furtively, beyond
The lawn, to see the monster, though she charged
Only the quota of her cold contempt.
Enthroned, immobile, she gave them eye for eye
Through the wide glass. The year turned, and the sun
Slanted each day closer to her chair,
And bored at last into that crystal ball,
A smoking beam that fell upon a page
Of one of the open books around her chair.
The paper blackened, and the flame at first
Was pale, almost invisible, but it leapt
From page to page, yellowing, dancing, dancing,
Like the doll at the end of the string, and fast flew round
The chair in a raucous ring, a ring of flames,
All gay and hot in a topsy world, a cheer
And a whirl, and "Hink!" she squealed, and laughed and laughed
Till she thought she'd die. "I've got you now, you brutes,"
She cried, and the tears streamed down and quickly dried.

The one world I knew how to love had died.

❯ Return to Love*

Shy at first but quick,
An alien thing in nature
Or lost last season's creature
Come back half well, half sick,
On poor leathern bat wings
Eager and creaking,
Blind still and still seeking
Where the thin sun sings –

Then strong in the array
Of an unhoped for season
That smoothes the winter lesion
Of snowbleeding earth away,
And bids bewildered grief
Remorselessly make merry
For sake of the coming berry
And the golden leaf.

* *Imitated from Robert Graves*

❯ Incident of May

My lovely lady stood in the wind
On the cresting hill by a damson tree,
And wind swept down like wind from the sea
Until the boughs seemed tossed and thinned
In the petals so thickly blown to me.

But at last she moved in the blossoms flying,
Down from the wind to my wondering touch,
And in fear I went to her, fain to clutch,
But that the flowers, flying, dying,
Seemed to say this would not help much.

❯ *November: Indian Summer*

The huge frostbank of the North
Leans over these few days.
Sunlight crumbles in haze,
Saffron of smell and color.
And the chickadees hold forth,
Thick in the ruined quince,
Scolding our complex dolor,
Talkative though long since
We came to a solemn season.
Close your eyes. The warmth
Of sun and the chickadee song
Will take you, against all reason,
To another time on the earth
That was idle and August-long,
When katydids twanged the skies
In peace, months past and more,
Far in your thoughts, as far,
Perhaps, if you close your eyes,
As the summer before the war.

❯ *The Sound of Snow*

Snow falls in the dusk of Connecticut. The stranger
Looks up to the glutenous sky, and it is remembrance
That tickles the end of his nose like the fingertips
Of a child and remembrance that touches the end of his
Tongue with the antique purity and coolness of the snow,
As if this were almost the beginning, the first snowstorm
Fluttering between his house and the serious hemlocks.

And best of all is the sound of snow in the stillness,
A susurration, the minute percussion of settling flakes;
And the stranger listens, intent to the whispering snow
In the fir boughs, earth's most intimate confiding,
And he thinks that this is the time of sweet cognizance

As it was once when the house, graying in old dusk,
Knew him and sang to him, before the house forgot.

In the last moments of day the earth and the sky
Close in the veils of snow that flutter around him,
Shutting him in the sphere of the storm, where he stands
In his elephantine galoshes, peering this way and that
At the trees in their aloofness and the nameless house
Vanishing into the dark; and he stamps his feet urgently,
Turning as if in anger away from an evil companion.

Yet when, like a warning just at the fall of darkness,
Yellow light cries from the window above in the house,
From the boy's room, from the old sixteen-paned window,
The stranger remembers the boy who sits in the light
And turns the glass sphere, watching to see the snowstorm
Whirling inside. And the stranger shivers and listens
To the tranquil and lucid whispering of the snow.

> *An Apology for Using the Word "Heart" in Too Many Poems*

What does it mean? Lord knows; least of all I.
    Faced with it, schoolboys are shy,
And grown-ups speak it at moments of excess
    Which later seem more or less
Unfeasible. It is equivocal, sentimental,
    Debatable, really a sort of lentil –
Neither pea nor bean. Sometimes it's a muscle,
    Sometimes courage or at least hustle,
Sometimes a core or center, but mostly it's
    A sound that slushily fits
The meters of popular songwriters without
    Meaning anything. It is stout,
Leonine, chicken, great, hot, warm, cold,
    Broken, whole, tender, bold,
Stony, soft, green, blue, red, white,
    Faint, true, heavy, light,

Open, down, shallow, etc. No wonder
    Our superiors thunder
Against it. And yet in spite of a million abuses
    The word survives; its uses
Are such that it remains virtually indispensable
    And, I think, defensible.
The Freudian terminology is awkward or worse,
    And suggests so many perverse
Etiologies that it is useless; but "heart" covers
    The whole business, lovers
To monks, i.e., the capacity to love in the fullest
    Sense. Not even the dullest
Reader misapprehends it, although locating
    It is a matter awaiting
Someone more ingenious than I. But given
    This definition, driven
Though it is out of a poet's necessity, isn't
    The word needed at present
As much as ever, if it is well written and said,
    With the heart and the head?

❯ Museum Piece

The eye which made this saw no pallor
But golden and blue paint;
Now on the dry wood the color
Is tenuous and faint.

Yet under the scratches our close study
Retrieves for our curious eyes
God raising the small from the larger body,
And there the new Eve lies.

Would we smile fondly in our pride?
Ours is a long descent,
Worked in the flesh of a tiny bride
Scarce fit for ravishment,

And she, discovering she was woman,
Measured her strength of will,
By which we estimate the human
And sorrow and courage still.

But listen. Beneath the veiling scratches,
Time's ancientest filigree,
Eve in a little girl's voice beseeches
Someone to set her free.

› *The Birth of Venus*

Surely we knew our darkling shore.
None doubted that continual roar
Of gray waves seething, cold and huge,
None misconceived that beach, those reeds
Wreathed in the dark, dead, dripping weeds.
No fiction there, no subterfuge.

Came she then, borne from such sea-bed?
We think so. Clouds in violent red
Shone on her warmly, flank and breast,
And some remember how the foam
Swirled at her ankles. Other some
Look shrewd and smile behind the rest.

She gave us beauty where our eyes
Had seen need only. We grew wise,
For how could wisdom fail the gift
Bestowed in that superb undress,
Value devised as loveliness
From ocean's riches, ocean's thrift?

But, Love, then must it be the sea
That makes you credible? Must we
Bear all to one phenomenon?
True, certainty is our seacoast,

The landmark of the clearly lost
Whose gathering waves drive on and on.

Great queen, an ignorant poet's heart
Is all his faith, yet still his art
Can prick your source to tell the truth.
So teach him, lady. Then always
Among the people here who praise
Your powers, one will be Carruth.

« II »

from

THE NORFOLK POEMS OF HAYDEN CARRUTH [1962]

In Tobey Woods

At noontime under the very tall pines
Heat is a half-light and nothing moves
Unless it is one deathly shell-white moth
Fluttering, fluttering.

And the woods are very quiet, unless
It is one vireo idiotically tzekking,
Tzekking.

Stillness; the deep stillness.

I wish my mind would not revert
To that time I was a bedlamite
At chess with the blushing Irish nurse
While the coprolaliac young lawyer
Cursed his father the judge in words
I would not whisper into a pit.

Maureen, Maureen, why did I not go
To meet you in the clean fields of Ireland?

The Wild Swans at Norfolk

To begin with there are
No wild swans at Norfolk,
This other Norfolk
Where James Laughlin lives
With his red-haired Ann.

There are towhees and wrens
And soft yellow sapsuckers
And Blackburnian warblers
And gray owls and barred owls
And flickers but there are
No wild swans
I can invent the swans.

They wheel on thunder's
Hundred throbbing wings
Down the sweet curve
Of Tobey Pond, pounding
The blocks of air
As trains in my childhood
Pounded their rails.

They are real wild swans;
And even though this summer
I turn forty and am deserted
By the young woman I love,
I have grown sick of emblems.

I have seen this place
On the map, and the names of
The people of Norfolk appear
On voting lists and tax rolls.

Hear how the swans converse
(As they break wing for landing)
In a rude, lightning tongue.
I cannot understand,
But clearly the swans know
What they are talking about.

> ❭ *Meadow House*

No house should ever be on *any hill or on anything. It should be* of
the hill, belonging to it, so hill and house could live together
the happier for each other. — FRANK LLOYD WRIGHT

This is a poem for you, Ann. Impromptu,
Falling out of my precipitate brain faster
Than light dropping through a torn cloud.

And the typewriter lags. Catch up, I say!
How the wood and stone must have lagged for
Wright looking at a trance-house on a hill.

At least you and I have the advantage of not
Being architects, who fret in houses they build
And go thoroughly mad in houses they do not build.

You can live in a house. Wright wouldn't have liked
Meadow House, his style being something different,
But Meadow House lives on the hill naturally.

As naturally as the birches. And Mr. Wright
With his artist's complacency could not believe
That houses grow and very seldom are built.

(Poems too. As the light grows when it plunges
Through the torn cloud like a taproot seeking
The needed humane sustenance for heaven.)

The house grew on the hill, the woman grew
In the house, the birches grew in the meadow,
The hill is growing, I see it change every day.

No one knows why. Growing is a word
That has never been defined, not even in
My huge thirty-five-dollar dictionary.

But the end of growth, which never really ends,
Is always perfection, even if ugly or sore,
Because growth proceeds by means of balances.

(And the end of growth is always a phase
To be left behind. And real ugliness
Does not grow but arises from destruction.

Of course Meadow House has nothing ugly;
Only balances, arrangements in which I move
Without seeming to make any displacement.

I hope there is none, because this is what
I knew many years ago and then forgot,
Forgot. It is the service of friendliness.

❯ Ho-Hum Again

Having lost the woman I loved
    I am of course heartbroken,
In a dying summer embarked on war
When many good folk are heartsore
    And one heart is a small token.

Too small to be taken seriously.
    Death creeps in the air like pollen,
Seeding amazement in lovely eyes,
Hers too that were my enterprise
    When reason had not fallen.

❯ Comparative Iconography

Give it what name you choose,
In all lands the female symbol is a hole,
And where I come from the people use
The eye-socket of a skull.

❯ Purana, Meaning Once Upon a Time

Only the gods may act with perfect impudence –
That is, irrationally. Listen while I retell
A story from a book as old as the Tobey Woods.

It fell on an autumn night, when the forest leaves
Moved like small rustling animals over the moss
And Jumna flowed with a sure deep-running strength,

That Sri Krishna played his flute by the riverbank
And the moonlight dripped like rain from tangled trees.
The music of love came liquidly to the village

Where gopis, who were the milkmaids, drank willlessly,
Their souls tipped to the song in unimagined thirst;
And soon they ran unresistingly to the forest,

One by one, and in groups, tripping and hurrying,
Leaving parents, brothers, sisters, husbands behind,
Leaving their babies whimpering in the cradles.

They said: "Ah, heavily love-laden we will give all."
Conceive the bewilderment in their eyes when Krishna,
Surrounded, the good looks of him bruising the girls,

Rebuked them, saying: "What! Have you come in the night?
Through the forest? Then you care nothing for tigers?
Shame! Respectable girls running after a lover

In the night, sacrificing your lords and your parents,
Your brothers and sisters and children. Pretty girls,
Go back to your places, go back and be content."

Tears melted their eyes and their hearts were frightened;
They looked miserably at one another in their confusion,
And began to scratch the ground with their feet like deer.

At last they said: "Truly we must attend our husbands
And our parents and children, but O Sweet Lord,
When thou art husband, parent, and child is it not just

That we seek the pleasures of all of these in Thee?"
The All-One turned away and I think said nothing,
And sorely, wearily the milkmaids returned to the village,

Their question unanswered. The singing hermit thrush
In Tobey Woods has brought this to my mind.
The leaves are beginning to fall. Soon he will be gone.

❯ On Canann Mountain Meadow

Of course, mankind – and the brain of it, brawn of it;
Enormous, as I too have marveled many a time
And will again.

But today its littleness I would moderately disparage,
That makes the stone a thing that is less than stone,
A dolmen, a god.

I say the stone is a greatness, itself in its grain,
Meaning more than a meaning, and more than a mind
May diminish.

In the sun in the field in the churchly changes of weather,
The stone lies ample and smooth and warm and brown
And at the same time blonde.

I am stroking the stone with my fingers and my curved palm,
And it is as soft as linen, and flows like the flax
From the spindle.

I would lie on the stone, reaching my arms down strongly
To draw myself full to the stone and to fondle
The flesh-gloss below.

I would copulate with the stone until I became like stone,
A slow, long spasm of love, I working calmly in love
All summer.

❯ Naming for Love

These are the proper names:
Limestone, tufa, coral rag,
Clint, beer stone, braystone,
Porphyry, gneiss, rhyolite,
Ironstone, cairngorm, circle stone,

Blue stone, chalk, box stone,
Sarsen, magnesia, brownstone,
Flint, aventurnine,
Soapstone, alabaster, basalt,
Slate, quartzite, ashlar,
Clunch, cob, gault, grit,
Buhrstone, dolomite,
Flagstone, freestone, sandstone,
Marble, shale, gabbro, clay,
Adamant, gravel, traprock,
And of course brimstone.

Some of the names are shapes:
Crag, scarp, moraine, esker,
Alp, hogback, ledge, tor,
Cliff, boulder, crater,
Gorge, and bedrock.

Some denote uses:
Keystone, capstone,
Hearthstone, whetstone,
And gravestone.

For women a painful stone called
Wombstone, which doctors say is
"A calculus formed in the uterus."
Gallstone and kidneystone hurt everyone.
Millstone is our blessing.

I will not say the names
Of the misnamed precious stones.

But a lovely name is gold,
A product of stone.

Underwards is magma;
May all who read this live long.

❯ August 14, 1961

THE DAY THE BRANDENBURG GATE WAS SHUT

I put my book face down,
And so that I could know
The news while I ate lunch
Turned on the radio.

I heard. I've heard before.
Mike Mansfield asks for calm,
Half muffled in the cries
Clamoring for the bomb.

Sitwell had made the book
To praise the lordly way
Men lived in Angkor Vat.
I'll read no more today.

❯ Adolf Eichmann

I want no tricks in speaking of this man.
My friends deplore my metaphysical mind,
But now I am a plain and plain-spoken man.

In my life only two men have turned my mind
To vengefulness, and one was this man's chief,
Who was, I now think, probably out of his mind.

But this one is rational. Naturally a mad chief
Needs sane lieutenants. Both were named Adolf,
An ugly Teutonic word which means the chief,

And earlier, in the cold north forest, this Adolf
Meant the wolf, a favorite totem. Let disgrace,
I say, fall for all time to come upon Adolf,

And let no child hereafter bear the disgrace
Of that dirty name. Sometimes in my bed
I study my feet, noticing their disgrace,

For the human foot is an ugly thing. But my bed
Is nothing like the bed that I have seen
Where hundreds of unclothed bodies lay. That bed

Was for dead people, deeply dug, and whoever has seen
Their feet knows the real ugliness and in their voice
Has heard the only true language. I have seen

And I have heard, but my feet live and my voice
Is beautiful and strong, and I say let the dung
Be heaped on that man until it chokes his voice,

Let him be made leprous so that the dung
May snuggle to his bone, let his eyes be shut
With slow blinding, let him be fed his own dung,

But let his ears never, never be shut,
And let young voices read to him, name by name,
From the rolls of all those people whom he has shut

Into the horrible beds, and let his name
Forever and ever be the word for hate,
Eichmann, cast out of the race, a loathsome name

For another kind, a sport spawned in hate
That can never be joined, never, in the world of man.
Lord, forgive me, I can't keep down my hate.

> ## *A Leaf from Mr. Dyer's Woods*

I don't know why or how
Sometimes in August a maple
Will drop a leaf burned through
Its tender parts with coral –

A rare device of color.
When I found such a one
I acted the despoiler,
Taking it from the woods
To give a friend for a trifle,
But her mind was on good deeds
And I turned shy and fearful.

> ## Notes from Robin Hill Cottage

One small joy still left
To a writer who has grown wise
In his profession and swift
In the making of similes

Is to discover a word
He has not used before,
An ordinary one just heard
In its whole force and humor.

I think I have not written
The verb *to shed* in all
The twenty years I've given
To saving my wordy soul.

.   •   •

As, when I was a drunkard
And staggered to my bed,
Wholly looped and tuckered,
One by one I'd shed

My clothes upon the floor
Until at last, all naked,
I'd tumble with a snore
Into my loyal blankets,

So, when I was reformed
And stumbled onward yet,

Trembling, cold, alarmed,
Then one by one I shed

Each of my heart's desires
Like garments until I fell
Naked among these firs
In the embrace of these hills.

.   .   .

A man is like all earth's fruit,
You preserve him dry or pickled,
It's taking him in and out
That makes him come unbuckled.

.   .   .

Fir trees surround me here,
The deeper woods have ash,
Larch and oak and cedar,
The wild cherry and the beech.

Not mine; no more these walls,
The clapboard or the slate,
That house me on Robin Hill
And another man's estate.

You can't push a metaphor
And I won't speak of clothes,
But my best home so far
Is here in a borrowed house.

.   .   .

Older, yet I am cleanly,
Freer, yet fierce of mind,
And the mountain summer greenly
Calls winter close behind.

.   .   .

I keep a whiskey bottle
Unsealed on my kitchen shelf

For friends who come to tipple
And to tease me and to scoff.

Friends are so often blind,
Or scared to agree in public
That booze and a bullet-wound
Are one to an alcoholic.

We live alone in the cottage,
Married, the bottle and I,
Good mates going down in courage
To die independently.

      •   •   •

A bottle's a genial spouse
But in some precise respects
Does not make glad a house;
What manages that is sex.

Now I'm not vain nor choosy,
Miss Marilyn Monroe
I imagine would be a doozy,
Or La Belle Dame Bardot.

Sometimes such folk are married,
And sometimes not. Me too.
Is your husband shucked – or buried?
Drop by for an interview.

❥ *R. M. D.*

There's rosemary, that's for remembrance. . . .

Somewhere in the hour
Or two or three
While I was by this flower
Meaning constancy
Seven winds cried in a tower
Hollowly.

« III »

from

NOTHING
FOR TIGERS
[1965]

The Event Itself

A curious reticence afflicts my generation, faced with the holocaust;
We speak seldom of the event itself, but only of what will be lost;
We, having betrayed our fathers and all our silent grandfathers, cannot cry
     out for ourselves, the present and tempest-tossed.

But many things and all manner of things will be hurled
In a force like dawnlight breaking, and the billion bagpipes of our screams
     will be skirled
Stupendously month after month, the greatest pain ever known in the world.

There will be some instantly indistinguishable from the molten stone;
But most will have bleeding, burning, gangrene, the sticking-out bone;
Men, women, and little children will be made pregnant of the nipping crab
     whose seed will be universally sown.

In the screaming and wallowing one thought will make each eye stare,
And that thought will be the silence pressing down at the end of the air,
Soon to smother the last scream forever and everywhere.

For the last man in the world, dying, will not know that he is the last,
But many will think it, dying; will think that in all the vast
And vacant universe they are the final consciousness, going out, going out,
     going out, with nothing to know it has passed.

The Master, Grieved with Age

The master, grieved with age,
Said discourse of art and song
Is pastime for dotard men,
Love being for the young;
He said moreover they
Will not have it long.

At present hard between,
Hot-eyed but cold of tongue,

I try my critical mind,
I study the songs I've sung,
And all of them cry with grief
And all of them last too long.

› *Horologikos*

Could we like youth consume the stolen night?
You told me, "Darling, put away your watch,"
But said that I might keep the candlelight
Whose intimations lapped at throat and crotch.

And years did us this favor, that our crime
At last was none, but innocence in powers
Still fit for this good work, suspending time
To make – well, something, not just paltry hours.

Now dawnlights blanch our candle. We lie warm
And so completely well beloved and kissed
That mankind's sole sane head rests on your arm.
Tell me, what is it ticking in your wrist?

› *The Saving Way*

When the little girl was told that the sun someday,
In a billion years or a trillion, will burn out dead,
She sobbed in a fierce and ancient way
And stamped and shook her head

Till the brown curls flew; and I wondered how,
Given the world, given her place and time,
She should ever come in her own right mind to know
That it all may happen one day before her prime,

The lights go out in one crude burst
Or slowly, winking across the cold,

The last and worst
That the old time's craziest prophet had foretold;

And I wondered also how she shall come to find
The town whose monuments
Are the rusty barbed wire rattling in the wind
And the shredding tents

And the street where the bodies crawl
Forever and ever, our broken dead
Who arise again, and again and always fall
For a word that someone said,

Or how she shall seek the plundered isles
Adrift on the smoking seas,
Or the desert bloodied for miles and miles,
Or the privacies

Of Jews laid out in a snowy woods,
Black men laid in the swamp,
All in their sorrowing attitudes
Of inquiry; or how when the wind is damp

She shall come someday to the marble square
Where papers blow and her father stands
In idle discourse with a millionaire
Who will rape her later on with his own hands;

And I wondered finally how all this
Will be anything to secure
What she knows now in her child's instinct is
The sole world, immensely precious and impure.

My dear, will you learn the saving way?
And then can we go,
In keen joy like Lear and like Cordelia gay,
To invent our lives from these great days of woe?

❯ Burning Dawn

This day lies under glass,
A relic. Blear and wan,
Two feet wade up the dawn,
Tread and fall back like fish,
Two fish as blind as bone.
The sun, the sun beats down.
A vitreous, brittle sky
Expands to the breaking point
Like burnt glass being blown,
And the blind feet go on.
Nothing can keep it now,
This sky that splits apart,
For the cygnet and the swan
On striding wings have flown
Over the shallow hill,
Dripping across the lawn
Droplets of breaking laughter
Like that of the soulless girl
Who was here and has gone.

❯ New Orleans

I am a trombone. By the chinaberry tree,
Under virgin's bower in the purple air,
I made a dirty noise you could almost see.
Arabesques edged the house with care
And voices crumbled in a distant square.
O King of the Zulus, consecrate me!
Mamselle's gown was a laugh of lace,
Band played "Dixie" at a thumping pace,
Moon sprawled low with a fire in her face,
And I brayed just once, deliciously.
Man said, "Boy, don't you know your place?"
O King of the Zulus, consecrate me!

Anent Socrates, or Somebody

Old friend, it's easy. However you behave
The end's the same, you may as well be brave.
I wonder though, can good form now make up
For when you called me Sophist? Ah, the cup . . . .

Études de Plusiers Paysages de l'Âme

1

The storm came Monday night. On Wednesday we
Took wreaths to the point and flung them in the sea.

The sun shone, and the waves – oh, how they sparkled!
Even the gulls' shrillness seemed sweet that day.

Sweet too the piquancy upon the breeze
Of stranded whale, burnt oil, and ambergris.

2

Olive trees wrought from crude bronze. The sagged sky
Pebbly and rank, old
Lemon rind. A raped voice abrades the end of day.

Small animals, perhaps lizards and mice, the color
Of clotted blood, play
Dead. Do they move when no one's looking?

Some distance away the sea with great regularity
Clangs the land like a cracked
Gong. In the grass a vermilion plume, leaking.

The voice chafes in time with the sea: "Tell this
To Alcibiades,
We'll raze all Greece before we yield an inch. . . ."

3

I strolled the waves from Tampa to St. Pete
While flying fishes swarmed beneath my feet
Like green grasshoppers. Bits of antic foam
Were daisies nodding in the fields of home.
The sky's impearled loudspeaker arched the bay
And Lester Young boomed changes all the day.

4

At dawn the desert turns to porcelain.
Upon a dune-rim stands a skeletal horse,
Head down, forehoof cocked, cropping glazed sand.

The stars blanch like goldfish in a frozen pond.
A lizard darts from the F-hole of a violin
That lies in perfect syntax on the sand.

Sunrays set the horse on fire. Behind
A giant cactus a shy Indian screams
Century after century in his death pains.

❯ *Billie Holiday*

Here lies a lady. Day was her double pain,
Pride and compassion equally gone wrong.
At night she sang, "Do you conceive my song?"
And answered in her torn voice, "Don't explain."

❯ *Algeria*

Years gone by in Chicago once
The Chalk Man came on an April day's pastel,
And ever since
My business has gone ill.

Because one day as I came home from school
A trilling woman spilled from an untuned house,
Thrusting her child
Into my arms; it jiggled, looking droll,
And she was wild
And ran beside me like a wounded horse.

The doctor said what could be said;
The thing I had been carrying was dead.

It was heavy;
Resilient, rubbery, collapsible;
Unbalanced inside like a bowl of gravy
Or a water-filled rubber ball.

That was an image of death.
And my waxen father orated in his casket.
And during the war
The crashed bombers had people underneath,
Though they really were not people any more.
We fished them out and put them in a basket.

Now I am thinking of the lovely land
Where palm trees more beautiful than herons
Sleep and stand
One-legged by the waters, and the flowers
Caress the old men in their barrens,
Pouring out splendors upon forgotten powers.

They also have bodies there,
And blood on the paving stones,
A bad smell in the mountain air,
Dead bodies, dead bodies, old meat and bones.

And the white-capped seas grope down the coast,
Pale hands beseeching, cold and lost –
So many. Yet the sea is blue
And all that red has vanished long ago.

For God's sake, stop, please stop.
Isn't this good faith
In your bodies' breath
All you can hope?

> ## *Ontological Episode of the Asylum*

The boobyhatch's bars, the guards, the nurses,
The illimitable locks and keys are all arranged
To thwart the hand that continually rehearses
Its ending stroke and raise a barricade
Against destruction-seeking resolution.
Many of us in there would have given all
(But we had nothing) for one small razor blade
Or seventy grains of the comforting amytal.

So I went down in the attitude of prayer,
Yes, to my knees on the cold floor of my cell,
Humped in a corner, a bird with a broken wing,
And asked and asked as fervently and well
As I could guess to do for light in the mists
Of death, until I learned God doesn't care.
Not only that, he doesn't care at all,
One way or the other. That is why he exists.

> ## *Existence Before Essence*

We rolled apart on the forest floor
(Remember?), each in a sighing terror,
As Hector after one battle more,
Sighing, turned to the armor-bearer
With his black lance in that black war.

Darling, then as the leaves plunged down
I knew the peril of such deep giving

(Leaves of aspen, leaves of rowan)
And the uselessness of such retrieving
Under a woods gone all nut-brown.

› *Alive*

I used to imagine we were a fine two-headed
    Animal, unison's two-tongued praise
Of fastened sex. But no, though singly bedded
    We went separately always.

When you burned your finger and mine smarted
    We had neither one body nor one soul,
But two in bright free being, consorted
    To play the romance of the whole.

It was good, else I had surely perished.
    In change may a changeless part survive?
As it is, crippled in the sex I cherished,
    I am full of love, and alive!

› *Essay on Marriage*

Snow came to us in the week of Thanksgiving.
I was studying Dr. Williams on the "variable foot"
    And Hölderlin on the necessity
        For writing one more poem,

And my wife and I had been married twenty-two days.
Not long, but considering the nature of
    Joy it was long enough. Because
        We each had known

Many bitternesses and disloyalties, and so
Recognized the advantage that loving brought to us
    After the ugly hope of solitude,
        We were very successful.

I was content to die. And when we went walking
We discovered many images of death: the gaunt and
   Skeletonized forest spreading its arms
     To gather cold flowers

From the sky, a pine seedling four inches tall
Mortified by a few ounces of frozen crystals,
   The trail vanishing among arcades
     Of snow-laden branches

Into the vague, expressive curtains of snow. Death
Was so deeply interpenetrated by purity and beauty
   That we clung together, whispering
     In awe, though no one

Could have heard us if we had shouted out
Love, love, love at the tops of our voices.
   By the time we returned to our cottage
     Rose Marie was crying

Inconsolably, for love, joy, the twenty-second day,
And perhaps, though she did not say so, for death . . .
   Measure, symmetry, these were ours. Yes,
     In each eye-turning

Down the forest's snowy avenues, and yet –
Has there ever been an invariable foot?
   Here I had wished a nude oak torso
     Fallen the other way,

And there the brookside to break more amiably.
Even Rose Marie, who is a good-looking woman
   By any standard and almost unbearably
     Beautiful by mine,

Nevertheless pouts and looks away because one breast
Is a quarter inch more marvelous than the other.
   And why should I write one more poem?
     Will it save the world?

Will it save Rose Marie? I expect to write
Hundreds, but no great good will come of them.
      Poetry, poetry, how many proud will die
            In thy service!

Poems will come inevitably like the seasons,
Imperfect and beautiful like the deathly woods,
      Expense of labor and expense of time,
            Like seasons and woods,

Like mechanisms, parts of a universe which means
Nothing, I guess, but simply moves, on and on,
      Imperfect and beautiful as only things
            May be that have no minds.

The meaning is all in my Rose Marie's tears.
We are grateful for their evanescence, creating
      Her the infinite wife, perfect and true,
            And me the infinite husband.

❯ *Godhulivela*

The poets of the Land of Indra write
Godhulivela, end of day, "the hour
The cows make dusty,   and a lotus flower
In my eyes lays its petals to the light

Of August evenings. Simply, this is how
The word in darkness lain two thousand years
And experience lost for thirty, hemispheres
Falling each way divisive of the two –

As we say, worlds apart – at last may join,
Something won back from chaos though by chance,
Godhulivela. The muddy cows advance,
Flicking their tails, Sad Udder, Bony Loin,

And Rolling Eye following one by one
Around the knoll, the duckpond, past the stile,
My lumbering, lowing, suffering, lingering file.
The saffron dust of evening cloaks the sun.

The poets of the Land of Tophet know
The word, could write it if they were inclined
To call that fading resonance to mind;
Their children would not understand them though.

The poets of the Land of Indra may
Consider this a mute and frightening end,
Something far too remote to comprehend,
But doubtless it will come to them someday.

❯ *Light in the Locust Tree*

My father was Menelaos, that homely king
— ST. AGISTHOS OF SAMIS

Light in the locust tree
Blown white, men say,
Was that lovelock; that eye
Was break of day;
Troy stares eternally
For those breasts' sway.

And maybe her mind was clean,
And maybe her sport,
But somebody was obscene,
Some crazy heart
Made beauty more than a man
And invented art.

She called the black bright ships
Dreaming to berth

Through all time's loom and lapse,
And then henceforth
A lie on a blind man's lips
Was woman's worth.

Ekstase, Alptraum, Schlaf in einem Nest von Flammen

Do not lecture me, doctor, about your science.
I sleep at night by a calm strong woman
Who dreams with her eyes deep-lidded in compliance
And with smiles, doctor, that appallingly illumine

Her sobs and contorted throat and thigh.
Doctor, her dreams are girl-breasts crushed to a rafter,
The rough wood, the held cry,
A rifle butt on the door and drunken laughter.

It happens, doctor, I am tired to death of your skill
Because I have given and given and have no more
To give in the cause of such a smile
For a crazed Slav hammering on a farmhouse door.

Spring Notes from Robin Hill

I

200,000 rhododendron blossoms I estimate
By multiplying the number seen
Through one pane of the "colonial" windowglass.
And I had wanted to show Rose Marie
A hummingbird, a most un-Silesian
Apparition: so she assures me.
Certainly one will come soon, I said.
Now the petals are almost gone,
Blown away like thoughts not written down,
And no hummingbird has visited us.
Probably they are becoming extinct.

2

The birches in front of the cottage
Bow like lissom queens at the emperor's court.
To whom?
To me naturally.

3

My German is awful, nine words mispronounced.
But a splendid language for bellowing.
When I find Tanio snoozing in a coil
Among my manuscripts, "Herauf!"
I proclaim, striking the air with my
Finger, "Herein, mein Herr Schlaffener!"
Nothing whatever happens. Tanio opens
One eye. "Kätze, was für hast du
Eine Attituden so gestinken!"

4

Two lesbians live on the far hill
And keep the most beautiful garden in town.
Hyacinth and lily-of-the-valley.

Brother Marcus, make something out of that.

5

Once we went walking in Tobey Woods
Leaving three loaves to bake in the oven,
And when we returned later than we had planned
The smell reached us some distance away.
"Oh – oh – my breads!" Rose Marie wailed.
"Ruined!" She fluttered her arms like a
Fledgling and hopped for home, clumsy
With the potbelly of her seventh month.

Not ruined at all, just good and firm
On the bottom.

6

Fierce storms this season. Tornado warnings
From the weather bureau, and a sure-enough tornado
In Waterbury; many wild storms in the hills.
One day lightning struck our weathervane,
Busted the cupola, scattered slates every
Whichway, split a rafter, blew out the radio,
Entered the plumbing, and knocked hell out of
The curb box, making a pretty fair geyser.
Scared? Not me, I'd just had too many strawberries.
Rose Marie says I must make an appointment
With the Rev. Hebard right away, to be
Baptized before anything more happens.
I'm not much on theology, but I bet
It's not that at all. It's those bombs
They keep exploding out there on the ocean.

7

A night in June. A new moon. Really,
On occasion the harmonies of the soul
Are too much.
                    Rose Marie walks under
The birches, and like them bending
Curtsies three times to the crescent
In thanks for a good conception, asking
That our child be beautiful and welcome.
So her mother had done before her
In a snowfield by the gray Oder, so
Her centuries-old grandmother had done
In the brown night of the Wendish forest.

Well, if it worked then, why not now?

8

I

  to be a child of history?

                    I

Determined by that tale of
   dutiful bloodletting?

However, let me speak now quietly
   without declamation
                  for I see
A fearsome thing will happen
   to my people –
Some lying at Concord or Shiloh
   or in France
                  and some others
Having also caught the grave-fever
   like cadavers well pleased
   and eyelessly rejoicing
                  in death.

See how they grow talons and
   lynx-tufted ears
                  – my people
   red-lidded in the night!

But Rose Marie was born on a
   crook of the Oder contested by
   three nations for three centuries
And she has the gentleness of the
   wood thrush in the cedar tree
   and no bitterness
                  though they
   drove her with pointed guns
   on the keen snowcrust.

In this cottage my history is –
   and my nation.
Quietly, quietly
   but with resolution
I will have no other.

9

Solomon's Seal and Adder's Tongue,
Five-leaves, Columbine, Whitlow-grass,
The misty *Maianthemum canadense*,
Indian Cucumber-root and Bluet,
Saxifrage, Foamflower, Sweet Cicely,
Trailing Arbutus, Fumitory,
Wakerobin and the lovely *Trillium*
Undulatum and the Lady's Slipper,
Marsh Marigold, Bloodroot, Jacob's Ladder,
Bitter Cress, Toothwort, small Coltsfoot,
The Wayfaring Tree and the Horse Gentian,
My gracious, delicate *Trientalis*,
Rose Marie's honest Partridgeberry –
And boo to you, Tom, Dick, and Harry.

> *The Smallish Son* ✓

A small voice is fretting my house in the night,
a small heart is there . . .
                    Listen,
I who have dwelt at the root of a scream forever,
I who have read my heart like a man with no hands
reading a book whose pages turn in the wind,
I say listen, listen, hear me
in our dreamless dark, my dear. I can teach you complaining.
My father, being wise, knowing the best rebellion is at forty,
told me to wait; but when he was sixty
he had nothing to say. Then do not wait.
Could I too not tell you much of a young man's folly?
But you will learn. When you play at strife-of-the-eyes
with existence, staring at the fluorescent moon to see
which of you will go under, please, please
be the first to smile. Do not harden yourself
though it means surrendering all, turning yourself out
to be known at the world's mercy. You will lose your name,
you will not know the curious shape of your coat,
even the words you breathe, spoken out so clearly,

will loosen and disperse forever, all given over
to the wind crying upon distant seas. Moment of horror:
the moonlight will name you, a profile among fallen flowers.
Yet you may survive, for many have done so. You need
only to close your eyes, beautiful feminine gesture;
and do not be afraid of the strange woman you find
lying in the chamber of your throat. When a silver bird
strikes at the shutters of your eyes with his wings
admit him, do not attempt to tame him, but as he swoops
in the tall glimmer of your intricate room
admire his freedom; and when a silver mouse
scurries twittering through the passageways of your blood
consider his beauty. So it will be: dark, a long vigil,
far among splendors of despair, this creation
in the closed eye. Everything will be true, pure,
your love most of all, and your flesh in the drunkenness
of becoming a dream. Lingering among the revenants
who still bear your name, touching and kissing,
dancing among their tatters of skin and splintered bones,
noticing the song of the tomb, how it soars in dream,
you in your sovereignty condescending to song,
permitting your myth – what awareness then, what ecstasies
in the shimmering dark pool, what marvels of the dark stair!
But now, please open your eyes again. Have we not said
down with all tyrants, even our own? Especially our own!
Open your eyes; they will glitter from long sleep
with the knowledge of the other side of the world.
Their light then will be of such a quiet intensity
that smiles and frowns will fall away like shadows
of wild birds flying over. No complicity, no acquiescence;
and yet a degree of affection remaining, as when one finds
an old bible in an old cupboard of an empty house.
So it is, so, freedom and beauty. Do not be modest,
wear the delicate beauty of those crippled at birth
who earn the grace of their maiming. Do not be afraid,
assume the freedom of those born in their captivity
who earn the purity of their being. All one and all many,
but remember, never the two alone, falsely dividing
in the mind's paralyzed divorce. This is our meaning

under our true rebellion, this is the dark where we
may venture without our dreams. In the dreamless dark
where I await you, the dark light of my eyes
may still be darkly burning when you come.
You must look and you must seek
for my eyes will answer but I think they will not summon.
And if you do not find them, turn away.

❯ *The President's Speech*

Before supper we had seen three grazing deer
in the frost-burnt asters at the forests edge;
we watched them from the kitchen window; then we ate
our good meat and bread like any husband and wife,
and listened to the President in the radio under
the kitchen shelf. The night moved the mountain.
The box rattled, the voice told our exact danger,
taking course among waves of world-destroying violence
like a small craft sailing infuriate seas. We had,
we two, gone driven far about on the world's misery,
much shaken, but had come at last in blind luck
to settle at this way station by the woods. We shivered
again tonight, but consumed our meal somewhat hungrily.
"God save the deer," Rose Marie said.

                                   Indeed, sir,
now I am alone and I am obliged to ask,
can you say, please, can you tell us what this is
that is necessity held in our sad hands? Innocence
will save the deer, I think, and all things loved
by Rose Marie; the quail whistling on Canaan Mountain,
the fox in his laurel, the gentian rusting by the brook;
innocence will almost save Rose Marie. No, not, dear sir,
their bodies or their souls committed to black fire
and the carious wind, but their minds that are their own.
Come, sir, man to man, now at one in the morning
before we walk out to the blast, would not this salvation

which we cannot, being men, esteem, nevertheless
be something? More than the appointments of history?
For once to think their thoughts and ask no due
in all the world of thoughts and things, nor take dominion?

> *Freedom and Discipline*

Saint Harmony, many
years I have stript

naked in your service
under the lash. Yes,

I believe the first
I heard (living, there

aloud in the hall) was
Sergei Rachmaninoff

set at the keys like a
great dwarf, a barrel

on three spindles,
megalocephalus, hands

with fourteen fingers,
ugly as Merlin, with whom

I was in love, a boy and
an old man; a boy nodding

and an old man sorrowing
under the bushfire of the

people's heart, until he
coolly knocked out the

Prelude in C# Minor. Second
was Coleman Hawkins

in about 1934 perhaps.
I, stript and bleeding,

leapt to the new touch,
up and over the diminished

in a full-voiced authority
of blue-gold blues. I

would do nothing, locked
in discipline, sworn to

freedom. The years shrieked
and smothered, like billboards

beside a road at night.
I learnt how Catlett

drove the beat without
harming it, how Young

sped between the notes,
how Monk reconstructed

a broken chord to make
my knuckles rattle, and much

from oblivion: Newton,
Fasola, Berigan, my

inconsolable Papa Yancey.
Why I went to verse-making

is unknowable, this
grubbing art. Trying,

Harmony, to fix your beat
in things that have none

and want none – absurdity!
Let that be the answer

to any hope of statecraft.
As Yeats said, *Fal de rol*.

Freedom and discipline concur
only in ecstasy, all else

is shoveling out the muck.
Give me my old hot horn.

« IV »

from

THE CLAY HILL
ANTHOLOGY
[1970]

October. Twilight
flutters like cloth of silver
caught in tall dark elms.

.   .   .

Coarse leaf, alder leaf,
turnest thou now mauve, and soft,
when the rest are brown?

.   .   .

Excellence requires
leaf-rakers to sweep one spot
nine times. Nine, not eight.

.   .   .

Tsar, who knew you? Who
knows you? Time like an arch fell
on its own keystone.

.   .   .

Fathers die, but sons
catch the grave chill, looking in
at lost forgiveness.

.   .   .

Imagine bird bones
walking in green grass, tiny
perfect skeletons.

.   .   .

The Sanskrit root word
for "war" means literally
"desire for more cows."

Electroshock. Bang –
no, not bang. Yes, *not-bang!* . . . God!
And headache after.

· · ·

They gave me in trust
this pouch of starshine, saying,
"Your turn to carry . . ."

· · ·

Ducks, waking at sea
on greasy billows, taste life
in the fog and brine.

· · ·

Niobe, your tears
are your children now. See how
we have multiplied.

· · ·

He: Life is an old
casino in the park. I:
Well, well, saxophone!

· · ·

Why speak of the use
of poetry? Poetry
is what uses us.

· · ·

She lay like a book
in moonlight: open and bright
but too dark to read.

No, I was wrecked here,
this rock is my raft. The sea
must be somewhere else.

.   .   .

Trees, the naked trees,
stopped in their tracks, so peaceful
talking together.

.   .   .

Am I wrong? The roads
have begun to squirm. Shame, shame,
you dishonored land!

.   .   .

Because in the heart
of darkness I could not see,
I began looking.

.   .   .

Emptiness – you know
what I mean? Moonlight howling
in the room like snow.

.   .   .

Over and over
and over and over and
over and over.

.   .   .

The shadow sprang out
blackly, then faded. No change . . .
except for someone.

Have you ever seen
someone watching a burning
candle and laughing?

·   ·   ·

I live where Frost lived.
So? It's a free country. Don't
jump to conclusions.

·   ·   ·

Again on dark looms,
dark shuttles. The wind weaving
a chiffon of snow.

·   ·   ·

You – Spanish-speaking
peoples of the world, lovely
revolutionists!

·   ·   ·

Against the wall he
gropes like ivy, you pray, I
cling like windblown leaves.

·   ·   ·

The last year of youth
was – when? 'Sixty? 'Fifty-nine?
Funny, I missed it.

·   ·   ·

Reversions, always
reversions. When wet, dogs smell
fishy, wives doggy.

Today my poems seem
only the spells I muttered
while waiting for poems.

•   •   •

The wise child is born
like spring in Vermont, too late,
too cold, too fragile.

•   •   •

Forward! You must. Keep
nothing. Possess not what you
have, but what you had.

•   •   •

All my life that's been
the watchword: Resist! Resist!
– cried deep in the world.

•   •   •

Sigh, you seven seas,
you four winds, sigh for the child
found today at dawn.

•   •   •

For your love given
ask no return, none. To love
you must love to love.

•   •   •

Omens, we despise
them. But have a look, will you?
– at that wind-wrenched pine.

Of course make love not
war. But then how will you stop
killing each other?

.   .   .

Parting up/down from
one on the shore, two egrets –
a white severance.

.   .   .

Women like new brooms,
men old. Absolute fact. Why?
God knows. Don't quote me.

.   .   .

Ideas hit life like
planks hitting water. Some skim.
Some plunge and shoot back.

.   .   .

"Ecstasy is the
disaster of pleasure": this
is worth repeating.

.   .   .

Look, a cypress tree
explaining why it always
wears a shred of fog.

.   .   .

Out of the garden,
down the sea-wall, I found this
obscure moss-grown stair.

One ant turns backward
along the file. The others
pause and hurry past.

.　　.　　.

Therefore to us, time's
final lesson: be content
with no monument.

.　　.　　.

Steeple bush, hardhack:
the eye's name and then the hand's.
When you speak them, think.

.　　.　　.

Hey, Basho, you there!
I'm Carruth. Isn't it great,
so distant like this?

.　　.　　.

Always this special
secret feeling, the failure
of reality.

.　　.　　.

Shirt, britches, paper
to write on, what more's a man
need . . . in Mexico?

.　　.　　.

True, I happen. So
put "I" in. But randomly,
I am not the song.

A hard journey – yes,
it must be. At the end they
always fall asleep.

.   .   .

The mansion burned. Maids
ran from window to window
shaking cloths of fire.

.   .   .

Dawn. Hoar on the grass,
deer knee-deep in crispness. Ah
baby, snuggle down.

.   .   .

There! Whitman's skull –
so elegant, sensitive,
cynical, and cool.

.   .   .

Well, beat on, beat on,
old ark, don't go down now. God,
what a stink! Beat on . . .

.   .   .

Let my snow-tracks lead
on, on. Let them, where they stop,
stop. There, in mid-field.

from

FROM SNOW
AND ROCK,
FROM CHAOS
[1973]

› *Dedication in These Days*

What words can make
seems next to nothing now
a tune a measure

Yet
I have seen you with
your eyes wet
with pleasure for their sake

For this then
these few
for now for you
again

› *I Could Take*

I could take
two leaves
    and give you one.
Would that not be
a kind of perfection?

But I prefer
one leaf
    torn to give you half
        showing

(after these years, simply)
love's complexity in an act,
    the tearing and
        the unique edges –

one leaf (one word) from the two
imperfections that match.

> *French Hill*

Tell, acquaint me
why they care,
men, if they lie

here or there
in finality?
Tell how come

they are so hot
to put the cold bones
they will have got

in this or another
remembered spot?
And if nearby or far

stone stand or
urn repose, tell
how they'll know it –

will they not
have gone all beyond
what knows and what's known,

meadow or grove or any
glory of mount
or glimmering plot?

For inside the skull
if it be winter
what is memory

but the mere ice that will,
before the ash leaves grow,
thaw and rot?

Here's ash in a knot
of smoky wild rose
above the valley

over the river –
is it a green tree
on midsummer day?

Tomorrow it will not
be a smoking ruin
– imagination is done! –

nothing, nothing
it will be
no thing.

Tell, acquaint me
half-dead mind
why

after all the tear-
drenched years
you'd still

when ice
frizzles your jelly
lie

high above valley
and over river
with the ruined ash

and the burnt rose
the rain and the winter
and tell me why

it is any use or good
if a stone certify
the name of nothing

up here above
that house known
for love?

> *If It Were Not for You*

Liebe, meine liebe, I had not hoped
to be so poor

        The night winds reach
like the blind breath of the world
in a rhythm without mind, gusting and beating
as if to destroy us, battering our poverty
and all the land's flat and cold and dark
under iron snow
                the dog leaps in the wind
barking, maddened with winter, and his voice
claps again and again down the valley
like tatters of revolutionary pennants
                      birches
cry and hemlocks by the brook
stand hunched and downcast with their hands
in their pockets

Liebe, the world is wild
and without intention

        how far
this might be from the night of Christmas
if it were not for you.

Down the reaching wind
shrieks of starlight bear broken messages
among mountains where shadows plunge
                    yet our brightness
is unwavering
        Kennst du das land
wo die zitronen blühn, im dunkeln laub

die goldorangen . . . liebe
art thou singing

It is a question partly
of the tree with our stars and partly
of your radiance brought from the land
where legends flower to this land
but more than these our bright poverty
is a house in the wind and a light
on the mountain

Liebe, our light rekindled
in this remoteness from the other land,
in this dark of the blue mountain where only
the winds gather
    is what we are for the time that we are
    what we know for the time that we know

How gravely and sweetly the poor touch in the dark.

> ❯ *Speaking for Them*

    August. Hear
    the cicadas
    splitting their skins.

    The bleeding cow
    has rubbed her neck on barbed
    wire against the flies,

    which return, crawling
    in her eyes. She looks up,
    a sorrow, raising her great
    head in slowness, brown eyes rising
    like pools in the earth.

    Then the elms. There marching
    down the knoll by the fence slowly,

a dead march. Shall we have

Memorial Day for the elms,
those veterans? Here are the oldest,
stricken and proud, lifting

poor broken arms in sleeves
of ragged bark.

Blackeyed susans bow their heads,
crazy swallows
turn somersaults in the air.

❯ *To Artemis*

The fog is departing, let it go. Odor
of the south, carrying what seems your last
intercession,   your final statement –
flakes of light whirling away, a shower –
     moonflakes, sparks
     scurrying through dark trees.

          And the solid cold air
of the Arctic is sliding around us.

Higher now – bright – you assume your
     mystery, a kind of indwelling
     light that looks sourceless
though it is not. Like alloy, bronze, pewter,
so changed, autonomous, remade: the source
becomes unimportant.

     Snow-lined, the branches of trees
vanish, leaving these jagged streaks,
calligraphic light.   The forest
     startles us.

          Tonight there is

no intercession, no power, but only
mystery. We call you queen but that
does not say what you are.   We try
to be like you; help us if you are able.
Whatever we are, these reflections, let us
change them now, let us be silent, cold,
let us be autonomous, bright,

in this place so remote and altered.

❯ *Tabula Rasa*

There, an evening star, there again. Above
The torn lovelace of snow, in the far sky
That glows with an afterlight, fading,

The evening star piercing a black tangle
Of trees on the ridge. Shall it be our kiss?
Can we call its sudden singleness,

Its unannounced simplicity, its rage
In the abhorrent distances, its small viridine,
Ours, always ours? Or shall we say

This wintry eloquence is mere affect
Of tattered snow, of tangling black limbs?
Everything reproaches me, everything,

Because we do not stand by Leman's water,
By the onyx columns, entablatures, all
The entablatures, watching the cygnets fade

With Sapphic pathos into a silver night.
Listen, the oboe and the little drum
Make Lulliana where the old whores walk . . .

Do men and women meet and love forthwith?

Or do they think about it? Or do they
In a masque play fated figures en tragique?

Perhaps they are those who only stand
In tattered snow and dream of fated things.
The limbs have snatched the star, have eaten it.

Another night, we've lost another day. Nothing
Spoke to us, certainly nothing spoke for us —
The slate is clean. Here therefore is my kiss.

❯ *Concerning Necessity*

It's quite true we live
in a kind of rural twilight
most of the time giving
our love to the hard dirt
the water and the weeds
and the difficult woods

ho we say drive the wedge
heave the axe run the hand shovel
dig the potato patch
dig ashes dig gravel
tickle the dyspeptic chain saw
make him snarl once more

while the henhouse needs cleaning
the fruitless corn to be cut
and the house is falling to pieces
the car coming apart
the boy sitting and complaining
about something everything anything

this was the world foreknown
though I had thought somehow
probably in the delusion

of that idiot Thoreau
that necessity could be saved
by the facts we actually have

like our extreme white birch
clasped in the hemlock's arms
or our baybreasted nuthatch
or our mountain and our stars
and really these things do serve
a little though not enough

what saves the undoubted collapse
of the driven day and the year
is my coming all at once
when she is done in or footsore
or down asleep in the field
or telling a song to a child

coming and seeing her move
in some particular way
that makes me to fall in love
all over with human beauty
the beauty I can't believe
right here where I live.

❯ *The Ravine*

Stones, brown tufted grass, but no water,
it is dry to the bottom. A seedy eye
of orange hawkweed blinks in sunlight
stupidly, a mink bumbles away,
a ringnecked snake among stones lifts its head
like a spark, a dead young woodcock –
long dead, the mink will not touch it –
sprawls in the hatchment of its soft plumage
and clutches emptiness with drawn talons.
This is the ravine today. But in spring it
cascaded, in winter it filled with snow

until it lay hidden completely. In time,
geologic time, it will melt away
or deepen beyond recognition, a huge
gorge. These are what I remember and foresee.
These are what I see here every day,
not things but relationships of things,
quick changes and slow. These are my sorrow,
for unlike my bright admonitory friends
I see relationships, I do not see things.
These, such as they are, every day, every
unique day, the first in time and the last,
are my thoughts, the sequences of my mind.
I wonder what they mean. Every day,
day after day, I wonder what they mean.

❯ *Homecoming*

A road that had wound us 20,000 miles
stops, with a kind of suddenness, at home.

At home and in midsummer. The snow has gone.
July murmurs its dark momentous tones.

The butternut is heavy, heavy the fruit
hung like genitals under the pleated leaves.

Weeds (we call them), marguerite and gromwell
and Queen Anne's lace, stand tall in the garden,

and one last foxglove stands among them, with one
magenta cloche hung darkly among the lace.

It does not move in the dark unmoving air
yet we almost hear its tolling. Knell on knell

broaden across the haze of afternoon,
conscious indecencies of ceremonious sorrow.

Two deaths, two abstractions. Our absence
was spooked somehow; changes in spite of us

done in the part of the world we had left locked
in safety. One was a favorite pine and the other

was old Steve Washer. The pine stood shining
in snow when we last saw it, but the rust

took it, and now even in death it is beautiful,
a russet tree in the dark woods. Eventually

its use will serve our fire; we cannot mourn it long.
But Mr. Washer's dying was not like this.

It has no beauty, no usefulness, it is
ugly and stupid, nothing but stupid. It hurts us.

Eighty-five years is long enough to live,
people say; and he was vigorous to the end.

And truly he was, as these said things are true
and good and wise, and in no way disguises,

since the very ones who say them shake their heads
over their own indecent and ceremonious words.

Mr. Washer was a free-born man
who in the toil of self-creation probably wished

he wasn't often enough, and so was like us all;
his loss, as ours will be, is irreplaceable.

That is understood. The man is gone. And then . . .
the type is almost gone, the tough hardminded Yankee

who loved John Locke and let John Bunyan go.
Mr. Washer was the only person who ever respected

our privacy, not partly, not indifferently, but absolutely;
yet was eager to share if asked, our labor or luck

as our need demanded. He was a small man, and lean;
weighed 130 in his prime and somewhat less

toward the end, but could heap grain sacks in the loft
faster than the mill boys could heave them up,

and could walk switchback behind his team all day
in the high fields. He was doing it last July.

Mr. Washer is gone, and in any useful sense
his virtues are gone with him. Our absence

has returned to absence. We walk in our high grass,
restless and petulant among weeds and spiderwebs.

The day is quiet, dark, and hot, but it will not rain.
After all the bell in the garden is silent.

❯ *Once More*

Once more by the brook the alder leaves
turn mauve, bronze, violet, beautiful
after the green of crude summer; galled
black stems, pithy, tangled, twist in the
flesh-colored vines of wild cyclamen.
Mist drifts below the mountaintop
in prismatic tatters. The brook is full,
spilling down heavily, loudly, in silver
spate from the beaver ponds in the high
marshy meadows. The year is sinking:
heavily, loudly, beautifully. Deer move
heavily in the brush like bears, half drunk
on masty acorns and rotten wild apples.
The pileated woodpecker thumps a dead elm
slowly, irregularly, meditatively.

Like a broken telephone a cricket rings
without assertion in dead asters and
goldenrod; asters gone cloudy with seed,
goldenrod burnt and blackened. A gray trout
rests under the lip of glacial stone. One
by one the alder leaves plunge down to earth,
veering, and lie there, glowing, like a shirt
of Nessus. My heart in my ribs does what it
has done occasionally all my life: thumps and
heaves suddenly in irregular rhythm that makes
me gasp. How many times has this season turned
and gone down? How many! I move heavily
into the bracken, and the deer stand still
a moment, uncertain, before they break away,
snorting and bounding heavily before me.

❯ *The Cows at Night*

The moon was like a full cup tonight,
too heavy, and sank in the mist
soon after dark, leaving for light

faint stars and the silver leaves
of milkweed beside the road,
gleaming before my car.

Yet I like driving at night
in summer and in Vermont:
the brown road through the mist

of mountain-dark, among farms
so quiet, and the roadside willows
opening out where I saw

the cows. Always a shock
to remember them there, those
great breathings close in the dark.

I stopped, and took my flashlight
to the pasture fence. They turned
to me where they lay, sad

and beautiful faces in the dark,
and I counted them – forty
near and far in the pasture,

turning to me, sad and beautiful
like girls very long ago
who were innocent, and sad

because they were innocent,
and beautiful because they were
sad. I switched off my light.

But I did not want to go,
not yet, nor knew what to do
if I should stay, for how

in that great darkness could I explain
anything, anything at all.
I stood by the fence. And then

very gently it began to rain.

❯ *Emergency Haying*

Coming home with the last load I ride standing
on the wagon tongue, behind the tractor
in hot exhaust, lank with sweat,

my arms strung
awkwardly along the hayrack, cruciform.
Almost 500 bales we've put up

this afternoon, Marshall and I.
And of course I think of another who hung
like this on another cross. My hands are torn

by baling twine, not nails, and my side is pierced
by my ulcer, not a lance. The acid in my throat
is only hayseed. Yet exhaustion and the way

my body hangs from twisted shoulders, suspended
on two points of pain in the rising
monoxide, recall that greater suffering.

Well, I change grip and the image
fades. It's been an unlucky summer. Heavy rains
brought on the grass tremendously, a monster crop,

but wet, always wet. Haying was long delayed.
Now is our last chance to bring in
the winter's feed, and Marshall needs help.

We mow, rake, bale, and draw the bales
to the barn, these late, half-green,
improperly cured bales; some weigh 150 pounds

or more, yet must be lugged by the twine
across the field, tossed on the load, and then
at the barn unloaded on the conveyor

and distributed in the loft. I help –
I, the desk-servant, word-worker –
and hold up my end pretty well too; but God,

the close of day, how I fall down then. My hands
are sore, they flinch when I light my pipe.
I think of those who have done slave labor,

less able and less well prepared than I.
Rose Marie in the rye fields of Saxony,
her father in the camps of Moldavia

and the Crimea, all clerks and housekeepers
herded to the gaunt fields of torture. Hands
too bloodied cannot bear

even the touch of air, even
the touch of love. I have a friend
whose grandmother cut cane with a machete

and cut and cut, until one day
she snicked her hand off and took it
and threw it grandly at the sky. Now

in September our New England mountains
under a clear sky for which we're thankful at last
begin to glow, maples, beeches, birches

in their first color. I look
beyond our famous hayfields to our famous hills,
to the notch where the sunset is beginning,

then in the other direction, eastward,
where a full new-risen moon like a pale
medallion hangs in a lavender cloud

beyond the barn. My eyes
sting with sweat and loveliness. And who
is the Christ now, who

if not I? It must be so. My strength
is legion. And I stand up high
on the wagon tongue in my whole bones to say

woe to you, watch out
you sons of bitches who would drive men and women
to the fields where they can only die.

The Far-removed Mountain Men

No salt here, old sea father, holy giant.
We season our nauseous venison
with its own blood.

No cape, no black rock
gleaming in spume, no promontory
touching the eternal waters.

No shifting waterlights far out when a storm
breaks into pieces and the mist
scatters like leaves in windy sunlight.

No grace of gull-flight over our mountains,
no spangle of sea wave below,
no song of a long wind in the dunes.

No tides!
– flood, ebb, spring and neap, beating slow heart,
the measure we dream, the measure we almost feel.

How the seine must rock in that dance!
How the molluscs must snuggle
in their concordant drumming blood!

Snow seeps in our cove. Our starving owl
hunts blind by day, battering the pines.
All night the hours squeak across our sky.

At least will you come to us, old one,
in the spring rains, will you walk
in our fog, surgent among moist firs?

Bring us the great spring-tide mounting
and the salts of love-sweat again.

› The Insomniac Sleeps Well for Once and

rises at five, just when a late moon
rises, huge, out of the snow cloud

at the end of the garden. You sleep.
Coming so tired and worried to middle age,

you'll sleep ten hours if we let you,
yet now, slept nearly out, you lie as if

this moon had brought from far in the east,
Silesia, your old self who you really are

come to inhabit you, girl of the rye fields
silver and green, and here comes another

moon, another, another, the snow gleams,
and each one brings something

so that your eyes smoothen as if for love,
your fine bone rises under your skin,

you move and smile in the sleeping knowledge
of yourself, as the spirit of this house moves

smiling from mirror to mirror in brightness,
and oh my god look at the sky full of moons,

look at the snow, the girl, look at the day!

› This Song

In an afternoon bright with
September, or in an old dissension
bright with fear, I went wandering where
there was purity in white lady's tresses,
hiddenness in peeping bluebottle gentians,

and where many species of goldenrod
and asters made funeral for the lost
summer world, and ferns, taken by frost,
made russet the fields and turned
the waysides yellow and brown.

It struck me that I had wandered all my years
like this, half a century, searching
for the touch that heals, but there is
no touch; searching everywhere for the
look that says *I know,* but there is

no look. This is Vermont, the land
hidden from violent times, far from the center
of life, they say. I walk by the gray brook,
around the knoll, through the pines. Winter
is coming. Searching, searching with my hand,

I feel September's little knives, and with my eyes
I see bright spattered leaves in the matted
grass. I hear this song, if it be a song. these
insistent little bright fearful hesitant
murmurs from high in the old pine trees.

› *The Birds of Vietnam*

O bright, O swift and bright,
you flashing among pandanus boughs
    (is that right? pandanus?)
under the great banyan, in and out
the dusky delicate bamboo groves
    (yes? banyan, bamboo?)
low, wide-winged, gliding
over the wetlands and drylands
    (but I have not seen you,
    I do not know your names,
    I do not know
    what I am talking about).

I have seen the road runner and the golden eagle,
the great white heron and the Kirtland's warbler,
      our own endangered species,
and I have worried about them. I have worried
about all our own, seen and unseen,
whooping cranes, condors, white-tailed kites,
and the ivory-bills (certainly gone, all gone!)
the ones we have harried, murdered, driven away
as if we were the Appointed Avengers,
      the Destroyers, the Wrathful Ones
out of our ancestors' offended hearts
at the cruel beginning of the world.
But for what? for whom? why?
      Nobody knows.

And why, in my image of that cindered country,
should I waste my mourning? I will never have
enough. Think of the children there,
insane little crusted kids at the beckoning fire,
think of the older ones, burned, crazy with fear,
sensible beings who can know hell, think
of their minds exploding, their hearts flaming.

I do think. But today,
O mindless, O heartless, in and out
the dusky delicate groves,
your hell becomes mine, simply
and without thought, you maimed, you
poisoned in your nests, starved
in the withered forests.
      O mindless, heartless,
      you never invented hell.
We say flesh turns to dust, though more often
a man-corpse or woman-corpse is a bloody pulp,
and a bird-corpse too, yet your feathers
      retain life's color
long afterward, even in the robes
      of barbarous kings,
still golden the trogon feather,

still bright the egret plume, and the crest
of the bower bird will endure forever
almost. You will always remind us of what
    the earth has been.

O bright, swift, gleaming
in dusky groves,
I mourn you.
O mindless, heartless, I can't
help it, I have so loved
    this world.

> ## *The Baler*

You tourist composed upon that fence
to watch the quaint farmer at his quaint task
come closer, bring your camera here
or fasten your telescopic lens
if you're too indolent, all I ask
is that when you go home you take
a close-up among your color slides
of vacationland, to show we pay the price
for hay, this actual panic: no politic fear
but tumbling wild waves down the windrows, tides
of crickets, grasshoppers, meadow mice,
and half-feathered sparrows, whipped by a bleeding snake.

> ## *I Know, I Remember, But How Can I Help You*

The northern lights.   I wouldn't have noticed them
    if the deer hadn't told me
    a doe   her coat of pearls   her glowing hoofs
            proud and inquisitive
            eager for my appraisal
and I went out into the night with electrical steps
    but with my head held also proud
            to share the animal's fear

and see what I had seen before
a sky flaring and spectral
greenish waves and ribbons
and the snow   under strange light   tossing in the pasture
like a storming ocean caught
by a flaring beacon.
The deer stands away from me   not far
there among bare black apple trees
a presence I no longer see.
We are proud to be afraid
proud to share
the silent magnetic storm that destroys the stars
and flickers around our heads
like the saints' cold spiritual agonies
of old.
I remember   but without the sense   other light-storms
cold memories discursive and philosophical
in my mind's burden
and the deer remembers nothing.
We move our feet   crunching bitter snow   while the storm
crashes like god-wars down the east
we shake the sparks from our eyes
we quiver inside our shocked fur
we search for each other
in the apple thicket –
a glimpse, an acknowledgment
it is enough and never enough –
we toss our heads   and say good night
moving away on bitter bitter snow.

❯ *This Decoration*

Blue light, morning
glory color, driven
through green fir boughs,

bright as crow-caw
on the next to last day
of October. You've given

me this decoration
made from dried pasted
flowers inside the cap

of a cottage cheese
carton. Beautiful
flowers, unrecognizable

flowers, at which I stare
with a blue-green feeling,
delighted and ignorant,

until you tell me you
made them up. One
is scales from a pine cone

flattened, with a tuft
of silverrod seedfluff
in the center. Another

from a dried panicle
of millet with petals
of mapleseed. Now

I see burrs, bark, a
snip of duck feather. How
exquisite, flowers

of imagination from this
real world, made and given
for lovingkindness. I

go out, wordless, walking
the stubble rows; and here,
high, comes this black

crow, above the furrows
high and straight, flapping,
as if from a great

distance, from eternity.
Caw caw, loudly. And back
from beyond the firs comes

the answer, *caw*, way off, far
although near too, and wordless,
as real things always are.

› *Too Tenuous*

Thirty yards apart, they face
not each other
but both in the same direction,
and yet could not be more together,
these sandhill cranes near Ruby Lake, Nevada,
two russet paleographic curves, slender
Chinese brushstrokes among tan reeds –
the composed and oriental splendor
of this world. Bo, my son,
you grow as this grows rarer.
We know what the cranes are facing. Already
I am a collector
of such precious fragments and you will become
perhaps a connoisseur, driven in love and wonder
to pedantry. Turn away, dear Bo.
Love will not keep in such a dwindled order
too tenuous to know.

❯ *Rimrock, Where It Is*

Ruined, time ruined, all these once good things.
The structure of many rooms built in the sun,

a refuge from sun; but its parts have gone
wandering, there down the hillside in flowers.

A few doorways remain, arched gently, open
to a white-hot sky, but through them the spirits

long since ceased to pass. Ladders mount the walls
rung by rung to nowhere. The city of desolation,

creviced for the scorpion, is pierced everywhere
by sun, whose mindless immitigable command

beats down with the same force as when its liege folk
listened: generate, generate. Only scorpions hear,

the female eating the male's head while they couple.
Nearby in a refuge of poured concrete and glass

a small woman, small as a girl, black with time,
lies and lies, always raising her head, her charred face,

always raising her knees in a mock of childbirth,
always opening her mouth that is gagged with dust,

always screaming. It reverberates, wave on wave,
the desert's pulse. And the blind albino

fish, relic of a once vast species, that swims
in the lake at the bottom of the deepest cave

in Arizona, in darkness or in glittering rays
of flashlights, goes round and round and round.

❯ Song

Summer burns on the edges of day
  and nothing changes.
The sea like an old thin opal
  clasped by a thin golden shore
turns past the broken stones of a temple
  on which the butterflies
perch and turn like slowly branching flame.
  A cankerworm spins in the quince tree.

Nothing changes. The woman stares
  outward, holding
one hand to her hair as always,
  her pale eyes
burning. The man searches his pockets
  or tosses his head
like a kite launched in the fiery wind.
  A cankerworm spins in the quince tree.

No word has been spoken. Her eyes are
  the same pale stars
as ever, and she will open to him
  with almost the same smile.
But the day burns as if a thread of fire
  in summer's tapestry
had severed the unicorn from the virgin.
  A cankerworm spins in the quince tree.

Nothing changes. The butterflies
  flare and subside,
the sea rubs sparks from the shore,
  the woman stares
at the gulls far on the fiery wind
  drifting her eyes over and out,
the man rubs flame from a match.
  A cankerworm spins in the quince tree.

O masters of revolution, don't you see
    what is the way of change?
Take this man to your cause quickly
    for he is desperate,
and listen to the names he is muttering
    against reality.
He changes the world, the world is changed.
    A cankerworm spins in the quince tree.

❯ *Twilight Comes*

AFTER WANG WEI

Twilight comes to the little farm
At winter's end. The snowbanks
High as the eaves, which melted
And became pitted during the day,
Are freezing again, and crunch
Under the dog's foot. The mountains
From their place behind our shoulders
Lean close a moment, as if for a
Final inspection, but with kindness,
A benediction as the darkness
Falls. It is my fiftieth year. Stars
Come out, one by one with a softer
Brightness, like the first flowers
Of spring. I hear the brook stirring,
Trying its music beneath the ice.
I hear – almost, I am not certain –
Remote tinklings; perhaps sheepbells
On the green side of a juniper hill
Or wineglasses on a summer night.
But no. My wife is at her work,
There behind yellow windows. Supper
Will be soon. I crunch the icy snow
And tilt my head to study the last

Silvery light of the western sky
In the pine boughs. I smile. Then
I smile again, just because I can.
I am not an old man. Not yet.

❭ Abandoned Ranch, Big Bend

Three people come where no people belong any more.
They are a woman who would be young
And good-looking if these now seemed
Real qualities, a child with yellow hair, a man
Hardened in desperate humanity. But here are only
Dry cistern, adobe flaking, a lizard. And now this
Disagreeable feeling that they were summoned. Sun
On the corrugated roof is a horse treading,
A horse with wide wings and heavy hoofs. The lizard
Is splayed head down on the wall, pulsing. They do not
Bother to lift their binoculars to the shimmering distance.
From this dead center the desert spirals away,
Traveling outward and inward, pulsing. Summoned
From half across the world, from snow and rock,
From chaos, they arrived a moment ago, they thought,
In perfect fortuity. There is a presence emerging here in
Sun dance and clicking metal, where the lizard blinks
With eyes whetted for extinction; then swirling
Outward again, outward and upward through the sky's
White-hot funnel. Again and again among the dry
Wailing voices of displaced Yankee ghosts
This ranch is abandoned to terror and the sublime.
The man turns to the woman and child. He has never
Said what he meant. They give him
The steady cool mercy of their unreproachful eyes.

« VI »

from

DARK WORLD
[1974]

"What a good and bright world this is if we do not lose our hearts to it,
but what a dark world if we do!"

– RABBI BARUKH OF MEZBIZH,
as recorded by Martin Buber in *Tales of the Hasidim.*

> Eternal City

Day turning to night
without flare, end of day
and first of night
held between
one air and another air,
a significance of light
in which a figure leans
against a pillar, weeping
under a great roof
in the midst of the city,
a figure that wears
a flat-crowned, flat-brimmed
hat tilted down
such as women have worn
in some times and places.
This is a man, weeping.
His hand, heavily veined,
falls beside veined stone.
Is he weeping? His face,
withheld, hidden beneath
the tilted hat-brim,
nevertheless is the center
of the city, the cathedral,
the web of evening mist.
He is weeping. Everything
we know, that turned our steps
this way, through these old
twilit streets, past these
gardens and courtyards,
affirms his weeping.

> The Chase in Spring

A forest of pine darkness. Shadows
are moist in the early spring
and wounded snow bleeds. I am

trying to investigate this butterfly,
something I had not thought to do
again, bright wings in gloomy light,
saffron and orange, and I am filled
with heaviness, wet shadows have buried
my fleetness. I perceive
only bits of butterfly, shed
like code flashing in its erratic
swiftness. When it lights it folds
its wings upright, showing me dull
undersides, the brightness hidden.

> ## *In Russia*

Somewhere in Russia I have heard
under a stony hill with a monastery
on its dark crown two rivers flow
and meet and join and continue on

but their currents are different. One
has yellow water while the other
is blue-green,
and although they meet and join

they do not mingle but run
side by side together, divided yet held
between the same banks of a single
channel, yellow and blue-green

out from beneath that monastery
into the brightness of sun
which drenches the long cool upland prairie
far from the sea.

I'd like to behold it but I never will.
Sometimes it seems as if all I know
is that any blood-soaked field will grow corn.
But in Russia the mind's desire is born in a hill.

⟩ *The Existing Pool*

Begin with a pool. The deepening
bed of a mountain brook
will do, where swift water quietens.
Ours is the Sheep Hole

where years ago, before the sheep
and their herdsmen all went west,
the flocks were driven
each springtime

for a good dunk before they were shorn.
It lies
below the Shinglemill Bridge
where a wheel once took the fall

at the pool's brim
to drive sawblades for shingles
years ago
before the cedars were exterminated.

But any pool will do. Let
it be clear, quiet,
and if, like ours,
it is guarded by yellow birches and elms

whose overleaning branches
darken the surface near the edge
leaving the center clear,
so much the better.

Look now, lean closer, see
down to the brook-bed, the pebbles there,
mosaic of intricate antique,
green, gray, red,

and then above them, between
you and the water
like a window
or like another eye encompassing your eyes,

the gleaming reflected sky.
How this light clings to the surface!
A triumph, so tactile
you could peel it

or turn it like a page,
and yet what is it?
The pebbles below, green, gray, red,
gleam as before. Throw

two more pebbles – left, right.
Ripples shake the light
and reflections dance
like new mosaic dappling

above the fixed
mosaic beneath, or like thought
dancing upon the face
of reality.

Poof, a poor figure with neither originality
nor grace, and the others too,
these inventions of yours,
guardian trees, mosaics, windows, dancing –

all absent. Reality and unreality
are your ways of looking into the pool
for the pool has neither.
The pool "has" nothing at all.

Some of you make your looking
into marks on a page and call it an object,
but see, it is absent, a memory,
perhaps a premonition,

and if it have
beauty or meaning, so
will the cedars
not growing in our woods.

A long time I have looked
in the pool. The surface
is placid again.
It has gathered together,

unformed, the light
that shines above the pebbles.
It will always
gather together.

› *Spring 1967*

The agitations of April in the sky
call down to you and earth quivers
underfoot as if the Eighth Avenue express
burrowed all the way to Vermont. Rain
soaks the fish-scale snow, the bloom
of beer cans emerges beside the road.
Another spring. You can think of nothing
that is not rotten, see nothing
not hideous. The sprung wicker chair
scarred with ice wrenches its way
in hysterical inaction across the yard.
You laugh, calculating the nostalgia
of people fifty years from now. Your mind
wrenches across the world, tearing the dirty
shimmer of blossom from every bough. Shedding
protoplasm, down on one leg, you strain
in the bloody mire, in the hysteria
of inaction . . .

Everything you make is taken from you,

repainted and displayed in the national exposition,
every word is stripped from you in the national tirade,
every gesture is absorbed in the national arm,
whatever you are disposed to think is already explained
in the national advertisement, and your being,
if you let yourself be,
is rung up *ping-ping* on the national cash register.
Your innocence is like cold spit in your mouth,
eject it or swallow it – you cannot
use it.
Your insane feet march
and numbers crawl on your skin. Everywhere
the spring lies darkening,
a monster birth whose besotted mother
stuffs it in the hole of time. April, May –
the green world shrivels like a napalm scab.

❯ *Coming Down to the Desert at Lordsburg, N. M.*

Stand there on the rock
of the mountain top
you man with a beard
so soon white-shot

you woman with pity
as old as the wars
you child with eyes
as young as the stars

behold this wind
southwestern sprung
that wrenches the desert
all month long

that blows out your pity
and blows out your eyes
and bleaches your beard
like the noon moonrise

behold the sand
the burning cloud
blown on the desert
like ash like gold

behold each other
your tender bones
strung in the wind
so long from home

then go down plunge
to the purge of sand
vanish together
hand in hand

❯ *Thaw*

. . . SONNET FOR ALLEN GINSBERG

fuzzed snow browning in lastyear's haystubble, the pasture's winter-starved moss
lionskin flung rumpled, moist, eaten, crushed eyes in the mange-fur
old leaves, world-flakes, eddy and sparrow-dance, get up they whimper
matter underfoot, sun's hairs, abandoned nests, coarse littleness, litter
mouse cry, shrew cry, snake-cry breaking against my ankles, set agony of small
      things, their glasslike sex
the stone's huge fame also, crevice-speaking, ancient in lichen, menhir for what
      slow generations gone –
and again I see the universe around me, decaying vision, mine so long and long,
      the filth of it
blowing mindless trash of stars, comets gasping down, space-dust
clouds of broken magnetism, bones of god-eaten nebulae
stirred in this warmish foreign wind, futile, useless – what good in it, ice will
      come again!
say
allen-what-do-they-call-you
mindpetal, spectre, strangest Jew, cityboy
farther from here than purple tao (far!), your little mousetrap books
clapping love insistent, my own fingers pained and pinched again after this time

look out, peer down, street under your high small window
greasy ginko, acacia, rubble, I don't know, not mine – do you see a wind? –
straw-rasp of papers, twigs shining? – what flows in your city, what stirs?
speak of it one more time for me, heart's cataclysm in the worn riffs of my years
in the beat of rote-pulse this new, this lifting, my pure impulse here
litany cracked open, wind across distance, a poke-through, such long ways
so that ragged solitude be warm, this pasture right for being –
right, right, and just, some cognizance, humanly, anything but heart-gape, void of
    misplacement –
this wind's connection come growling now low in the hills like the cityvoice,
    many-toned, horns and angers, terrors, far echoes, proceedings, prowling this
    way in lethean twistings, whispers among firs and spruces
or like smoke on the long wind, like pieces of the rims of circles come rippling up
    this long inlet –
yours dominantly there now, gingerly, your tender cupbearings, self-song, not
    strange to me
soft breathings hard against fact, sudden, like ben webster once, and valid,
    magnanimous –
o poet, ragged heartsinger, stranger and friend of mine!

❯ *Re-Acquaintance*

Kevin, Kevin Rooney, is it you?
come back like this in a title –

"For K. R. Who Killed Himself
in Charles Street Jail"

a poem by Gregory Corso/

            you, Kevin?
That day 15 years ago, front page *Mirror*
the unforgivable pix, you hanging there
face down in the barred iron corner
like a sad flag, you 'child of dark'
Corso calls you, and I say it too, Child of Dark –
I wanted to write something then for Chicago's sake,
nights of your most handsome Irish head asking

for poems nobody could write, nobody, such sorrows.
You held the automatic to your temple and pulled the
WHAM! – nothing happened, the damn thing wouldn't fire
so you waited two years, moved to the Village, and
did it in Charles Street with your belt.
                    I stood
reading the *Mirror*; not reading, looking; ward six.
You had written once to the asylum, a forlorn letter.
Now what could I write there, that wordless place?
I had a lousier day than usual, and a week later
electroshock wiped you out – until now –
now, Kevin, my Child of Dark. Drooped Flag.

❯ *Stepping Backward*

I waken and
    lean and look out
        to see the darkness
flee,
    sunken westward
        over curving earth,
departed
    like the long ocean
        running in tide
so fast and far
    it can never return
        or darken
this wide shore.

The last green star
    dies
        and the trees
lean in their green leaves
    westward
        as if in yearning
and then they straighten.

        I rise
            from my window
                thinking now

        the new words I must say
            as I step backward
                into day.

❯ *Green Mountain Idyl*

    Honey   I'd split your kindling
        clean & bright
    & fine
        if you was mine

    baby baby
        I'd taken to you like my silky hen
    my bluetick bitch my sooey sow
        my chipmunk   my finchbird
    & my woodmouse
        if you was living at my house

    I'd mulch your strawberries & cultivate
        your potato patch
    all summer long
        & then in winter
    come thirty below & the steel-busting weather
        I'd tune your distributor & adjust
    your carburetor
        if me & you was together

    be it sunshine be it gloom
        summer or the mean mud season
    honey I'd kiss you
        every morningtime
    & evenings I'd hurry
        to get shut of the barn chores early
    & then in the dark of the night

I'd stand at the top of the stairs & hold the light
for you   for you
    if you'd sleep in my room

& when old crazy come down the mountain after you
    with his big white pecker in his hand
you would only holler
    & from the sugarhouse
the mow   the stable
    or wherever I'm at
I'd come   god I'd come running to you
    like a turpentined cat

only in our bed
    honey
no hurting
    but like as if it was
git-music
    or new-baked bread
I'd fuck so easy
    sweet-talking & full of love
if you was just my daisy
    and my dove

> *Poetical Abstracts*

I. CHRONOLOGICAL
this moment/ 26th Sept/ snowdrops
blooming I suppose in Tasmania
& Zululand, and notes
of a nightinggale sprawling like waterdrops
down a bright valley floor
in Anatolia, somewhere a gibbon cries,
a cold surf beats

somewhere

all those possibilities once
calling,   and I knew
I would go, and now

losses, losses

He said, "Memory, the rose of time." She said,
"Ach, my mother, that old whore, believe me."
The poet said, "Hear the word 'poem' fraught
with time." And we listened, we heard it,
that's true, echoing, we listened courteously

to the undistinguishable roar like bees or stars
or a wailing in the loins. And the child said,
"Well, if it means all that to you, I will –
I'll pray for you. Is once a week enough?"
The bird said, "Look, look at my wailing
as it falls,   bright
    down the valley floor."
The old man said nothing.

"Nothing."

        a mote wriggling in a sunbeam
that falls through a bay window
among geraniums between white muslin curtains
onto a faded title behind the parlor glass
Mr. Britling Sees It Through

and the cat

2. METAPHYSICAL
fascination
o' jack-o'-lanterns

round livid fruit already dulling
sagging

on an autumnal doorstep
in a stone wind

leaf-waste and the chill
discussions of dust

the light inside gleaming
at all four windows of life

laughing
gusts of light

flickering, now guttering
and ah the darkness – but

it brightens and again
life quickens, comic

intelligence leaps out
a quirk on the dark until

it can leap no more
falls, the darkness

rushes in, tidal
over the smell

of snuffed wick and sweet
flesh overheated.

3. CLASSICAL

what the hen does
after
the axe falls

running like that
close to
the tilting ground

an athlete
pumping
spouting blood

one wouldn't say
it's her
most meaningful act

but what has she
ever
done more

winding down, toppling
wings crushed
meanwhile here's her head.

4. Rhopaloceral

When these two butterflies flutter upward toward the blue-white agatine sky, defining in their dance of sex the loose twining rope that gleams with vacancy in

the sun, my eyes frankly sink back and cannot climb with them: back to this end of the rope where the noose coils, dangles, calls.

Peculiar glitter, as of something false, associated with all symmetry. These two perfectly inversive wings; so bright, so fair to see. And those figures there, man and man, a face intent upon the surface of the pool.

Once a white butterfly made mirror-dancing with a white duck feather floating down the brook. Did I imagine that?

Two small azure butterflies dancing in a pool of dust by the road; from hill to opposing hill two chainsaws dissenting.

Wide blue sky. How many hundreds of centuries have men thought this the mirror of earth, as if our niggling particularities could be so smoothed and fused, instead of the mirror of what lies under the earth? We on the surface are in between, caught in a mighty reverberation of nothingness, shaken. Superficies. Powerless to deflect the organ tone that riddles us.

These are strange butterflies, brown and blue with spots of ivory; strangeness attracting special notice. Why not? I look into their symmetry as into a huge dim hall hung with tapestries on either side. I see that my imagination is the mirror of what lies there, out there; a mirror put into me like a foreign object. My being suffers anaphylaxis and tries to expel the irritant, but without success. It is I who am alien, I who am excluded. Symmetry is the sign of irrelation and death.

The function of self-consciousness is to carry, I mean literally to transport, these butterflies of the nonself. Can one think of any other? It is enslavement, granted. Why am I unconsoled to hear that my burden is only a butterfly?

When I thought to escape them they danced just outside the open window high over the city street, or rested opening and closing on the windowsill. When I hoped to join them they teased my clutching eyes across the country meadow, through the umbrageous woods.

Where am I? Not locus, but substantiation; not wherein nor whereon, but whereof. The crystal of windowpane contains, transports, transmits. I am "in" the lens of my eye. I am the veriest point of passage and reverberation.

O blue-brown-ivory twining upward into the wide sky, how marvelous that you sustain my dead weight hanging here!

5. INTROSPECTIONAL
of the shadow cast by earth in the sun's light
way way way far away away across

the void

and of the shadow cast by earth in the light
of a far faint opposing star, cast
like a pin   in
the depths of the sun

rise & turn & sit down & raise my head
& smile   and the dog
raises his head

& howls

« VII »

from

THE BLOOMINGDALE PAPERS

[1975]

(written in 1953)

In the exiled poet's room
Where Fear and the Muse keep watch by turn
while night comes on
that has no hope of dawn. . . .

– AKHMATOVA

> This all begins on a November day.

       •   •   •

I know there is a country where we go
Only adventuresomely, where the bears
With summer in their bellies sink to sleep,
Abatement, a subsidence of the will
Into warm lures and ardors of their dreams.
And here the wind veers to the cold northeast.
Another oak leaf makes a silent parting
And circles downward like a swinging gull
To the sea below. And everywhere this is
The time for shoulder-turning carelessly
After a pondering glance, the withdrawing time,
Time for the turning in and inward, time
For the long, long scrutabilities of the fire.
So rich and fearful are the dreams of winter
We never mourn the filmy world outside,
We even turn our anger from the door
That opens only for someone else's key
And from the windows and their iron bars.
Prison grows warm and *is* the real asylum.
And all the terrors of our inward journeys,
The grave indecencies, the loathsome birds,
Are goads to the strange bravery we muster,
We crippled, unbrave ones; and our hard days
Become as perilous as our quilted nights.
Into quiescence we pursue our killers;
Into fell lassitude we fight our way.
And never in our drowsy eyes appears
For an instant any boredom but the sharp
Unwearying tedium of this great despair.
These are the fascinations of our winter.

       •   •   •

       'Tis a fine deceit
To pass away in a dream; indeed, I've slept
With mine eyes open a great while.

・　・　・

In the hot high summer I came.
The heaven fumed, the earth seethed,
The leaves of the trees hung heavily,
So many moist hands.
For ten days we lived in a cauldron.
From the hot food we turned away.
And I was under constant observation, as we say;
I couldn't take my dull stomach
Off to the healing solitude of sorrow.
Or my dull heart.
Misery was deep and everywhere
Like a sea smothering us.
And even now I ask how I came here.
The shock, looking up to see these bars.
We, the new ones, milled elusively,
Watching each other for the dangerous sign,
Wondering who among us was the one who was truly mad.
And the heat burned through the night,
As burned the attendant's light where he watched,
Through the night spying our shudders,
Hearing our sighs . . .

The night broke with a scream, not mine.
But the possibility terrified me.
My belts and neckties were numbered and locked up at night,
My glasses taken away.
"Won't you play bridge?" asked the nurses.
"Checkers?" "Shuffleboard?" "Croquet?"
And the heat burned on through September.
The sun burned, the grass was burned.
Each morning we woke to terror and hid our heads.
At evening
Moths stove in hundreds against the screens.

The walls are of old brick, umber, tightly laid so that from a little distance one sees
        no mortar; the roofs are slate.

The windows are barred, but with grilles of curved ironwork to look less
     forbidding.

On the grounds are many trees; I have seen hemlock, spruce, white pine and
     scotch pine, white oak and red oak and blackjack, sassafras, tulip, elm,
     swamp maple and Norway maple, ironwood, birch, locust, shagbark
     hickory, apple and plum, and willows in the distance.

Virginia creeper, the institutional vine, clambers the walls and for a week in
     October looks like the longed-for fire.

Among the things which inmates are not permitted to possess are: razors, knives,
     matches, bottles, jewelry (even wedding rings are taken from those who wear
     them), cigarette lighters, tobacco cans, soap, or anything made from metal
     or glass.

Inmates must always ask for a light to be provided for their cigarettes, just as they
     must wait for a key to open every door; which makes for a great deal of
     business.

Inmates are prohibited from the use of the telephone, and all outgoing mail is read
     by the doctors.

The grounds, I am told, comprise 250 acres and include flower and kitchen
     gardens, an orchard, a golf course (for the staff), a pond (not in view)

The hospital is a large building with many wings which sprawls northward and
     southward for perhaps a quarter of a mile. It is divided between the Men's
     Side and the Women's Side.

All told, four hundred inmates or thereabouts and seven hundred employees
     compose this community.

At first there are no visitors; later the doctors usually allow members of the family
     to visit between 2:00 and 5:00 on Mondays and Fridays.

Next to the rare occasions of genuine thought and feeling, the particulars, remote
     from a beautifying image, of a way of life are important; the incidental reflec-
     tions are what we ought to do away with.

We rise at seven and go to bed at ten.

During the night there are inspections by the night-dwellers; we wake and jerk upright in the flashlight's glare.

One of the senior doctors, accompanied by the supervisor of nurses, makes an inspection round each morning and evening. At first the inmates greet the doctors with smiles, an attempt to seem cheerful and healthy; later they are sullen and silent and resentful; at last they are really exceedingly bored with all these good mornings and good evenings.

The Men's Side is separated into wards called "halls": numbered Eight, Seven, Six, Five, Four and Two.

Hall Eight is for the murderous ones, the hall of packs and jackets to which attendants from other halls are sometimes curtly summoned.

Hall Seven is for "disturbed" folk, the hall of voices and shadows.

Hall Six is the convalescent ward, where those who have been shocked or worn into uniformity and submission wait and wait; intolerable waiting. Tempers are short on Hall Six, and often inmates are sent back to another hall.

Hall Five is the hall of the aged, the senile; it is the nursery in which those singular children play for a time before they fall back to the womb.

Hall Four is the admitting hall, where everyone goes first. Some remain there many months.

Hall Two is the "open" hall; inmates there are given the freedom of the grounds (during the day only and in a restricted area not including the golf course), and many receive "passes" on weekends.

There is an "Annex" too, somewhat mysterious. For the rhapsodists, the wolf people?

The Women's Side – the other side of the moon.

Pity not Ulysses, but the ear-stopped rowers.

The Shock Room is next to the Hydrotherapy Room.

Each hall is equipped with a radio and a television set and about 25 inmates; some
have pianos and billiard tables.

Many are committed here through the courts, and we have much talk of lawyers
and writs and injunctions to restrain. We have many sea-lawyers.

The others commit themselves, so wretched are they.

"Hey Gin-head, twenty points for a pack of butts!" – an invitation to billiards.

·   ·   ·

> Aw, Dylan, have you left us? Have you gone?
> An evil day it is. A day unblest.
> My skin crept with the shiver of the air
> This morning, it was a dark, reluctant dawn.
> Another morning nohow the stars did stare
> When our daft company jollified the west.
> But Jim went south, and Harry's God knows where,
> I'm in the loony bin, and you are gone.
>
> Aye, Dylan, tides there are to waft us all,
> But you especially that blood and ink
> Named for the seas your christening was your call.
> They say you died at St. Vincent's. Is it so?
> I'd have sworn you perished in the bloody drink.
> But deeper oceans flood the land; we know,
> We crazy ones, how strong those waters flow.
> If only you hadn't tried to drink it all.
>
> And, Dylan, if the hills and woods of Wales
> Still sound, as I've been told, with ancient song,
> If winds there sputter Merlin's prophecies,
> That is the land where Welshmen all belong.
> It is an upland country, steep and strong,
> Stemming a sea whose changing voice assails
> The solitary heart. I think you please
> To rest now in your song at home in Wales.

. . .

The diagnosis is
Anxiety psychoneurosis
(Chronic and acute)
Complicated by
Generalized phobic
Extensions and alcoholism.
Which is meaningless,
Even in clinical usage.
No doubt the files
Contain a description
In more precise language.
The fact is I am here,
Having collapsed, because
I can't be anywhere else –
The case with most of us.
And because the terrors
Which clutch and shake me,
The drink which wards them off,
Equally reduced me
To inaction, paralysis,
And extreme pain. I came
To the bin for the same
Essential reason anybody,
Injured in a fortuitous
Blast, goes to hospital. This
Place is supposed to help me.
But it's difficult, obtuse.
I may be walking in
Some placid sunny street,
Perfectly free and at ease,
Nonchalant you might say,
When the terror strikes –
Or rises or debouches or whatever.
It seizes me, whop!
Very fast. First, tension
In legs and neck, the flutter
Of hand to head; then

The general tremor, upheaval,
Sense of wobbling, falling;
Then panic, desperation.
To run, to fly, to sink —
To escape: an absolute command.
Fear of screaming, the sound
Bulging in the throat.
Heart-gasp and darkness
At the edge of the eyes.
Fear of fear. Terror is
Such a humiliating spectacle.
In busses, offices, theaters,
Shops, country roads and
Lonely woods, everywhere
But in beds and barrooms.
William James spoke
Of the experience and ascribed
It to an acute perception
Of evil — or some such;
I have no books. Yes,
Perception is involved,
A sharp sensory receptivity
To almost hidden things,
And evil of course is also
Involved for you learn quickly
In fear nature's rapacities.
But it is more and less
Than that. More, because you
Track it down the fathering
Years as through a labyrinth
And encounter details,
So many inflowering
Centripetal courses of
Behavior, all related, all
Parts of a dreadful design
Which you can annotate
In terms of debasement and
Analyze in terms of cause

And effect. Less, because
You lose the powerful image,
The demon, the worm; you are
An ignoramus after all;
Worse, you are an ignoramus
Superior to James.

                .   .   .

To dig at Luxor, to peer
At the sky from Mount Wilson,
To hunch in Paris over
A Sumerian fragment or in
Princeton over the eternal
Deceptions of measurement –
These are the occupations
Of men I admire and envy.
These are the dreams in which
Men lose themselves, the dreams
Of objectivity. Vanity
Becomes so needful to them
That no one calls them vain,
And they themselves think
To add something to the cubits
Of the world. Fascinating
And in no way criminal,
That mode of life, and weakness
Asks no more.
                    Herodotus
Saw farther than most without
Really looking very hard.
It's what one wants that counts.

I don't mean to say
There weren't good times.
The bad predominated.
Booze helped immensely.
Work also, but not,
Unfortunately, writing.
Friends and parties and lovers

Lent ease to my unease
Sparingly. The doctors kept
The anxious pot aboil.
So passed the years.
When I say they were filled
With disaster I am not
Joking, not by a damn sight;
Tragedy hasn't gone from
Our lives, even if the meanness
Of the cultural environment
Prevents us from believing it.
The disasters were seen by many,
The consequences are palpable.
Time healed nothing.
Nor has it ever, though death
Has. The two are not to be
Confused. The years passed.
After the hurts, the fears,
After the fears, the escapes,
After the escapes, the despairs.
My solicitous friend, Dr. Gin,
Came often to my house.
The house closed in; I,
My cat, and my poor girl
Watched the world gibber
And clung to the tilting floor.
The birds swam dreamily
Past the windows, and somewhere
A siren wailed incessantly.
The city was enormous,
And our cell broken down and
Unnoticed in all the wreckage.
But at last a dear lady
Of mercy came to help me.
And I found myself here
In the hot time of the year.

•   •   •

December now. Winter deepens and darkens. Stars
Shine distantly in the trees when we return
From Gym at five o'clock, reminding us,
Not of our smallness – only abstractions are large –
But of our loneliness on this lost planet.
And in the morning hoarfrost lies on the hemlocks,
And white rime glitters on my window's bars.
The winds roam endlessly among our wings and ells,
Massive old choirs singing their desolation.
Within, the drafts play coldly through our halls.
I write in my small cell at a table placed
Before the window, the only space I have,
And my hands are stiff and cold. Mongolia where
These winds originate seems bleak and hostile.
Thin snow sifts on the hard pavement there,
Stone buildings rise like towers of ice.
Bitter, bitter blows the wind in those streets,
Freezing poor faces like anesthesia,
Blinding poor eyes with winter's tears. I see
The girls with thin-clad legs and hunched shoulders
Who scurry and jitter and tremble and stand and weep:
How unlovely they are, all bleary and pinched.
I think of their clay-cold breasts and their blue knees.
The men too, with drops at the ends of their noses –
Their hands hurt, as if they were made of money.

The age of wonders. Who would have thought the dream
Of luxury could live in those freezing heads?

What shall I say? What shall I do?
The place I call Mongolia is home.
There I was born, there I remained for more
Than thirty years, not different from the others.
I also walked those freezing streets, and the cold
Sank in my skull and swished against my ankles.
I found sometimes a curious joy in knowing
The pain of life, in being one of the many
Who tinkled grimly down the cold steps to hell
On the Lexington Avenue line.

The bitcheries of Madison Avenue
Where I lost my mind, where pigs that learned to read
Talk moneywise around the urn of love;
The stink of certain senators that reaches,
As in Chicago every nose perceives
The stockyards on a foggy day, across
The country, fouling every wind; the creamy
Excrement of Hollywood; the noise
Which fulsome sentiment emits in moans
And wailings – falsely imitating war –
Wherever our sick young assemble; the goads
And insults of the advertising writers;
The insipidities of bread and beer
And all the goods of this commercial era;
The slattern minds that waste away the schools
And foul the house of thought with personal lust –
The catalogue of our misfortunes, oh
How long it is, so have the false men prospered!
Yet for the sight of red-winged blackbirds in
The spring, and for their song, and for
The sight and song of love, I kept at home
And said Mongolia was my proper country.

But leaving, had that country, I look back
With loathing deeper than ever I thought to feel.

•   •   •

The rule of the majority is
strictly enforced in all matters
concerning the television set.
Whereas one might suppose that
we should look at "Suspense"
nine times and something else
once, in fact we see "Suspense"
ten times – those who can bear

to see it. The sound reaches
to the farthest cell. No less
than sedition to suggest that
the damn thing be turned off.
Listen, fossils, the faucet
drips other distractive meters.
Could a wrench stop tears?
I'd tighten my eyeballs
sideways. But everywhere
white dominates, like hate
in a quiet woman full of waiting.

Prizefight. Heavyweight
championship. We are permitted
to stay up past curfew, a special
occasion. Dark room, spectral
light. How tension grips me,
violence without and within.
Heart hammers, heaves. Images
flare in a gust of light.
Long before knockout I retreat
and lie in my cell in the dark
hidden, trembling, the loser.

⋅　　⋅　　⋅

Once on a night in spring
                    I remember
I sat at the end of the long curving jetty
whose base is attached to the city of Chicago –
that is to say, it bends into Lake Michigan
                    from North Avenue.
I had turned my back to the city
                    and I watched the stars.
It was a night to think of poems to write.
Then, weary of poems, I sprawled back
letting my head hang upsidedown from the pier.
I looked toward Chicago, the lake was above me.
In the watery sky the city shone and glimmered.

Up, up it reached, tower on tower, into
the black depths
where fishes with alien intelligence kept
motionless company.
And earth below me was strewn with stars.
Oh it was a dancing delicate rippling world,
so bright, gaiety beyond noise and laughter,
in the water of all souls' drowning.
Deeply it rose, darkly it shone, and I drew
breaths of cool water, coming alive in that world.
But magnificently a fish jumped, and the city
flew apart, sparks in the wind,
and only the stars were still.

. . .

Expectantly and fearfully I sing.
A bird must walk that has a broken wing.

. . .

For thon demgeorne dreorigne oft
In hyra breostcofan bindath faeste.

The gathering fog closes. Rust,
The winter's disease, spreads
Like a cloak of blood on the metal.
Little waves stir under the wharf.
Only the terns work, plying
A swift traffic outward and inward.
The bell-buoy chimes in the harbor,
January's song, and the fog is cold.
We fear the coming of ice to our harbor.

One has spoken to me of conflict.
He has scarred my mind with his voice.
His hands made structures in the air.
Somehow he has found an old diary
I wrote and had forgotten,
Stiff pages and a childish scrawl.
Of provenance he spoke, and growth,

And he told me in his soft voice
Of the wasted years, the losses
Mounting when I strove and loved.
I listened, too weary to protest.

Vanity hath betrayed me.
Yes, I dreamt of deeds.
I ventured, I journeyed.
I dreamt of the love of fair ladies.
I found them, I wore their scarves.
My dreaming, hours by the iris when sun
Awakened the marshland
And the red-winged blackbird sang,
Were the attainable contentment,
Had I been content. Vanity hath
Destroyed me, fierce seignior.
Thy will hath destroyed me.

Striving for goodness against
The evil within me,
Striving for love against
The hatred within me,
Striving for peace against
The hunger within me,
I waged honorable war.
I am the victor. I established
The right. My spoils were sorrow.

As a great nation wars,
Mustering all citizens and all wealth,
To rescue those who are truly
Pitiable, even at the expense
Of many lives, of anguish, perhaps
Of smaller nations; so the
Individual makes conquest
Of himself, coercing the base animal
To right action, and the victory

Destroys his fortitude, his balance,
And perhaps those he has loved.

Retreat. Pray for forgiveness.

All you whom I have violated
Out of your great goodness forget me.
You whom I have destroyed . . .

Remember, we concurred, we agreed.

After the battle the wounded rest,
And useless honor is accorded them.

.   .   .

In deep winter the sea roams
Menacingly under the fog.
It roars through the quick gaps in the whiteness,
Then is muffled again.
Icebergs may loom, waves of mountainous force,
Ghosts may inhabit the fog.

The anchor-chain creaks.
The terns cry in the fog,
Voices of distress, dying
A flower of drenched feathers
Comes in on the sloping tide.
The sea gives us many mementoes.

Memories circle and sweep outward and die.
Each tide brings to this harbor
Many corpses. And the harbor folk
Give flowers to the sea,
Wreathes flung to the vagrant waves.

On this ship the rust grows
Like moss on a ledge by the forest.

Fog lies on the sea and the deck.
Sound of lapping water, sound
Of rats' teeth busy. Candles
Saved from their ravening
Illumine a white face.

Shuffle, deal. Patience by candlelight.
The world rocks on the swinging sea.

    •   •   •

Hall Five

The window bars are spider webs
    Where live our ancient folk,
The clock no longer keeps the time
    And chimes with a random stroke.

The faces gathered in that gloom
    Are often wet with tears
For joy and melancholy rise
    Quickly at ninety years.

And Georgie beats the tom-tom, Dick
    Draws horsies in the dust,
And Buddy Boy from San Antone
    Sings songs of his deep disgust.

The millionaire looks up, surprised
    That this should come to men,
And cries until the nurse can come
    And make him dry again.

The Palace of the Doges hangs,
    A tinted photograph,
Above the broken lamp that looks
    Like a tumbledown giraffe.

The boo lives under the billiard table
    And makes his gentle moan,
At night the wambus flies the hall
    Where he has always flown.

So much has been forgotten that
    We sometimes think perhaps
They have forgotten everything,
    But no, the little lapse

From dreaming lets a memory in,
    And then the old men swoon
And say, "Dear friend, come easily,
    And please, dear friend, come soon."

                .   .   .

Words for My Daughter from the Asylum

Alas, that earth's mere measure strains our blood
And makes more airy still this parentage.
The bond is all pretending, and you sleep
When my affections leap
And gasp at old hope vainly in my night's cage.

Dear marvelous alien snippet, yes, you move
Like a down-raining cloud in my mind, a bird
Askim on low planes under lightning thought,
An alter-image caught
In gossamer seed, my most elusive word.

There must be some connection, more than mood,
The yearning wit of loneliness, and more
Than meets the law on that certificate.
Strangers do not create
Alliances so deep and dark and sore.

Yet we are strangers. I remember you
When you began, a subtle soft machine;
And you remember me, no, not at all,

Or maybe you recall
A vacancy where someone once was seen.

I can address you only in my mind
Or, what's the same, in this untouching poem.
We are the faceless persons who exist
Airily, as a gist
Of love to twist the staid old loves of home.

Strangers we are, a father and a daughter,
This Hayden and this Martha. And this song,
Which turns so dark when I had meant it light,
Speaks not at all of right
And not at all, since they are dim, of wrong.

Distance that leaves me powerless to know you
Preserves you from my love, my hurt. You fare
Far from this room hidden in the cold north;
Nothing of me goes forth
To father you, lost daughter, but a prayer.

That some small wisdom always may endure
Amidst your weariness; that lovers may
Be kind to you; that beauty may arouse
You; that the crazy house
May never, never be your home: I pray.

from

BROTHERS,
I LOVED YOU ALL
[1978]

> *The Loon on Forrester's Pond*

Summer wilderness, a blue light
twinkling in trees and water, but even
wilderness is deprived now. "What's that?
What is that sound?" Then it came to me,
this insane song, wavering music
like the cry of the genie inside the lamp,
it came from inside the long wilderness
of my life, a loon's song, and there he was
swimming on the pond, guarding
his mate's nest by the shore,
diving and staying under
unbelievable minutes and coming up
where no one was looking. My friend
told how once in his boyhood
he had seen a loon swimming beneath his boat,
a shape dark and powerful
down in that silent mysterious world, and how
it had ejected a plume of white excrement
curving behind. "It was beautiful,"
he said.

The loon
broke the stillness over the water
again and again,
broke the wilderness
with his song, truly
a vestige, the laugh that transcends
first all mirth
and then all sorrow
and finally all knowledge, dying
into the gentlest quavering timeless
woe. It seemed
the real and only sanity to me.

❯ When Howitzers Began

When howitzers began
    the fish darted downward
to weeds and rocks,
    dark forms motionless
in darkness, yet they were
    stunned and again
stunned
    and again and
again stunned, until their
    lives loosened, spreading
a darker darkness
    over the river.

❯ August First

Late night on the porch, thinking
of old poems. Another day's
work, another evening's,
done. A large moth, probably
Catocala, batters the screen,
but lazily, its strength spent,
its wings tattered. It perches
trembling on the sill. The sky
is hot dark summer, neither
moon nor stars, air unstirring,
darkness complete; and the brook
sounds low, a discourse fumbling
among obstinate stones. I
remember a poem I wrote
years ago when my wife and
I had been married twenty-
two days, an exuberant
poem of love, death, the white
snow, personal purity. Now
I look without seeing at

a geranium on the sill;
and, still full of day and evening,
of what to do for money,
I wonder what became of
purity. The world is a
complex fatigue. The moth tries
once more, wavering desperately
up the screen, beating, insane,
behind the geranium. It
is an immense geranium,
the biggest I've ever seen,
with a stem like a small tree
branching, so that two thick arms
rise against the blackness of
this summer sky, and hold up
ten blossom clusters, bright bursts
of color. What is it – coral,
mallow? Isn't there a color
called "geranium?" No matter.
They are clusters of richness
held against the night in quiet
exultation, five on each branch,
upraised. I bought it myself
and gave it to my young wife
years ago, a plastic cup
with a 19¢ seedling
from the supermarket, now
so thick, leathery-stemmed,
and bountiful with blossom.
The moth rests again, clinging.
The brook talks. The night listens.

❯ *That I Had Had Courage When Young*

Yet had I not much
who went out – out! – among those
heartless all around, to look
    and talk sometimes and touch?

In the big lunatic house
I did not fly apart nor spatter
the walls with myself, not quite.
    I sat with madness in my mouth.

But never was it ever enough.
Else how could all these books
I did not write bend down my back
    grown now so old and tough?

❯ *Essay*

So many poems about the deaths of animals.
Wilbur's toad, Kinnell's porcupine, Eberhart's squirrel,
and that poem by someone – Hecht? Merrill? –
about cremating a woodchuck. But mostly
I remember the outrageous number of them,
as if *every* poet, I too, had written at least
one animal elegy; with the result that today
when I came to a good enough poem by Edwin Brock
about finding a dead fox at the edge of the sea
I could not respond; as if permanent shock
had deadened me. And then after a moment
I began to give way to sorrow (watching myself
sorrowlessly the while), not merely because
part of my being had been violated and annulled,
but because all these many poems over the years
have been necessary – suitable and correct. This
has been the time of the finishing off of the animals.
They are going away – their fur and their wild eyes,
their voices. Deer leap and leap in front
of the screaming snowmobiles until they leap
out of existence. Hawks circle once or twice
above their shattered nests and then they climb
to the stars. I have lived with them fifty years,
we have lived with them fifty million years,
and now they are going, almost gone. I don't know
if the animals are capable of reproach.
But clearly they do not bother to say good-bye.

The Joy and Agony of Improvisation

There, the moon, just appearing
over dark pines, heavy and round,
the color of old parchment; and indeed
it seems archaic. What does it mean
in our histories, yours and mine,
except a myth no longer altogether
necessary, a theorem proven in another
millennium? This is a peculiar night,
uncomfortable. Well, it is like most moments
of the present, it doesn't fit us.
The low night wind, shifting, directionless,
moves the pine boughs, as if – so you say –
we were in the midst of voices in some
obscure contention. Of course we are.
But not obscure, only fruitless, stupid,
and very dangerous. Come,
let's go in the tent and sleep.

Later
we waken, knowing the night has changed.
It's a high wind now. Strange how the voices
have turned to song. Hear
it rising, rising, then breaking, then
rising again, and breaking again. Oh, something
is unutterable, the song cannot reach it.
Yet we know it, know what we cannot
hear – out on the night's great circle,
the circle of consciousness with its far rim always
hidden, there where suffering and joy
meet and combine,
the inexpressible. How the song is striving
and how beautifully failing – the measure
of beauty, beyond plenitude,
never but always enough. Come
outside again, under tossing pines
and the racing clouds. This
is more than we could ever have meant

in our kiss; it is the gathering of our love
into all love, into that suffering and joy.
And see, up there in the sky, uncovered now
as the clouds stream away,
the moon,
so new, so clean and high and bright and true.

❯ *My Hut*

AFTER TRAN QUANG KHAI

Built long ago, old
sills rotting in mud,
filled now with soft ash
from a thousand fires that warmed me,
ash settled indelibly
on these books, never
to be clean again,
and on these shoulders
and hands.

❯ *In Memoriam*

This warmish night of the thaw
in January a beech chunk
smoldering in my Herald
No. 22A box stove suddenly
takes fire and burns
hot, or rather I suddenly
who was reading the sweet
and bitter poems of Paul
Goodman dead last summer
am aware how my shed
becomes a furnace, and taking
my shovel I ladle
a great mush of snow
into the stove's mouth

to quieten it
and then step quickly
outside again to watch
the plume of steam rise
from my stovepipe straightly
and vanish into the mist.

❯ *The Little Fire in the Woods*

Even these stones I placed crudely once,
black now from many fires, bring me
a little knowledge, things I've done,
times endured, saying I am this one, this
person, as night falls through the trees. I see sand
darkening by the edge of an ocean, lights
on the rim of a galaxy, but I have not planned

my visions. I wish I could. We used birch bark
and spruce cones for tinder tonight, in which
a spark rambled until it met itself, flaring then
and leaping, throwing shadows among the trees.
Now punky gray birch smolders. Held
in the roots of our great spruce, I hold
my son, and the darkness thickens. It isn't

the cares of day I think of any longer.
True, I got this bruised belly when the machine
kicked this afternoon in our troubled potato patch
where the earth too cried out for justice,
justice! I tauten my muscles; the pain
is good and I wish it could be everything. But
larger errors are what we think of now

that have flared and leapt and thrown these shadows
of extinction among our objects. Or is the error
necessity, a circle closing? Son, in nature all
successions end. How long and slow is chaos.
Anywhere I am I see the slow surge of fire –

I, a diffraction, nothing. My son moves
closer. "Pop, how does the fire make heat?"

He does not see the fire I see, but I know
he knows a terror that children have never
known before, waiting for him. He knows.
Our love is here, this night, these woods, existing;
it is now. I think how its being
must emanate, like heat in conversion,
out beyond the woods to the stars, and how

it joins there in the total reckoning. It *must*.
Could anyone resist this longing all the time?
Oh, I know what I know, and I cannot
unknow it, crying out too for justice,
while the fire dwindles and shadows rise and flow.
But listen, something is here in the forest. Listen.
It is very clear and it whispers a little song:

       Sweet Bo I know thee
                  thou art ten
       and knowest now thy father is
       five times more again
                  and more
       and most gone out of rhymes
       sweet Bo
             for thou dost know me.

       And thou old spruce above us
       many are they of comrade and kin
       who love us
                so that their loving proveth
       everything
                although their way hath not
       the same compassion
              as thy nonloving.

       Sweet Bo good night and hold me
       hold me close

```
                    the good firelight
        is dying
                the woods are sighing
        and great is the dark
                        grateful
        am I for thee sweet Bo
                            good night
        good night.
```

❯ *The Mountain Cabin*

Hour by hour the storm deepened. He read,
not much, less than most days, and watched

the wind driving the snow in its circle,
mountain to mountain, forty miles around.

He was o.k., nothing wrong. But he knew
– and knew he could not stop knowing –

he was trapped, couldn't go down, would lose
his trail in storm, the red-gashed blazes

blown out. He'd end in the lowland thickets,
frozen. Today what he had chosen

had chosen him. He tended the stove,
refilled the kettle with snow, drank tea, watched

blue smoke from his stovepipe twist downward
with writhing swiftness into the trees,

recounted his cigars, shuffled the letters
he'd brought to answer. Whiteness

trickled under the door, hoarfrost grew
on the nailheads. He tested the harness

of his snowshoes, cold greased leather.
At sunset unexpected color-of-pewter

shone for five minutes in the western notch.
Then he lit the lamp. It flickered, teased

by the wind hunting through the walls,
so that the glass blackened and the flame,

without shrinking, became remote, an orange
specter. He listened. Now at night

the storm seemed unrelated, an absolute,
the unseen whole of otherness out there.

His light was a dusky ovoid floating
at the top of the lamp on darkness.

In time he got up, stiff and cold,
and leaned over the lamp and blew it out.

❯ *Family Reunion*

Gathered at the time of thanks; and the harvest
is gathered in, and earth and sky are cold,
the standing weeds are brown; and the lady

of the house is tremblingly brown and old
who had once grown like a flower, and the third son,
in his rich suit as soft as summer, smiles

his dear smile, and smiles and smiles, till it fades
to the haggard smile of freezing and pallor
and deep hidden pain, and the second son

moves heavily and laughs heavily, the gray
specter of the lady's husband who is dead,
and the first son who has come the longest way

smiles awkwardly in a head gone out of true
and made of fearful crookedness, and he wonders
what harvest, what harvest now; and the children

are forgotten upstairs in God knows what old games,
and the wives recede adroitly to another room,
and the dog walks among the smiles, sniffs them

for their aroma of things found in the field
and rolls in them; and later, when all is done,
the first son sits under the family clock on the mantel

that is older than them all, and he looks in the dark
window to see whose face is there, and the clock
walks in its place, a dreadful steady tread,

step, step, step, where it has always walked,
and the first son looks at the ashtrays, the glasses
redolent of ceremonial whiskey and wine,

the chairs out of their places, and the lines of his head
plot strange diagrams on the window; and thanks,
he says, thanks, thanks, not said but shouted

in the outcry of hours, protesting stars and the moon,
and the sleepless clock says it too, thanks once,
thanks twice, thanks three o'clock, and the man,

who is the sleepless first son from farthest away,
says thanks, thanks again, thanks just the same.
What more could he, what more would you have him, say?

❯ *The Mountain*

Black summer, black Vermont. Who sees
this mountain rising nearby
in the darkness? But we

know it there. On the other side
in a black street of a black city
a man who is probably black

carries a Thompson
submachine gun, and don't
tell me how that feels

who carried one two years
in Italy; blunt-barreled power,
smooth simple unfailing mechanism

– the only gun whose recoil
tugs you forward, toward
the target, almost

like love. Separated
by this immense hill we share nevertheless
a certain knowledge of tactics

and a common attitude toward reality.
Flickering neon, like moonlight in beech leaves,
is fine camouflage. To destroy

can be beautiful.
I remember Mussolini's
bombed statues by the *dopo lavoro* pavilion,

thick monsters transformed to elegance
by their broken heads and cut-off
arms. Let the city be transformed.

A man with a submachine gun is
invulnerable, the sniper's
sharp little steel or the fist

of a grenade always
finds him surprised. Hey,
look out, man! What you

trying to do, get yourself
killed? They're everywhere, everywhere,
hear? – the night's

full of them and they're looking
for a dead nigger – so watch it,
go on fox feet and listen like a bat:

remember everything I told you.
You got to be smart enough
for both of us now.

But are you there? Are you
really there?

❯ *Essay on Stone*

April abomination, that's what I call
this wet snow sneaking down day after day,
   down the edges of air, when we
     were primed for spring.

The flowers of May will come next week – in theory.
And I suppose that witty sentimentalist,
   Heine, saw this same snow falling
     in the North Sea

as into the Abyss. I look out now across
this pasture, the mud and the matted grass,
   the waving billows of it, where
     the snow is falling

as into our own abyss. I stand on Marshall's
great rock, to which I have returned, fascinated,
   a thousand times. I stand as if
     on a headland

or on an islet in the midst of waves,
and what is this fascination, this cold desire?
    Once I wrote a poem about
      making love to stone

and a whole book in which the protagonist,
who was myself, carried a stone with him
    everywhere he went. I still like
      that poem and that book,

and yet for all my years of stone-loving
I've learned not much about stone. Oh, I
    can tell slate from quartz from sandstone –
    – who couldn't? – and here

in this district we even have an exotic
stone, the talc, that feels warm and bloody
    in one's hand, but basically I am
      ignorant. Let

the geologists keep their igneous pyrites
to themselves. I don't even know if
    this great rock, projecting
      bigger than a barn

from the slope of the pasture, is a free
boulder that may have come here from the top
    of Butternut Mountain who knows
      how many eons ago,

or part of the underlying granite of Vermont.
I stand on its back, looking into the abyss.
    At all events the fascination
      is undeniable. I

always said there could be no absolutes,
but this is stone, stone, stone –
    so here, so perfectly
      here. It is

the abyss inverted, the abyss made visible.
Years ago when I wrote that other poem
   I might have taken pleasure from this,
     I think I would have. Now

I am fifty-three going on fifty-four,
a rotten time of life. My end-of-winter clothes
   are threadbare, my boots cracked, and how
     astonishing to see

my back, like that figure in Rembrandt's drawing,
bent. I shift weight on my walking-stick
   and the stick slips in wet lichen
     and then my boots skid too,

and down I go – not hurt, just shaken.
And what a hurt that is! Is it consoling
   to know I might have fallen
     into the abyss?

All this in silence, every word of it spoken
in my mind. The snow falls. Heine,
   there must be something wrong with us.
     I've heard this pasture

moaning at my feet for years, as you heard
that gray sea, we two shaken and always
   unconsoled by what we love,
     the absolute stone.

  ❯ *Valentine*

     That you should still send
     yourself to me, that you should
     arrive and attend like this
     when there is no reason, when
     actually there may be

contrary reasons, remains
the one phenomenon to me
most wonderful. Please,
lie back a moment, raise
your arm. I love to see

how the heart buries its
point in your groin, so dearly,
though it would be nothing
without its upward rounding
and flectioning over your

belly. Don't you believe
what you've been told, that now
valentines are grievous, all
the more for those as old
as we are? Still you come,

still you present this heart
with its swelling curves.
In wintertime I work
all night for quiet and then
go out to watch the dawn,

how February's bright stars
fade so that only knowing –
the mind – can tell they're there.
Strange that the light should be
a concealment. Yet I think

that's how it is with us, we
who are "enlightened," who know
sex and the hurt of sex,
yes, the era's learning, so
necessary. But still the older

and farther, farthest lights
shine behind the day, there
for our minds, or something

in us, to remember. Sweetly,
smilingly, when I come in

you throw the covers back,
an unconcealment, sending
from sleep your valentine
in the light the windows shed,
ice laced, on your warm bed.

❯ *Once and Again*

The peace of green summer lay over this meadow so deeply once
that I thought of England, cows lazy on the sward, the great elm
rising above them in diaphanous arches, the meadow that Marvell might have
    seen
from his study window but that I have never seen, yet I saw it
here. It *was* here, but that so long ago. And now the elms
of this region have mostly died, it is mid-November, the gray season,
purple on wooded hills, the meadow is gray and bare, the cows
are in their barn. I thought of England because so many things I love
have come from England, many images in my memory, although
I have never been there and have little hope that I will ever go.
I stand in the grayness, searching, looking for something without knowing what,
until I remember the great elm that used to be. To believe in the God
who does not exist is a heroism of faith, much needed in these times,
I agree, I know, especially since the hero is and must always be
unrecognized. But to love the God that does not exist, to love the love
that does not exist, this is more than heroism, it is perhaps almost
saintliness, such as we can know it. To discover and to hold, to resurrect
an idea for its own sake. Ah my heart, how you quicken in unrecognized energy
as hard little pellets of snow come stinging, driven on the gray wind.

❯ *November Jeans Song*

Hey, hey, daddio,
Them old jeans is
    Going to go!

Rose Marie done put in a new
     Valve cover gasket,
Them jeans good for a whole nother
     10,000 mile.

Man the wood them jeans cut,
And split and trucked and stacked,
     No wonder the axe
Been yearning and drooping
Like the poor lone gander
     For them old jeans.

Look out, get set, let
     The woods take warning.
     Come six in the morning
     Me and them jeans is back,
What I mean *ready*,
We going to go
And don't care nothing for nobody,
               baby,
     Not even the snow.

❯ *Simple*

Looking back 25 years I
     imagine it simple
(the reality being so
     uselessly complex),

how we made a pier, a jetty
     of lights, a brightness
in that fantastic dark,
     down which we took our way

to the vessel that lay in the
     shadows. We stood
a moment, looking here or there,
     and then you stepped aboard

as if this were perfectly
    natural, and I turned
back into the knowledge of going
    crazy from loneliness.

The lights went out, the pier
    vanished, the vessel
became a kind of legend
    of a ship beating

Oriental seas. Looking
    back I imagine
how I retired to a room
    I built, perhaps

a kiva lit by reflections
    of the moon, where I
celebrated over and over
    the trembling mysteries

of loss. I became a living
    brain in an effigy
of reeds and cloth and paint,
    completely insane.

❯ *John Dryden*

Dry they call him, and dry is what he hopes
never to be, though springwater is all his drink
six nights after the welfare comes, and most
all his feed too, I sometimes think – though once
I saw him bring down a hare at seven rods
with a stone, and it didn't look lucky either.
When I asked him if he knew a famous poet
had the same name, he looked at me not quite
contemptuously; and yet I took a while to see
his scorn wasn't because he was smarter than I'd
credited – for a fact he can't read but about

half what's printed on the welfare check – but rather
because he'd been asked so damn many times before
and he figured I should have known. I should have too.
Dry is not dumb. He's only crazy. Well, anyway
that's the general impression around the Plot,
which is what they call this section. My neighbor
rounds up her kids and locks her door when Dry
comes striding and caroling up the hill from town
in his outsize rummage pants with a carton
of grub held like an offering in both arms and his coat
gone slantywise from the fifth of sauterne
in his pocket. Paranoid, I'd say. There's more
than a few in these mountains, and sometimes I'm not
just certain about myself. But I know Dry.
I know he hasn't worked four consecutive days
on any one job in fifteen years. That's
indicative. Once we were haying up at Marshall's
and Dry took offense because a car with a shield
on the door drove in the barnyard and Dry thought
Marshall was telling the CIA on him, and he
came after Marshall and me with his hayfork,
chasing us round the tractor, his face dead white
like snow that's thawed and frozen again; he did,
and it wasn't funny either. My kidneys ached
for two hours after from thinking about that fork.
Finally he saw he couldn't catch us. He thew down
the fork and marched off, straight as a bee, over
the meadow, the pasture, the orchard, the fence, and was gone.
That year Marshall and I made the rest of the hay
alone. One time Gilbert told how he and Dry
were cutting sugarwood for old man Saunders
up toward Codding Hollow, and Dry took one
of his spells and came after Gilbert with the axe,
and Gilbert yanked quick on his chainsaw string and remarked,
"Dry, you damn fool, listen here – just you set down
that thing, or by the jumping Jesus Christ
I'll cut off both your arms." Dry set it down,
about three inches into a black birch stump, and marched
straight as a bee over brakes and brambles,

hobblebush and thornapple, and he was gone.
Which may be indicative too; he can be "took"
right sudden, but when he's licked he knows it.
And he's a fair hand at marching. He told me once
how it was here forty years back. "Them days
was cruel," he said, "awful cruel. Things was
turning on a slow reel" – and he made a motion
like so, like the bobbins down to the woollen mill
when they run half-speed. "Why, hell," he said,
"I had one of them five dollar gold certificates,
you remember? I felt like I was rich, and I was too,
but I spent it running the cunt. And it come back,
and I spent it again, and it come back again,
so help me over and over till the damn thing
wore itself out – I carried the pieces for years.
But they're gone now." One time Dry vanished,
clean gone, no on knew where and don't know yet,
but when he came back I met him up in the woods
and he stood on a spruce log and threw out his arms
and said, "God, Hayden, it's Moxie in the can,
being back on this here goddamn mountain again!"
And he laughed. The last what you could call steady
job Dry had, as far as I know, was 1945
down at the rendering plant in Burlington where he
slugged cows with an axe and pushed their guts
through a hole in the floor all day. "Stink? Jesus,
I guess I stunk! Like a she bear in whistling time,
but I made good money. Forty a week, and that
wan't bad in them days; but I spent it all
running the cunt, every dime. Why, I got
throwed out of five flea-bag rooming houses
and I wan't even drunk, just owed the landlady
a week or two." Well, running's what we say
a bull does when you turn him out to pasture
with the cows, so you can see how Dry felt about that –
at least providing you've ever watched a bull
in action. "But now, goddamn it" – Dry spit
and grinned sly-like with his uppers, which is all
the teeth I've ever seen him wear – "now

you could lay a slobbering big juicy one right there,
right there ready and open" – him leaning and making
a kind of slicing gesture along the log –
"and I couldn't do nothing, I couldn't touch it,
couldn't hardly spit on it," and he spit and grinned.
"It'd be all wasted, Hayden. I'm fucked, fucked,
and I ain't but fifty-nine – how old are you?"
That's Dry all right. The nailhead every time.

Well, he lives up in the old Connell sugarhouse now
that he's shingled all over with sap bucket covers
to keep the wind out, till it looks like a big tin fish
in among the pines near the brook, and there's plenty
more he could tell you, like how he got bit that time
by the cattle grub and took the "purple aguey,"
or how he has a buckshot in him that keeps going
round and round in his veins, catching him sharp-like
on his cotterbone when he don't expect it
every now and again, or how he eats forty aspirins
a day and hears sweet patooty music in his ears,
or how he fell in a cellarhole at blackberrying time
and landed on a bear – "I says, 'Whuff, old bear,
get you away from me,' and then I climm the hell
out of there" – or how . . . but have you noticed
I can't talk about him without talking like him?
That's my trouble. Somehow I always seem
to turn into the other guy, and Dry's the kind
that brings it out the strongest. But *his* trouble
is what I'm telling about now; for it's not
just buckshot in his blood, it's worse, a whole
lot worse. His reel is turning slower and slower,
no mistake. Crazy? I reckon he is. I sure don't
want to be there when he's took bad, even now –
if he's got a fork or an axe within grabbing distance.
But I'll go up to call on him in his sugarhouse.
I believe old Dry is preparing to march again,
or anyway preparing to prepare. And I believe
he'll go straight as a bee, white as a squall of snow,
knowing what he damn well knows, over

the goldenrod, the birchwoods, the pines and hemlocks,
over the mountain. And he'll be gone. And then
Marshall and I shall make this hay alone,
by God, and curse old Dry. But in our thoughts
we'll remember and remember how that man could march.

› *Johnny Spain's White Heifer*

The first time ever I saw Johnny Spain was
the first time I came to this town. There
he was, lantern jaw and broken nose, wall-eyed and
fractious, with a can of beer in one hand and a
walkie-talkie in the other, out in front
of the post office. And I heard someone saying,
"Johnny, what in hell are you doing?" "I'm looking,"
he answered, in an executive tone, "for me goddamn
white heifer." "Run off, did she?" "Yass,"
he said. "Busted me south-side fence, the bitch –
if some thieving bastard didn't bust it for her."
"You reckon she's running loose on Main Street?"
Johnny looked down, then up, then sideways, or possibly
all three together. "Hell, no," he growled.
"She's off there somewheres." He swung his beer can
in a circle. "Me boys is up in the hills, looking
I'm di-recting the search." Then he turned away
to a crackle on the walkie-talkie.
                              And that
was how Johnny liked it. He wasn't much
on farming, although his farm could have been
a fine one – closest to town, up on the hillside
overlooking the feed mill. But Johnny's curse
was a taste for administration. The "farm" was no more
than a falling-down barn, some mixed head
of cattle, and a flock of muddy ducks. Johnny
was the first man in the volunteer fire department
to have one of those revolving blue lights
set up on top of his car, and Johnny Spain

was always going to a fire. When he came down
off that hill of his in that air-borne '65 Pontiac –
look out! It was every man for himself
when Johnny was on the highway.

> I used to think
sometimes I had a glimpse of that white heifer
that Johnny never found. "A goddamn beauty,"
he'd say. "By Jesus, she was. Why, I give
five whole greenback dollars cash and a pair
of Indian runners to Blueball Baxter for her
when she were a calf – there wan't a finer heifer
in the whole goddamn county." I'd see a flash
of white in the balsams at the upper end of the pasture
or in the thickets across the brook when I looked up
at twilight; but I never found her. Probably
all I saw was a deer-tail flashing.

> After
they changed the town dump into a sanitary
landfill operation the selectmen hired Johnny
for custodian, and they gave him a little Michigan
dozer to bury the trash with. Johnny loved it.
"Dump it over there," he'd holler. "Goddamn it,
can't you see the sign? Tires and metal
go on the other side." One time he even
inaugurated a system of identification cards,
so people from Centerville and Irishtown
would quit using our dump, and by God
you had to show your pass, even if Johnny
had known you for years. Part of the deal
was salvage, of course. Johnny could take
whatever he wanted from the accumulated junk
and sell it. Trouble was he mostly didn't
or couldn't sell it, so it wound up in his
barnyard, everything from busted baby carriages
to stacks of old lard kegs from the diner,
up there to be viewed by whoever cared to look.
And the one with the best view was Mel Barstow,
son of the mill owner, who lived on the hill

above the other side of town. There they were,
two barons above the burg, facing each other
at opposite ends, like the West Wind and the East Wind
on an old-time map. Mel had everything
he thought he wanted – a home like a two-page spread
in *House and Garden,* for instance, and a wife
that was anyone's envy, and a pair of binoculars
with which he liked to watch the gulls flying
over the river. Of course he'd seen Johnny's place
many a time, but one evening he focused down
on that barnyard, then quick got on the phone.
"Johnny, why in hell don't you clean up that mess
over there? It's awful. It's a disgrace." Johnny
didn't say much. But a couple of nights later,
maybe about an hour past dark, he phoned up Mel.
"Mel," he said, "I got me a pair of them by-
nockyewlars over to Morrisville this forenoon,
and I been a-studying them goddamn birds out there,
and what I want to know is why in the hell
you don't tell that good-looking female of yours
to put some clothes on her backside when she's parading
up and down behind that picture window? Picture, hell –
I'll say it's a picture! It's a goddamn frigging
dis-grace, if you want to know the truth."
                                            Well,
I expect for a while Mel's wife was the one
that would have liked to get lost, and maybe
Mel too, because it's a cinch you can't go down
to buy even a pack of Winstons at the IGA
without running into Johnny Spain, and of course
Johnny's the one that knows exactly, exactly
how to keep the sting alive, winking wall-eyed
both ways at once, grinning that three-toothed grin.
But Johnny Spain's white heifer was what was lost.
She wasn't found. Wherever she is, she's gone.
Oh, I'm not the only one who thought they saw her,
because reports kept coming in, all the way round
from the Old Settlement clear up to Mariveau's
gravel pit. But that's all they were, just

reports. She'd have made a first-rate cow,
I reckon, if a man could have caught her, only
of course somewhat more than a mite wild.

› *Lady* ˅

Lady they calls me, Lady, and they always has
my whole life long. And I hated it – God, how I
hated it! You know? But you can't go hating
on a thing like that forever. One time I says,
"What the hell's the difference?" Now they call me
Lady, same as ever, and that's o.k.,
now my belly don't even twitch like it used to.
Hating. That's for those other downcountry folk,
that's for your city folk. What does it get them?
Gut-ache. Anybody knows that.
                              Well, what I've got
is this nice old house now, big barn and the shed,
a first-rate meadow, some fair hill pasture,
and a woodlot that's good enough for what I need.
And my horses, my Arabians, every one bred
by my own stallion; yes, and them there silver
whoduddies you see on the mantel for showing
all over the state. I got me my Herefords too,
registered, fourteen head. And I got me a job,
to make up what the horses and beef won't bring,
down to the hospital in Waterbury. You know?
The *mental* hospital. Don't get the idea I'm one
of those movie battleaxe types neither. I'm not.
I work at the ward for the chronics on the midnight shift,
and there's a good lot of them poor bastards in there
as can't sleep when it comes night, and I know why.
Believe me, I know why. I treat them right,
I talk to them, make them tell me their stories,
and then sometimes they can sleep. Sometimes.
Then I come home and do my chores and sleep
myself. Later I make hay, or mend fence, or tend
the foals, or whatever needs doing. i got me

a Ford 3000 tractor, a baler, mower, side-rake, a Dodge
two-ton platform truck, and when I need something else,
like a tedder or a teakle rig, I borrows it.
We're neighborly round here, we have to be. Why,
we switch off labor for all our big jobs. Yes, sir.
And I do my share.
                       One time I was spreading
manure down in the lower pasture, next the spruces.
It was late, see, past sundown, because I can tell you
I got to run seventy minutes to the hour to work
this place. And of course that had to be the time
the damn spreader jams, so there's nothing to do
but throw out the stuff by hand. I was just climbing
off of the tractor with the dung fork in one hand
when this old she bear come out of the trees. Popped
right out of there, coming right at me, big
as a spruce-oil kiln, she looked, and black as a stove.
I whooped, let me tell you, and threw my fork
and climm back on that tractor in a kind of a hurry,
breathing a mite hard. And when I got back to the barn
I found I had more manure than I started out with.

I told Jasper the next day. He owns that
gone-to-Boston-looking place over the hill
with the ham-o-gilly in the dooryard. "Jas,"
I says, "I was plain *scart* – scart of that old she bear.
I shit my britches." Jas, he looked straight and soft-like.
"Lady," he says, "I don't blame you none. 'Twas me
I believe I'd of shatten too."
                          That's one thing –
small, it don't mean much. You asked me who I was.
I'm Lady. I'm what some folk might call
uncommon, a speck maybe. Well, I get along,
a good neighbor to good neighbors. There's all kinds
living round these mountains. I raise beef,
a little, and I raise some damn fine horses, here
on this hilltop farm, then I work out nights
in the loony-bin. That's all, mostly. Though sometimes
it does seem funny, don't it, the way things happen.

> *Marshall Washer*

They are cowshit farmers, these New Englanders
who built our red barns so admired as emblems,
in photograph, in paint, of America's imagined
past (backward utopians that we've become).
But let me tell how it is inside those barns.
Warm. Even in dead of winter, even in the
dark night solid with thirty below, thanks
to huge bodies breathing heat and grain sacks
stuffed under doors and in broken windows, warm,
and heaped with reeking, steaming manure, running
with urine that reeks even more, the wooden channels
and flagged aisles saturated with a century's
excreta. In dim light, with scraper and shovel,
the manure is lifted into a barrow or a trolley
(suspended from a ceiling track), and moved
to the spreader – half a ton at a time. Grain
and hay are distributed in the mangers, bedding
of sawdust strewn on the floor. The young cattle
and horses, separately stabled, are tended. The cows
are milked; the milk is strained and poured
in the bulk tank; the machines and all utensils
are washed with disinfectant. This, which is called
the "evening chores," takes about three hours.
Next morning, do it again. Then after breakfast
hitch the manure spreader to the old Ferguson
and draw it to the meadows, where the manure
is kicked by mechanical beaters onto the snow.
When the snow becomes too deep for the tractor,
often about mid-January, then load the manure
on a horse-drawn sled and pitch it out by hand.
When the snow becomes too deep for the horses
make your dung heap behind the barn. Yes, a good
winter means no dung heap; but a bad one
may mean a heap as big as a house. And so,
so, night and morning and day, 365 days
a year until you are dead; this is part

of what you must do. Notice how many times
I have said "manure?" It is serious business.
It breaks the farmers' backs. It makes their land.
It is the link eternal, binding man and beast
and earth. Yet our farmers still sometimes say
of themselves, derogatively, that they are "cowshit
farmers."

2

       I see a man with a low-bent back
driving a tractor in stinging rain, or just as he
enters a doorway in his sheepskin and enormous
mittens, stomping snow from his boots, raising
his fogged glasses. I see a man in bib overalls
and rubber boots kneeling in cowshit to smear
ointment on a sore teat, a man with a hayfork,
a dungfork, an axe, a 20-pound maul
for driving posts, a canthook, a grease gun.
I see a man notching a cedar post
with a double-blade axe, rolling the post
under his foot in the grass: quick strokes and there
is a ringed groove one inch across, as clean
as if cut with the router blade down at the mill.
I see a man who drags a dead calf or watches
a barn roaring with fire and thirteen heifers
inside, I see his helpless eyes. He has stood
helpless often, of course: when his wife died
from congenital heart disease a few months before
open-heart surgery came to Vermont, when his sons
departed, caring little for the farm because
he had educated them – he who left school
in 1931 to work by his father's side
on an impoverished farm in an impoverished time.
I see a man who studied by lamplight, the journals
and bulletins, new methods, struggling to buy
equipment, forty years to make his farm
a good one; alone now, his farm the last
on Clay Hill, where I myself remember ten.

He says "I didn't mind it" for "I didn't notice it,"
"dreened" for "drained," "climb" (pronounced climm)
for "climbed," "stanchel" for "stanchion,"
and many other unfamiliar locutions; but I
have looked them up, they are in the dictionary,
standard speech of lost times. He is rooted
in history as in the land, the only man I know
who lives in the house where he was born. I see
a man alone walking his fields and woods,
knowing every useful thing about them, moving
in a texture of memory that sustains his lifetime
and his father's lifetime. I see a man
falling asleep at night with thoughts and dreams
I could not infer – and would not if I could –
in his chair in front of his television.

    3

                    I have written
of Marshall often, for his presence is in my poems
as in my life, so familiar that it is not named;
yet I have named him sometimes too, in writing
as in life, gratefully. We are friends. Our friendship
began when I came here years ago, seeking
what I had once known in southern New England,
now destroyed. I found it in Marshall, among others.
He is friend and neighbor both, an important
distinction. His farm is one-hundred-eighty acres
(plus a separate woodlot of forty more), and one
of the best-looking farms I know, sloping smooth
pastures, elm-shaded knolls, a brook, a pond,
his woods of spruce and pine, with maples and oaks
along the road – not a showplace, not by any means,
but a working farm with fences of old barbed wire;
no pickets, no post-and-rail. His cows are Jerseys.
My place, no farm at all, is a country laborer's
holding, fourteen acres "more or less" (as the deed
says), but we adjoin. We have no fence. Marshall's
cows graze in my pasture; I cut my fuel

in his woods. That's neighborliness. And when
I came here Marshall taught me . . . I don't know,
it seems like everything: how to run a barn,
make hay, build a wall, make maple syrup
without a trace of bitterness, a thousand things.
(Though I thought I wasn't ignorant when I came,
and I wasn't – just three-quarters informed.
You know how good a calf is, born three-legged.)
In fact half my life now, I mean literally half,
is spent in actions I could not perform without
his teaching. Yet it wasn't teaching; he *showed* me.
Which is what makes all the difference. In return
I gave a hand, helped in the fields, started
frozen engines, mended fence, searched for lost calves,
picked apples for the cider mill, and so on.
And Marshall, now alone, often shared my table.
This too is neighborliness.

4
                    As for friendship,
what can I say where words historically fail?
It is something else, something more difficult. Not
western affability, at any rate, that tells
in ten minutes the accommodation of its wife's – well,
you know. Yankees are independent, meaning
individual and strong-minded but also private;
in fact private first of all. Marshall and I
worked ten years together, and more than once
in hardship. I remember the late January
when his main gave out and we carried water,
hundreds and thousands of gallons, to the heifers
in the upper barn (the one that burned next summer),
then worked inside the well to clear the line
in temperatures that rose to ten below
at noonday. We knew such times. Yet never
did Marshall say the thought that was closest to him.
Privacy is what this is; not reticence, not
minding one's own business, but a positive sense

of the secret inner man, the sacred identity.
A man is his totem, the animal of his mind.
Yet I was angered sometimes. How could friendship
share a base so small of mutual substance?
Unconsciously I had taken friendship's measure
from artists elsewhere who had been close to me,
people living for the minutest public dissection
of emotion and belief. But more warmth was,
and is, in Marshall's quiet "hello" than in all
those others and their wordiest protestations,
more warmth and far less vanity.

     5

                                  He sows
his millet broadcast, swinging left to right,
a half-acre for the cows' "fall tonic" before
they go in the barn for good; an easy motion,
slow swinging, a slow dance in the field, and just
the opposite, right to left, for the scythe
or the brush-hook. Yes, I have seen such dancing
by a man alone in the slant of the afternoon.
At his anvil with his big smith's hammer
he can pound shape back in a wagon iron, or tap
a butternut so it just lies open. When he skids
a pine log out of the woods he stands in front
of his horse and hollers, "Gee-up, goddamn it,"
"Back, you ornery son-of-a-bitch," and then
when the chain rattles loose and the log settles
on the stage, he slicks down the horse's sweaty
neck and pulls his ears. In October he eases
the potatoes out of the ground in their rows,
gentle with the potato-hook, then leans and takes
a big one in his hand, and rubs it clean
with his thumbs, and smells it, and looks
along the new-turned frosty earth to fields,
to hills, to the mountain, forests in their color
each fall no less awesome. And when in June
the mowing time comes around and he fits the wicked

cutter-bar to the Ferguson, he shuts the cats
indoors, the dogs in the barn, and warns
the neighbors too, because once years ago,
many years, he cut off a cat's legs in the tall
timothy. To this day you can see him
squirm inside when he tells it, as he must tell it,
obsessively, June after June. He is tall,
a little gray, a little stooped, his eyes
crinkled with smile-lines, both dog-teeth gone.
He has worn his gold-rimmed spectacles so long
he looks disfigured when they're broken.

6

                              No doubt
Marshall's sorrow is the same as human
sorrow generally, but there is this
difference. To live in a doomed city, a doomed
nation, a doomed world is desolating, and we all
are desolated. But to live on a doomed farm
is worse. It must be worse. There the exact
point of connection, gate of conversion, is –
mind and life. The hilltop farms are going.
Bottomland farms, mechanized, are all that survive.
As more and more developers take over
northern Vermont, values of land increase,
taxes increase, farming is an obsolete vocation –
while half the world goes hungry. Marshall walks
his fields and woods, knowing every useful thing
about them, and knowing his knowledge useless.
Bulldozers, at least of the imagination,
are poised to level every knoll, to strip bare
every pasture. Or maybe a rich man will buy it
for a summer place. Either way the link
of the manure, that had seemed eternal, is broken.
Marshall is not young now. And though I am only
six or seven years his junior, I wish somehow
I could buy the place, merely to assure him
that for these few added years it might continue –

drought, flood, or depression. But I am too
ignorant, in spite of his teaching. This is more
than a technocratic question. I cannot smile
his quick sly Yankee smile in sorrow,
nor harden my eyes with the true granitic resistance
that shaped this land. How can I learn the things
that are not transmissible? Marshall knows them.
He possesses them, the remnant of human worth
to admire in this world, and I think to envy.

❯ Crow's Mark

They don't say gully, cove, cut, gulch,
glen, dell, etc., around here,
they call it a gulf, meaning
something less than a notch but more
than a ravine, and my house sits
in the bottom of Foote Brook Gulf. Back
about a hundred twenty years or so
the house was a barn, more like a shed,
well, a utility building
attached to a sawmill on the brook.
All the mill that's left now
is part of the old foundation, but the shed
was converted into a house by tacking on a smaller
shed – I can show you where they toed in
the spikes through the two wall plates –
to serve as a kitchen. It still does.
The house is called Crows Mark. Don't ask me
why. I know, but I'm tired of telling.

It's a south-running brook, the Foote, rising
back up on the beaver meadows
on Butternut Mountain, which means
the Gulf runs north-south too,
roughly; and this in turn means the winter wind
that's usually more west than north sails
overhead – we hear it, a roar in the trees above,

but we don't feel it. Why, I've seen sheets
of snow flung over us, flopping and flapping,
and we dead calm underneath. Of course Marshall,
in his farmhouse up on the crest, gets it
full blast, so it's a good day's work to walk
from the house to the barn sometimes,
it seems as though. On the other hand,
still nights in winter the cold
spills down, over the pastures, the ledges,
into the Gulf till it's thirty-five
below on my thermometer, while Marshall
sits snug and comfy in the warmth
of the upper air where it's only twenty-five
under the zero, as I make sure
to point out to him next morning.
                                        And then sometimes,
usually ten or twelve nights a winter,
the wind veers round due north, straight
down from the pole, and when it hits the Gulf
it's like full choke on a twelve-gauge
barrel – compression, you know what I mean?
I mind one time
in January – 'sixty-eight, I think it was –
the wind blew the beam of my flashlight
twice around the maple by the woodshed
and wrapped it tight. You don't
believe me? Ask Marshall. The flashlight
was hanging there still next morning.
I let it stay till the batteries wore out
and it fell down.
                        Fortunately the wind
at Crows Mark sits mostly west by north,
through the Waterville notch, over our heads.

> The Poet

All night his window
shines in the woods
shadowed under the hills
where the gray owl

is hunting. He hears
the woodmouse scream –
so small a sound
in the great darkness

entering his pain.
For he is all and all
of pain, attracting
every new injury

to be taken and borne
as he must take
and bear it. He is
nothing; he is

his admiration. So
they seem almost
to know – the woodmouse
and the roving owl,

the woods and hills.
All night they move
around the stillness
of the poet's light.

> Essay on Love

Years. Many years. Friends laugh, including
even my best friend, Rose Marie, but they all
are younger, and I might laugh as well
to think how they will

come to know. Or tears might be as easy.
I used to drive this wedge in the maple blocks
　　　with pleasure; now I wouldn't care
　　　　　if I never saw another.

Yet the air so clear, utterly clear, and the blue
September sky arching the forest's bright crown
　　　so very deep; come, lean the sledge
　　　　　on its maple block

and walk away, slow, stepping by the little brook
where shad leaves turn coral and the turtlehead
　　　blooms, late this year, its petals
　　　　　still perfect and white.

See, ladies' tresses, right here where they always
were; kneel then to their fragrance, near
　　　to the cool of earth. And goldenrod,
　　　　　plumes of yellow

where yellow bees mumble, and asters, blue
and purple and white, New England asters
　　　that are our stars, and the small
　　　　　speckled asters, massed

at the edge of the clearing, that are called
farewell-to-summer; and there beneath them
　　　the peeping, deep, blue, shy eyes
　　　　　of the gentian,

so rare a color. Does that mean something? Count
the maple leaves if you can. Or those bluebirds
　　　perched, one by one, apart, on the wire
　　　　　over there, seven,

blue in the sunlight: are they a rarity? Then
count too, as one always must, the "rare" pains,
　　　hernia raving, bladder and penis
　　　　　in an acid flame,

arthritic hip – was it Plato said a man
is finished at fifty-five? And Rose Marie,
    my dear friend, whose spine is a pain
        that I see marching

often enough in her young eyes. What do
the bluebirds say? They don't know why they wear
    that rare color, or why they gather now
        on that wire to fly

tomorrow to Guatemala; they don't know,
nor do I. Those seven little blue machines
    look down from their pain on a somewhat
        larger machine

of a somewhat less determinate color, down
into the clearing among coral shadblow leaves
    and the red and golden maple leaves
        and the parchment leaves

of moosewood, the speckled banks of asters.
Years, years; seasons and changes. Time,
    which is nothing but the measure of change –
        nothing, no meaning.

Years, years I've driven this wedge with my big
hammer into these maple blocks for Rose Marie,
    to keep her warm and give her stovewood
        for her kitchen

all winter, firesticks wrenched, split, pried
apart, each with the thought of her. I see
    so clearly, precisely, with the keen
        eyes of dispassion,

the trees, flowers, birds, all colors and forms,
but what good is such seeing in this chaos
    we used to call our order? She
        is invisible now,

a purity, the greater loveliness for the greater
seeing. Back to the block then, back once more,
  pick up the sledge, eyes down, and bend
    to the labor

that is the only meaning. Farewell to summer.
Yes, let changes keep the time. I'll count
  no further, except these firesticks
    counted for her.

> *Missing the Bo in the Henhouse*

In here, caught by the storm. How the rain beats
on the metal roof! And the hens peck at my feet,

these my ladies, their mournful pessimism, ayie,
ayie, ayo, and my boy whom I have loved – how

shall I say it or sing it? – more than myself,
more than my poems (that are myself),

more than the world (that is my poems),
ladies, these thirteen years, and now

he is turning, turning away. I know
we are "carried about the sun," about and about,

this conglomeration, a higgledy-piggledy
planet, incomprehensible, I could not

be part of it. And I am.
Carried. Desire long ago beaten out,

so that I wanted small things only, a song,
a boy. No, it will not cohere, this "world";

relentless the years and it will not. Mind
cannot make it. Ladies, do you know ever

what it means to be carried? Woe, ladies,
the boy is turning. A current runs on the grass.

And the dark falls early. Come now, up to your roost
and let the evening dance begin, the slow sarabande –

aft by fore, or aft by aft, which
shall it be? – turning, turning in the cadence

of your song. Ayie, ayie, ayo. Slower
and slower. Good night, ladies,

in your hurtling house. The time of the mouse
has come, the rain strums on your roof.

Keep close and keep warm. Bless me if you are able,
commend me to the storm. Good night, good night.

❯ *Paragraphs*

I

Begin right here. The Campground Road. Some calls it the
Hogback, but that's up higher. Down here's the river.
And there's Vermont, all ridge and valley
and all cockeyed – seem'z'o. Over
acrost is the hayth-o-land, Whiteface and all,
Madonna, Mansfield. Butternut's back here. And Baldy
Langdell's uncle's place was right there,
him that set his house as square
as his own square Yankee head afore he died   and Baldy
     died and old
Jimmy   and Hank Rago
King, Malcolm, Jackson and all –
     all in a breath of years.
                              A cold wind,
                                        old and cold,
sprung these waterdrops from a bare birch bough,
these lightdrops scattering to the edge

of a pool of darkness. Or say we could glimpse
    Vivaldi's parchment now,
his hand flinging down a bright arpeggio . . .

2

Keep going. *There's nothing else to do.* Past
the few farms remaining, Manchester's, Jones's.
Past brutishness new since last
I drove here, sliced stone,
eviscerated hills. And then the worst,
these superadded trailers, this prefab, damned fashion
out of Monterey or Bronxville, God knows where –
the national mean taking over. Or
the mean nationals.

                          Keep going, Waterville
to Johnson. I'd have thought
(almost) this was too tough, they couldn't spoil it,
ridge and riverbottom, massed heights,
granitic Vermont.   But they've walked on Kailas
    and thrown
town dirt on snow-bright Sati,
    they've exulted
before Kali.   They've put their feet on the moon,

3

Ithiel Falls, below the Nazarene campground. A name
clinging to its old place. The falls were blown out
in a WPA so-called work program,
1934 I think, to avert
another flood like '27 that had been true bedlam,
death-night all over Vermont. Icy water, the flame
in the lungs. God!
                          Yet the dynamite
was a fool's work, wasted. What
caused the flood was a jam in the fall's crest
where the old covered bridges,

floating loose on high water, came to rest,
creating a dam. But then the new bridges
that replaced them were ironwork. Could *they* float?
Ah, Ithiel Falls, lovely cascading down ferny ledges,
and I never saw it.

Why were the falls blown out?

4

Why was the passenger pigeon exterminated?
Sometimes
I dream of those bridges; downriver on the flood,
shapes in dark water, awash and lumbering.
Why did the beatitude
who shot the last otter in Otter Creek come home
bragging? I dream how they yawed and stumbled,
how they wallowed almost but not quite like the huge
Jurassic animals caught in the deluge.
Why were the braves castrated, the stretched squaws
bayoneted up their vaginas?
Bridges are only bridges, that's all, bumping along,
    spandrel and truss,
post, brace, beam –
arks
of a minor people and a time too small for grief,
crunching, foundering, gone in the rain-drenched dark.
I grow old, my dreams are factual and brief.

5

Not night now. Dawn. Six o'clock, a November morning.
But raining still. I stop. In the blown falls the river
sinks on a long grade, curling
through the dogleg. I lower
my window. Rain hisses on the coarse snow remaining
from yesterday's freeze where broken stems of mullen
fence the ditch. A grove of popples,
grayish-green, is a drabness opposite,
with one stark white birch outstanding. A jay,

slanting tidily across the water
to a low branch, jeers as he goes. Way away,
way in the East, beyond our boarded up
Nazarenes, the sun struggles in a fog.

> Once at Walden
it was the "morning star" calling us to the order
of this world.

> Tell me   Henry David   are you still called?

6

The Lamoille River Valley otherwise known
as these objects jays trees snows that wont cohere
or where on the waters of darkness Apollyon
stalks to make this hour
dawn's awful madness in the Valley of Humiliation
and him the Angel of Death but Im no Christian
and first becomes last coherence fails
connections cherished 50 years and alls
lost no art more Ill write what I want how I want
dont bug me about my words
the vision is cold chaos and I need what warmth
my old mind knows I rub my beard
I crank my window closed but there there the Prince of Prose
Apollyon water-marcher his terrible swift regard
flinging look his icy pointed oldwords where he goes.

7

Arthritic gray snowlight hobbles down the valley westward.
It is day. Who also will choose my delusions and bring
my fears upon me? Engrafted words
I sing and sing and sing
upon blocky objects floating downriver, my days, while my godhood
ordains resolutions, a chaos of light, of flood,
a *catastrophe*. I turn the key, ram
the old truck in gear, and grind home
down the Campground Road toward the colorless, futile
dawn – past Farrell's

up Stearn's Hill, past the Whiting Lot. More trailers,
earth crumbling and eroding visibly
beneath the snowcrust, pines and birches massacred. I feel
nothing but cold. I catch my reflection on the wet window, alone,
a face old and broken, hunched over Ixion's wheel.

．　　．　　．

8

the one called Next steps up
to the wall. a face detailed
and well remembered. but
my voice won't call
when i try it. stuck. i shut
my eyes. i hear the gunbolts
slide home. i open
my eyes. my hands
are missing. i reach.
i have nothing but wrists.
the face falls down. i retch.
the next one is called Next.
so dream after dream they keep
going. yet i'm sound awake.
the world has gone to sleep.

．　　．　　．

9

It was the custom of my tribe to be silent,
to think the song inwardly, tune and word
so beautiful they could be only held,
not sung; held and heard
in quietness while walking the end of the field
where birches make a grove, or standing by the rail
in back of the library in some northern
city, or in the long dream of a tower
of gothic stoniness; and always we were alone.
Yet sometimes two
heard it, two separately together. It could come
nearby in the shadow of a pine bough

on the snow, or high in the orchestral lights,
or maybe (this was our miracle) it would have no
intermediary –
                a suddenness,
                              indivisible, unvoiced.

        •   •   •

10

"There was this girl   18, 19   and slight
the way they are in that country   (you know)   laying
by the others in the ditch   taking
the bullets
with her body/   with which she shielded
as best she could   both her little child
and her zillion-year-old grandmother"
                  hic divisio
facta est inter Teutonicos et Latinos
Francos circa 843 a.d./
                    or,
                    ahi serva Italia
di dolore ostello –
Dante who made it all ours and even more terrible
than perhaps it was   eloquence
so grave and so sweet,
                  "Her mouth was narrow
blood-choked/   we thought her eyes widened
more in incredulity than pain . . ."
                    Ahi
        thou inn of sorrow.

        •   •   •

11

Oh I loved you Pete Brown. And you were a brother
to me Joe Marsala. And you too sweet Billy Kyle.
You Sidney Bechet. And Benny Carter.
And Jo Jones. Cozy Cole.
Cootie Williams. Dicky Wells. Al Hall. Ben Webster.

Matty Matlock. Lou McGarity. Mel Powell. Fats Waller.
Freddie Green. Rex Stewart. Wilbur & Sid
de Paris. Russ Procope. And Sister Ida
Cox dont forget her. And Omar Simeon. Joe Smith.
Zutty Singleton. Charlie Shavers.
Specs Powell. Red Norvo. Vic Dickenson. J. C. Higginbotham.
Nappy Lamare. Earl Hines. Buck Clayton.
Roy Eldridge. Pops Foster. Johnny Hodges. Ed Hall.
Art Tatum. Frankie Newton. Chu Berry. Billy Taylor.
And oh incomparable James P. Johnson.

                    Brothers I loved you all.

          •   •   •

          12
I was watching the telly not serious you know just looking
with my wife there too and feeling all right after a dinner
at home together for once with our own cooking
and afterwards a whisky for sipping
and I really was feeling all right   Almost shocking
when you consider my age (65) and my line of work
(political) but even in the Trouble
you forget sometimes/ you have to   The doorbell
sounded/ Jenny bringing that big memo
to sign for the early pickup
I opened   It was a hooded man with a pistol
He fired three times/ there was a terrific
thud and I stood there watching a huge wall subside
under the pendulum stroke of a ball   while my wife's hysterics
drifted down the street like a shower of rain/
                    And then I died.

          •   •   •

13

And the water/ the rising water

                    nothing like it

    for force

moving everywhere   embracing every obstacle

        as if it were love

               carrying everything before it/

                  a miracle

of conversion

               See how it spreads out & across

the field

        making a nacreous sky-reflecting lake

           where geese

              in thousands

rest for four days

        on the long journey to Hudson's Bay

Rills rivulets streams springs ditches pools

               it's a watery world

all trace of the old order going fast/

                 it spills

          mud and the rich mould

      of its long astonishing suppuration

            and then

it's over

      all at once the movement has come full

and everyone

      puts on shirts of bright triumphant green.

     •   •   •

14

In filthy Puerto Rico lives a bird with no
legs and transparent wings, a somewhat small
bird whose flight is awkward and slow
yet it spends its whole
existence in flying. Luckily it knows how
to ride high currents above the eagles, hawks, crows
and all the preying host that seeks
its life continually. As long as it keeps

above them, soaring between them and the sun,
it cannot be seen, partly
because the predators are blinded by the exceeding shine
of brightness, partly because the heart
of the bird is the only thing that shows, a speck
in its transparency. High it flies, flies, flies, hungry and hurt,
until at last it falls on filthy Puerto Rico. And the name
    of this bird is blank.

          ·   ·   ·

    15

"I am a fanatic lover of liberty, considering it
the unique condition in which intelligence, dignity,
and human happiness may develop and grow;
not the purely formal liberty
conceded, measured out, and regulated by the State,
an eternal lie which in reality represents
nothing more than the privilege
of some founded on the slavery
of the rest; not the individualistic, egotistic,
shabby and fictitious liberty
extolled by the school of J. J. Rousseau and the other
schools of bourgeois liberalism,
which gives us the would-be rights of all men
as embodied in a State that limits the rights of each –
an idea which leads inevitably to the reduction

    16

of the rights of each to zero. No, I mean the only
kind of liberty that is worthy of the name,
liberty that consists in the full development
of all the material, intellectual, and moral
powers which lie hidden in every person; liberty
which knows no restrictions beyond those
determined by the laws
of our individual natures,
which cannot properly be regarded as restrictions

since they are not imposed,
but are immanent and inherent, forming
the very basis of our material, intellectual,
and moral being – they do not limit us, they are
the real and immediate conditions of our freedom"
– Thus, living light cast back from a burnt-out star.

     .   .   .

17
RAVAGE, v.t. To lay waste; to subject
to depredations; to work havoc or devastation upon;
to sack; plunder; despoil. *Syn.* –
RAVAGE, DEVASTATE, SACK
agree in the idea of despoiling or laying waste.
Ravage emphasizes the idea of violence; *devastate,*
that of waste or ruin; *sack,*
that of plunder or pillage. One *ravages*
or *devastates* a country, one *sacks* a town.

Unquote.
                               Please/
distinctions are important. There's still one man
who chooses with care. Anyone who agrees
may love me or not, but those condemning
my methods never will.
                              Regard the breeze
how it plucks bright autumn leaves
                    one after another
                            to expose the timber.

18
And so with paragraphics.
                            It was in summer
that lovely word chosen with care when I
first loved this valley where the river
was a curving ribbon of sky
lacing together the fields of every color

potatoes timothy mustard alfalfa clover
and purple widemarching corn. The farms
lay scattered in their places, a barn,
a house, fenced fields irregular. Their old
horse-drawn mowers
and manure spreaders rusted in the yards. Fold
within fold the darkening hills arose
toward glowing mountains. Here was a peacock, there
a Mongolian pheasant – no exotics, no more
than the useless horse or ox, for this was where

       19

all things lay in nature, even the plastic flowers,
the flowering plastics,

                 the plastic farmers . . .

                      Wordsworth!
thou should'st be living in this hour:
Vermont hath need of thee/

              Carruth

being at all events not up to it;

               the ancient power
of that vision is gone.

            Gone? Was I bemused? The scars
are not new, the macadam was here then,
half the forests lay in slashed ruin,
the river's blue was more likely not sky
but the paintworks in Hardwick
cleaning its vats again. And yet

              somehow
it was absorbed,   humanity sick
with greed, with loathing, somehow was taken in
by earth, water, mountain . . .

         No more! The weak
have conquered and the valley is their domain,

20

ugly, evil, dying. The old soft lines,
knoll and glen, mountain and river, that held
the farms like poems curled in time,
have been ripped out,

     raveled,

wrenched apart. The connections gone. It was dynamite
did it

   more than chainsaws or the great Cats, but –

     ahi

       it was men's minds

that did it!

     In this town, Johnson,
some have sold their own and everyone's
birthright to the ravagers, on our east and our west,
and particularly these two:
André Tournailler (*Anglice*, Toenailer) and Jacob Blesh.
Yes, townsmen, friends, I name *you*,
Andy and Jake, against every rule of Yankee decorum,
I name you in your public guilt. Here and now.
Look, the trailer park, filling station, plastic ranches, the rural

21

slums par excellence that were your farms! And all
for a hot pocketful of dollars.

      I don't say others
haven't done as much, Farrells, Hills,
Berrys, Lahouillers, Parkers,
and so on – the length of the valley, to Hyde Park, Morrisville,
Wolcott, Hardwick, or westward to Lake Champlain,
a shambles, ravaged, devastated, gone,
or going fast. All in the name
of "development." But good friends, where are your dollars
now? And who has profited?
Not farmers. Not (God knows) poets. None of us. The poor
play patsies again for mean-spirited
weaselly downcountry men, the capitalists, varmints,

come ravaging in our dooryard like the strange coyotes
come from the west.
                    And your *best* is what you gave them,
                            oh my friends –
                                    your lives, your farms.

                2 2

Now tell me if we don't need a revolution! Black
is the color of my only flag/
                                    and of man's hope.
Will revolution bring the farms back?
Gone, gone. The only crop
this valley will grow now is the great landwrack,
breakage, erosion, garbage, trash, gimcrack.
We burn it. The stink trails in the air,
a long thin smoke of floating despair
down the time of our valley. Someday we will be free,
someday when it's too late.
It's true, the real revolutionary is one who can see
all dark ahead and behind, his fate
a need without a hope: the will to resist.
The State is universal, the Universe is a state.
Now ask me if I am really an anarchist.

                •   •   •

                2 3

Another hard, hard morning with a hard snow
Falling small and fast. It is eight below.
Yet the ash pail brims. I must go
Out to the garden and sow
This remnant of value where the beans will grow
Next summer maybe. The goddamned gods bestow
And men . . .
                    are at best a paradigm
Sowing and reaping in the void of time.
Or say that one must do what one does as though

It might mean something, so –
Broadcasting ashes, swinging my shovel low,
Spreading this color that I don't know,
Dirty lavender, dirty pearl, row upon row,
Death upon death, "sowing the ashes," to and fro,
A *tour de force* in an abandoned studio.

·   ·   ·

2 4

And I was past caring   so many, too many men,
so many children/   body broken, slack
as the spirit   skin & bone
like a burlap sack
with a liter of rice in the bottom.
                                No one
wants lugging that around,
                        let the others run,
I said, and sat right down, there
where I was, and looked up into the air
to see it coming.
              And when it came (that spout
of flaming jelly)   I cursed
and then I made a great sound: no shriek, no shout,
more like an enormous croak – the worst
I had ever heard.
                  For once then   once   I knew
what I had done was the most
                        and maybe the first
human thing I had ever been permitted to do.

·   ·   ·

2 5

Reading myself, old poems, their inside truth that was
(is, is!) crucial, tree stark in lightning glimpse, hidden
mostly by the storm: complexities,
modes, names, manners,   words laden
with terror. What true voice? Where? Humiliated, in throes
of vacillation, roundhead to cavalier to ivy league to smartass –

never who I was. Say it plain:
death/beauty, loneliness/love, wisdom/pain,
they the simple coordinates. Was it shameful
to be insane, or so grotesque
to wrench lucidity out of nowhere? Yet my call
came a whisper, my sentence an arabesque,
my song falsetto. Put the book back on the shelf.
Gone goodness. Dear mother, dead father, what burlesque
of feeling phonied us, that made you make me hate myself?

              .   .   .

        2 6
A day   very solid   February 12th, 1944
cheerless in New York City (while I kneedeep
elsewhere in historical war
was wrecking Beauty's sleep
and her long dream)
                            a day (blank, gray) at four
in the afternoon, overheated in the W.O.R.
Recording Studios. Gum wrappers and dust
and a stale smell. A day. The cast
was Albert Ammons, Lips Page, Vic Dickenson,
Don Byas, Israel
Crosby, and Big Sid Catlett. (*And* it was Abe Linkhorn's
birthday.) And Milt Gabler
presided over the glass with a nod, a sign. Ammons
counted off
                        a-waaaaan,,,   *tu!*

                        and went feeling

his way on the keys gently,
                            while Catlett summoned

        2 7
the exact beat from –
            say from the sounding depths, the universe . . .

When Dickenson came on it was all established,
no guessing, and he started with a blur
as usual, smears, brays – Christ
the dirtiest noise imaginable
                          belches, farts
                                    curses
but it was music
                  music now
                          with Ammons trilling in counterpoise.
Byas next, meditative, soft/
                          then Page
with that tone like the torn edge
of reality:
                  and so the climax, long dying riffs –
groans, wild with pain –
and Crosby throbbing *and* Catlett riding stiff
yet it was music   music.
                                    (Man, doan
fall in that bag,
                  you caint describe it.)
                                    Piano & drum,

Ammons & Catlett drove the others. *And* it was done
and they listened *and* heard themselves
      better than they were, for they had come

      2 8
high above themselves. Above everything, flux, ooze,
loss, need, shame, improbability/   the awfulness
of gut-wrong,   sex-wrack,   horse & booze,
the whole goddamn mess,
And Gabler said "We'll press it"   and it was
      "Bottom Blues"
BOTTOM BLUES   five men knowing it well   blacks
      & jews
yet music, music   high

in the celebration of fear, strange joy
of pain: blown out, beaten out

                     a moment ecstatic
in the history
of creative mind *and* heart/   not singular, not the rarity
we think, but real and a glory
our human shining, shekinah . . .   Ah,
                   holy spirit, ninefold
I druther've bin a-settin there, supernumerary
cockroach i' th' corner, a-listenin, a-listenin,,,,,,
              than be the Prazedint of the Wurrurld.

from

IF YOU CALL
THIS CRY A SONG
[1983]

› *Words in a Certain Appropriate Mode*

It is not music, though one has tried music.
It is not nature, though one has tried
The rose, the bluebird, and the bear.
It is not death, though one has often died.

None of these things is there.

In the everywhere that is nowhere
Neither the inside nor the outside
Neither east nor west nor down nor up
Where the loving smile vanishes, vanishes
In the evanescence from a coffee cup
Where the song crumbles in monotone
Neither harmonious nor inharmonious
Where one is neither alone
Nor not alone, where cognition seeps
Jactatively away like the falling tide
If there were a tide, and what is left
Is nothing, or is the everything that keeps
Its undifferentiated unreality, all
Being neither given nor bereft
Where there is neither breath nor air
The place without locality, the locality

With neither extension nor intention
But there in the weightless fall
Between all opposites to the ground
That is not a ground, surrounding
All unities, without grief, without care
Without leaf or star or water or stone
Without light, without sound
                    anywhere, anywhere . . .

❯ I Tell You For Several Years of My Madness I Heard the Voice of Lilith Singing in the Trees of Chicago

1

Of waste and again of waste, and of the waste of wasting, o void, o desolation:
of the cruelty of the seed, of the unbearable force of the seed, o sinking sun:
of the vessel shattered and the vessel cast away, o oblivion.

2

Before the weak sister Eve who betrayed the serpent that had lived at peace in my
 cave, there I was:
before the strange sister Inanna who destroyed the huluppu-tree for a place to lie
 dreaming of Gilgamesh, there I was:
before the rushing and circling of the winds of the desert, yes, before God, there I
 was.

3

In the blink of the eye of the black crow in the center of the leafless tree:
in the knot of the wood of the tree, the knot ever unblinking:
in the potsherds broken in their brightness, scattered and shining beneath the
 furious sun.

4

For I was bitten, for I bear the insignia of the toothmark on my shoulder:
for I was thrown down and compelled to carry the sands of the earth in my womb:
for I was sold for a song, bought for a tablet of law, and my compassion was made
 my indenture.

5

How long, beside the waters, beside the moonlight, beside the stone:
how long, at the hot edges of highways, both the eastern and western:
how long, where the sewers foam and the black bayous rot.

6

Because my body resembled the wheatfield, they tilled it:

because my breasts were like the blossoming apple boughs, they broke them:

because the animal of my sex was wild in fugitive mystery, they tamed it for
  servitude.

7

O Batseba, who opened her knees to an harpist and took God's scorn for the song's
  sake:

o Batseba, who opened her knees to an hero and took man's pity for the deed's
  sake:

o Batseba, o beautiful and wise, o traitorous sister.

8

A woman's bone is bright as the tree of the olive in sunlight:

a woman's flesh is beat down like the unripe fruit:

a woman's death lies gleaming and twisted like a torn-out root in the early morning
  dew.

9

Therefore the awakened bird cries once in the night:

therefore the sweet fire sings when it reaches the knot:

therefore, o therefore Lilith her cry, and Lilith her curse and her detestation, and
  again I sing: therefore.

❯ *On Being Asked to Write a Poem Against the War in Vietnam*

Well I have and in fact
more than one and I'll
tell you this too

I wrote one against
Algeria that nightmare
and another against

Korea and another
against the one
I was in

and I don't remember
how many against
the three

when I was a boy
Abyssinia Spain and
Harlan County

and not one
breath was restored
to one

shattered throat
mans womans or childs
not one not

one
but death went on and on
never looking aside

except now and then like a child
with a furtive half-smile
to make sure I was noticing.

❯ *Anima*

FOR JANET

There she was. While the flare
of the August sky darkened
and twilight deepened, deepening
the field, while the evening star
came holily out, she tended
the fire by the edge of the woods,
a young woman both dark and fair,

moving among these natural
things, the fire, the woods, the star,
and the distant mountains, barefoot
and wearing a sweatshirt, a skirt
that fell loosely over her thighs,
she who was strong in her sex,
with her hair loosened, a figure
of sturdiness in the female way,
bending as she stirred the beans
in the blackened pot or walked
in darkening grass with a bucket
on her hip or split firesticks
with her axe; and I saw a scene
of ten thousand years ago or maybe
ten thousand to come; and she also
must have thought of time, for she
pointed to the star, and her voice
was distinct on the twilit air,
"Look at the star now, look
at a thing that was always there."

I do look. And I see her, and she
is there. Others too, her husband,
Rose Marie and the Bo; but for one
moment, or forever, I see only her,
her and the star and the fire
and the woods and the mountains,
a pure moment from an existence
in the other consciousness where time
is stilled and no fear is felt.
Firelight and starlight and woman,
complete and beautiful, for only
one place is known, ever, and this is
there, meaning beauty, meaning
all that is human in one fathoming,
the passion of mind, the reflectiveness
of spirit. I do not know, on this shore
of a shadowed field in the shadow of my
old age, what else a man lives for.

❯ *The Point*

In a broken
mirror you might
lie fragmented

a nipple paired
with an eye
and all your parts

strange in their
new arrangements.
And I might take

these fragments (if I
were so given)
in these selfsame

chances
and cement them
to that sunniness there

of morning wall
where you would be
a mosaic of your

random beauty.
Glittering
you would endure

for years and years
in time that will admit
no chances.

But the point is you
you looking out
a little unknowable

not wanting to be known

not in that way
not like a chance

but holding your own
like time   like stone
like leaping flame.

> ## *Two Romantic Pieces*

"Une Allée du Luxembourg," by Gérard de Nerval

There now, she's passed – that slight
One, just there and gone like a bird,
Holding a bright flower, humming
Some tune I almost heard.

Might she have loved me? Maybe
Hers is the last little light
In the whole world that could enter
My dark, darkening night.

But no. That time is over.
Good-bye, small light that shone,
Fragrance, woman, music,
Happiness . . . you are gone!

"Tristesse," by Alphonse de Lamartine

Once more let me go, I said, where that blest shore
Images Naples over an azure sea.
Palaces, hills, unmisted stars, the orange trees
Blossoming there under skies eternally pure!

What delays you? Come! I would see again
Vesuvius flaming, mounting from the very waves;
On her heights I would worship the inchoate dawn;
I would descend, as in a smiling trance, those slopes,
Leading the way for somebody I adore.

Follow me where the coast of that tranquil bay
Winds in and out; let us tread once more that path
Our footsteps knew so well, to the ruined Gardens
Of Cynthia, Virgil's Tomb, the Temple of Venus:
There, under orange trees, under the flowering vine
That twines so slenderly amidst the myrtle
And weaves a mantle of blossom above your head,
In the music of gentle waves or the murmuring wind,
There together, alone with our love, alone in nature,
Like the light our life will seem sweeter.

                                  Now
My days resemble the torchlight, acrid, guttering,
Little by little snuffed in the winds of anguish,
Or shedding sometimes, when in my heart the memories
Of you rekindle, a lurid and momentary glimmer.
I do not know if finally the gods will permit me
To complete my difficult journey here on earth;
My horizon contracts, and my bewildered eyes
Hardly dare search beyond one narrow season.
    But if I must die tomorrow,

If in this land once destined for happiness
    I must let fall from my hand
    The goblet that fate had seemed
To wreathe with rose petals fragrantly all
For my pleasure, I beg them only to lead me
Again to the shore that your memory still adorns.
There in a sad remoteness I may hail once more
Those sunny vistas, and die where I tasted life!

❧ *Bouquet in Dog Time*

A bit of yarrow and then of rue,
steeplebush and black-eyed susan,
one fringed orchis, ragged and wry,
some meadowsweet, the vetch that's blue,
to make a comeliness for you,

with dogbane, daisies, bouncing bet,
the clover red, the clover white,
walking the field before the night,
lazy under a lavender sky
(crazy and spent from the day of fear)
for one of every kind that's here,
sundew, burnet, thimbleberry,
all so simple, all so true,
like a bit of yarrow and of rue.

❯ *My Meadow*

Well, it's still the loveliest meadow in all Vermont.
I believe that truly, yet for years have hardly

seen it, I think, having lived too long with it –
until I went to clean up the mess of firewood

left by the rural electric co-op when they cut
my clump of soft maples "threatening" their lines,

this morning, the last day of September. My maple leaves
were spilled in the grass, deep crimson. I worked

with axe and chainsaw, and when I was done I sat
on my rock that had housed my fox before the state

executed him on suspicion of rabies, and then
I looked at my meadow. I saw how it lies between

the little road and the little brook, how its borders
are birch and hemlock, popple and elm and ash,

white, green, red, brown, and gray, and how my grass
is composed in smooth serenity. Yet I have hankered

for six years after that meadow I saw in Texas
near Camp Wood because I discovered an armadillo

there and saw two long-tailed flycatchers
at their fantastic mating dance in the air.

Now I saw my meadow. And I called myself all kinds
of a blind Yankee fool – not so much for hankering,

more for the quality of my looking that could make me
see in my mind what I could not see in my meadow.

However, I saw my serviceberry tree at the edge
of the grass where little pied asters, called Farewell-

to-Summer, made a hedge, my serviceberry still limping
from last winter's storms, and I went

and trimmed it. The small waxy pointed leaves
were delicate with the colors of coral and mallow

and the hesitating blush of the sky at dawn.
When I finished I stepped over my old fence

and sat by my brook on moss sodden from last night's
rain and got the seat of my britches wet.

I looked at my brook. It curled over my stones
that looked back at me again with the pathos

of their Paleozoic eyes. I thought of my
discontents. The brook, curled in its reflections

of ferns and asters and bright leaves, was whispering
something that made no sense. Then I closed my eyes

and heard my brook inside my head. It told me –
and I saw a distant inner light like the flash

of a waterdrop on a turning leaf – it told me
maybe I have lived too long with the world.

❯ Regarding Chainsaws

The first chainsaw I owned was years ago,
an old yellow McCulloch that wouldn't start.
Bo Bremmer give it to me that was my friend,
though I've had enemies couldn't of done
no worse. I took it to Ward's over to Morrisville,
and no doubt they tinkered it as best they could,
but it still wouldn't start. One time later
I took it down to the last bolt and gasket
and put it together again, hoping somehow
I'd do something accidental-like that would
make it go, and then I yanked on it
450 times, as I figured afterwards,
and give myself a bursitis in the elbow
that went five years even after
Doc Arrowsmith shot it full of cortisone
and near killed me when he hit a nerve
dead on. Old Stan wanted that saw, wanted it bad.
Figured I was a greenhorn that didn't know
nothing and he could fix it. Well, I was,
you could say, being only forty at the time,
but a fair hand at tinkering. "Stan," I said,
"you're a neighbor. I like you. I wouldn't
sell that thing to nobody, except maybe
Vice-President Nixon." But Stan persisted.
He always did. One time we was loafing and
gabbing in his front dooryard, and he spied
that saw in the back of my pickup. He run
quick inside, then come out and stuck a double
sawbuck in my shirt pocket, and he grabbed
that saw and lugged it off. Next day, when I
drove past, I seen he had it snugged down tight
with a tow-chain on the bed of his old Dodge
Powerwagon, and he was yanking on it
with both hands. Two or three days after,
I asked him, "How you getting along with that
McCulloch, Stan?" "Well," he says, "I tooken
it down to scrap, and I buried it in three

separate places yonder on the upper side
of the potato piece. You can't be too careful,"
he says, "when you're disposing of a hex."
The next saw I had was a godawful ancient
Homelite that I give Dry Dryden thirty bucks for,
temperamental as a ram too, but I liked it.
It used to remind me of Dry and how he'd
clap that saw a couple times with the flat
of his double-blade axe to make it go
and how he honed the chain with a worn-down
file stuck in an old baseball. I worked
that saw for years. I put up forty-five
run them days each summer and fall to keep
my stoves het through the winter. I couldn't now.
It'd kill me. Of course they got these here
modern Swedish saws now that can take
all the worry out of it. What's the good
of that? Takes all the fun out too, don't it?
Why, I reckon. I mind when Gilles Boivin snagged
an old sap spout buried in a chunk of maple
and it tore up his mouth so bad he couldn't play
"Tea for Two" on his cornet in the town band
no more, and then when Toby Fox was holding
a beech limb that Rob Bowen was bucking up
and the saw skidded crossways and nipped off
one of Toby's fingers. Ain't that more like it?
Makes you know you're living. But mostly they wan't
dangerous, and the only thing they broke was your
back. Old Stan, he was a buller and a jammer
in his time, no two ways about that, but he
never sawed himself. Stan had the sugar
all his life, and he wan't always too careful
about his diet and the injections. He lost
all the feeling in his legs from the knees down.
One time he started up his Powerwagon
out in the barn, and his foot slipped off the clutch,
and she jumped forwards right through the wall
and into the manure pit. He just set there,
swearing like you could of heard it in St.

Johnsbury, till his wife come out and said,
"Stan, what's got into you?" "Missus," he says,
"ain't nothing got into me. Can't you see?
It's me that's got into this here pile of shit."
Not much later they took away one of his
legs, and six months after that they took
the other and left him setting in his old chair
with a tank of oxygen to sip at whenever
he felt himself sinking. I remember that chair.
Stan reupholstered it with an old bearskin
that must of come down from his great-great-
grandfather and had grit in it left over
from the Civil War and a bullet-hole as big
as a yawning cat. Stan latched the pieces together
with rawhide, cross fashion, but the stitches was
always breaking and coming undone. About then
I quit stopping by to see old Stan, and I
don't feel so good about that neither. But my mother
was having her strokes then. I figured
one person coming apart was as much
as a man can stand. Then Stan was taken away
to the nursing home, and then he died. I always
remember how he planted them pieces of spooked
McCulloch up above the potatoes. One time
I went up and dug, and I took the old
sprocket, all pitted and et away, and set it
on the windowsill right there next to the
butter mold. But I'm damned if I know why.

❯ *Marvin McCabe*

First off, I have to say I can't talk good.
What's the use of saying it? Damned if I know;
nobody could miss it. But something always makes me
try to apologize. The talk machine's busted,
that's all. Connections all screwed up. Have you ever
wondered how it would be to have your thought
that's clear and shiny inside your head come out

like a mouthful of mud? As for simple things,
I say, "Ahwan ahg' abah'" – what does it mean?
I say it five times, "Ahwan ahg' abah',"
grimacing and smiling, *pleading*, and no one
hears me say I want to go to the bathroom.
I have to take a leak, for Christ's sake! – what
could be simpler? Well, for me, almost everything
if it doesn't require speech. That's why I have to
rely on Hayden. He's listened to me so much
he knows not only what I'm saying but what
I mean to say, you understand? – that thought
in my head. He can write it out for me. What
I'm thinking now – and most of the time – is how
I wish whoever invented beer had been stuffed
back and smothered in his mother's womb. That's
damn-fool wishing, of course. But it's the kind
a man in my fix can spend a lot of time on.

It was hard at home. I mean hard. We never
had a farm. Lived here and there, my old man
milking cows for other farmers or shoveling gravel
on the road gang; he did most anything. But what he was
was a trader. He'd go up to Canady looking
for auctions, in Knowlton or around Granby,
and he'd buy a team or a set of chairs or a
barrel full of old dishes or God knows what,
and he'd bring the stuff home and sell it. He'd
do it all right, I'll give him that; he was a
damn good trader – I never knew but one man that
took him in a deal. Yet he never made any
money, not to speak of. He was a *trader* –
do you understand what that means? It's a breed,
a special kind of a man, I think, or like some
craving or craziness in the head. Pa had it.
And he figured his boys should have it too.
It was the only way he could see that a man
might get somewhere; one good deal could set it
off, he thought, and then a couple more – no saying
how far a man could go. He used to tell us

how John D. Rockefeller started out peddling oil
door to door in a wagon. With me it was blankets.
One morning, the winter I was twelve, Pa hitched
our nag to the old sled and piled a dozen blankets
on behind. "Get going," he said, "and don't you
show your face till you've sold them." I did it.
Took me four days and three rotten freezing nights,
but I did it. And what I minded most wasn't
the selling or the cold, it was driving that horse
and that lousy sled. Somehow that stood for Pa,
as if he himself was standing there behind me,
sounding off in my ear. But I drove that horse
many a time more before I was through with it,
selling whatever Pa loaded on behind, junk
mostly.
 So you can see how I felt when I
turned sixteen and got my license. I felt
free. I was like a prisoner stepping out the door
of the jailhouse for the first time. I bought a car,
a wreck but I made it run, and I drove it
all over the countryside. And then of course
I discovered beer. All kids do, but can you
imagine what it meant after peddling away
my childhood behind that horse? The first time
I put a couple bottles of Bud inside me
it was – it was terrific. That buzz, like something
I dreamed of. Happiness. Christ, what a miracle,
I was free and happy too! Who could have foreseen
anything like that? Then I got a job, I got
a girl, I got her pregnant, the usual story
here in the mountains. I was married at seventeen,
and when the war came I went across and got
shot up – the usual story there too. What matters
is what came next: another car, a dark night,
a bellyful of beer, and that sharp turn on Rt. 15
just east of the gravel pit. I wish I'd died.
But they put a plate in my skull and pinned my arm
together with little bits of silver and wire,
and a year later I remembered who I was.

Marvin McCabe – I could hardly believe it.
That was twenty-eight years ago. I believe it now.
Marvin McCabe is a slobbering idiot: he talks
like one, so he must be one, mustn't he? And he walks
like one too, shuffling along with his cane.
Anyone who thinks the important part of his brain
is the part that thinks – well, let him take a look.
No, it's the part that controls the tongue and the other
motor functions. And mine's seventy-five per cent
dead.

     My wife was gone before I got back from the
hospital, gone and remarried – naturally. And I
had nothing to say about it, and wouldn't have said
anything if I had. But there's been no woman
for me in twenty-eight years; that's hard to take.
My boy used to come out to see me regularly
once a week, on schedule, which was a mistake,
of course, but one he rectified himself
when he was fourteen and ran away. I think
he ran off just to escape those afternoons
with me. For hours he'd sit there and say absolutely
nothing; but his looks would speak – how he despised me.
Naturally, and that was hard to take too.
And Pa, he despised me, and still does, old
as he is, though we've lived together this whole time.
He talks to me just like he talks to the dogs,
and when I try to answer he cuts in, "Shut up,
shut up that mumbling, no one can understand it."
When people come he tells them, "Look at me,
eighty-five years old and I'm looking after
a fifty-year-old man. Marvin's not worth
keeping, he's no good for nothing." And I just
smile. That's hard to take, believe me. But the hardest
of all was always this feeling that my thoughts
were shut inside me, that all I could do was smile.
I knew the words but couldn't say them – do you
see what that means? No one knew who I was.
It was like those people who believe your soul
can pass into another body when you die.

I was in the wrong body, but I hadn't died.
Can jail be worse than that? I wanted to die.
I would have if wanting could do it. But then
I came to see it doesn't make any difference.
If I spoke, what would it do? – my thoughts mean nothing,
my life means nothing, my death means nothing.
And everything means nothing. Sometimes I sit
here in this bay window and look out
at the field, the hills, the sky, and I see the boulders
laughing, holding their sides and laughing,
and the apple trees shaking and twisting with laughter,
the sky booming and roaring, the whole earth
heaving like a fat man's belly, everything
laughing. It isn't because we're a joke, no,
it's because we think we aren't a joke – that's
what the whole universe is laughing at. It makes
no difference if my thoughts are spoken or not,
or if I live or die – nothing will change.
How could it? This body is wrong, a misery,
a misrepresentation, but hell, would talking make
any difference? The reason nobody knows me
is because I don't exist. And neither do you.

❯ *Bears at Raspberry Time*

Fear. Three bears
are not fear, mother
and cubs come berrying
in our neighborhood

like any other family.
I want to see them, or any
distraction. Flashlight
poking across the brook

into briary darkness,
but they have gone,

noisily. I go to bed.
Fear. Unwritten books

already titled. Some
idiot will shoot the bears
soon, it always happens,
they'll be strung up by the paws

in someone's frontyard
maple to be admired and
measured, and I'll be paid
for work yet to be done –

with a broken imagination.
At last I dream. Our
plum tree, little, black,
twisted, gaunt in the

orchard: how for a moment
last spring it flowered
serenely, translucently
before yielding its usual

summer crop of withered
leaves. I waken, late,
go to the window, look
down to the orchard.

Is middle age what makes
even dreams factual?
The plum is serene and
bright in new moonlight,

dressed in silver leaves,
and nearby, in the waste
of rough grass strewn
in moonlight like diamond dust,

what is it? — a dark shape
moves, and then another.
Are they . . . I can't
be sure. The dark house

nuzzles my knee mutely,
pleading for meaty dollars.
Fear. Wouldn't it be great
to write nothing at all

except poems about bears?

❯ Song: So Often, So Long I Have Thought

FOR CYNTHIA TOKUMITSU

So often, so long I have thought of death
That the fear has softened. It has worn away.
Strange. Here in autumn again, late October,
I am late too, my woodshed still half empty,
And hurriedly I split these blocks in the rain,
Maple and beech. South three hundred miles
My mother lies sterile and white in the room
Of her great age, her pain, while I myself
Have come to the edge of the "vale." Strange.
Hurrying to our ends, the generations almost
Collide, pushing one another. And in twilight
The October raindrops thicken and turn to snow.

Cindy stacks while I split, here where I once
Worked alone, my helper now younger than I
By more years than I am younger than my mother —
Cindy, fresh as the snow petals forming on this old
Goldenrod. Before her, it was war-time. In my work
I wondered about those unarmed Orientals swarming
Uphill into the machine guns, or those earlier
Who had gone smiling to be roasted in the bronze
Cauldrons, or the Cappadocian children strewn —

Strewn, strewn, and my horror uncomprehending. Were they
People, killers and killed, real people? In twilight
The October raindrops thickened and turned to snow.

I understand now. Not thoughtfully, never;
But I feel an old strange personal unconcern,
How my mother, I, even Cindy might vanish
And still the twilight fall. Something has made me
A man of the soil at last, like those old
Death-takers. And has consciousness, once so dear,
Worn down like theirs, to run in the dim
Seasonal continuance? Year by year my hands
Grow to the axe. Is there a comfort now
In this? Or shall I still, and ultimately, rebel,
As I had resolved to do. I look at Cindy in the twilight.
In her hair the thick October raindrops turn to snow.

⟫ *A Little Old Funky Homeric Blues for Herm*

Knock off that hincty blowing, you Megarians,
I got a new beat, mellow and melic, like
warm, man. I sing of heisty Herm.

'Twas early dawn when somebody smashed the stars
and hardnose Herm was born. He lay there
on his cot a while, then he raised up and said:

"Ma – " that's Maybelline " – Ma, who's my daddy?"
"Him!" snorted Maybelline. "Yeah, but who is he?"
"He come in a white cloud." "Hah, I knows the kind –

them so big-balled." "Gully-low he was,
sure enough." "He live up Sugar Hill?"
"Up some hill somewheres, that's all I heard."

"I knowed it!" And hero Herm he laughed
and looked in the glass and smarmed to hisself:
"An eight-rock mama and a ofay pop –

hey, man, you got something coming sure!"
Then the window flashed with curious light.
"Ma, ma, what's that?" "Why just a car going by."

"Car – what kind of car?" "Hmm, it look like a
Jaguar." Horrid Herm flaked out in a fake of sleep,
but then rose up, unseen, and out the door,

down the dark hall where he found a rusty pipe
which cried out, "No, no! I too am an object of this world!"
But hectic Herm he said, "Bah, you nothing now."

And he killed it with one blow, and bent it,
and then and there, all by himself,
invented the tenor sax. O hippocrene Herm!

He blew, he strutted, he made the walls fall down
and then fall up again, with only 96 bars
of Hermetic Swan-shaped Blues; and bowed and departed.

Down the stairs, down the block, past fizz and fuzz
– "You mess with me, baby, I bite you ass" –
down Fifth, and down and down, till there it stood,

the great red Jag tethered tight outside
the pad of Apollonio. Apollonio the brave,
fair, friend to all, talented, liberal, who played

all day on his symphony orchestra.
Hoodoo Herm he fingered the secret switch,
and drove that Jag like a fist of fire

across the park, up Amsterdam, to a cave
on Morningside Heights. Wham! – it was hidden.
Hieratic Herm sat down and pulled his pud,

and then and there, all by himself, invented
man's sacrificial relationship to fate.
Twelve times he jetted to the twelve prophets in order.

Handsome Lake
Simon Kimbaugh
John Wilson
André Matswa
Muana Lesa
Kanakuk
Marcus Garvey
Enoch Mgijima
Wodziwob
Doctor George
Isatai
Makandal

And bowed, and said, "I done what you told me."
Then home, and slipped through the keyhole
In the form of a flatted seventh. Back to the cot.

Maybelline cried, "Where you been, child?"
But holy Herm: "Nowheres. How you expect
a little newborn baby going to go?"

Then Maybelline looked wise: "Little fucker,
I knows you. The day that big man
from up yonder stuck his thing in me

he got a heap of trouble on the world."
Then hijacker Herm he snuggled in his rildy
and answered: "Ma, you is quaker oats. Now listen,

ain't you heard about status yet? It's like powerful,
like being on top, but with class, no sweat, see –
and I aim to get me some. If nobody –

meaning that mister big on the hill –
give it to me, I gets it any way, that's all,
any way I can. Don't you worry none, I

blowing real sharp on this gig already."
And he fell asleep. Snuffling and snoring.
Then came the fuzz with Apollonio

to wake him up. "Boy, where'd you stash that Jag?"
"Jag? – Jag? – I don't know nothing about – "
but Apollonio lifted him and shook him hard,

and here's where handy Herm did his cleverest,
for he farted juicily inside his diaper
and topped it with a sneeze. Awed Apollonio

dropped him like a toad. Yet at last
they agreed to submit the matter to
the man on the hill, who smiled when he heard

of heretical Herm and the big red Jag,
smiled and said: "You got to give it back."
And haunted Herm said: "Shucks," and he said:

"Dadgumit," but what could he do? –
something tied his tongue. He was like a child,
he was a child. He had to give it back.

So haywire Herm and affable Apollonio
trucked down the avenue together,
until, after a ways, Herm unslung his horn,

the golden tenor, and with a groan and a squeal
bopped out the changes on Cora Banty's Ride,
and Apollonio's blond wig stood up

and he jigged, he twitched, he chuckled, and he perspired,
and at last he leaped and cried: "Oh, man, I dig you,
teach me to play that thing." "What!"

said hispid Herm, "you grunch and groan!
You dirty them fingers so lily-white!"
"I got to, man, I got to. Give me that beat again,"

cried Apollonio, down on his knees and rocking.
"What it worth to you?" "Anything, anything –
take my Jag, take my electronic wristwatch,

I got to have that horn. Oh Herm, we are brothers now."
And so hilarious Herm went home again,
grinning and gloating. But Maybelline

she said: "You too big for you britches, boy,
they going to fix you yet. Prince of Thieves
they calls you. Maybe you is and maybe you aint

but you know what they going to make you? –
Prince of Storekeepers, that's what, Prince
of Nickels and Dimes, Prince of Gouging and Niggling,

you going to be a rat just like them, little prince,
you hear? – squeezing and scrambling and squawking
just like them, just like them,

and the very best name they ever going
to call you is Psychopompos."
"Shit," said homunculus Herm.

> *The Mouse*

The mouse sharpens his teeth
    in my house, gnawing my timbers.
I hear him, a dry sound
    at night underneath
the moist wind in the pine trees.
    Night after night I hear him.
The mouse sharpens his teeth.
    Under the moist wind I hear him.
In the darkness I hear a dry sound.

> *The Line*

All my woods are
tangle. Ancient
spruce, bent birch,

popple broken and
maple springing
too tall and thin.

It's a wrangle
of fern and raspberry
canes and pokeweed.

Next to me my
neighbor, Mr. Davis,
is entirely red pine,

a stand of ranks
and files, bedded
in its own needles.

How loud my woods
with stirrings, callings,
chatterings and then

how peaceful there
in the pines! I
love to step over

the clear line
into my neighbor's
silence, where only

the high murmur
in tree crowns, far
and near, tells human

loneliness something
about itself.
It is so strange, so

awesome. It is
like stepping out
of reality into

a theater, a change
so sudden, a hush
so informative

and portending. Yet
I know I love
my neighbor's quiet

because it is his,
it belongs to Mr.
Davis, whom I've

never met (he lives
in Waterville),
and I can only

borrow that high
far murmur. At last
I must step

back over the line
to my own weedy
mixed-up clamor

where all the voices
proclaim their own.
And that is love

and I am home.

❯ Almanach du Printemps Vivarois

Am I obsessed by stone? Life has worn thin here
    where the *garrigue* slopes down to the fields,
to the *vignes* and *luzerne*. A meager surface
    covers the stone – stone so long my own
life and song – only gray tufts of grass, moss,
    the thyme just beginning in its rough
tangles to glitter with little purple blooms,
    the summer savory so very
fragrant now, the *piloselles*, the broom, the first
    poppies and thistles, with no more than
a few *cades* and *chênes verts,* scrubby and prickly,
    to make shadows; yes, a sparse surface
and the stone shows through, flakes, grits, fragments, sharp shards
    littering the ground, or the outcrop
of smooth bedrock here and there, and then the huge
    escarpment across the way, looming
over the valley. The stone gleams, pale gray. Life
    has worn thin here, washed always down. Ah,
republica de misèria, so sang
    one poet in the olden tongue, *lo*
lenga d'oc, a song of dole, and he meant it
    to be taken hermetically
both ways, of spirit and body; *trobar clus*
    for the oppressed and loving people.
Now one tractor, small in the distance, rumbles
    below in its *sulfatage,* spraying
the vine-rows, while nearby a wall that someone
    a couple of hundred years ago
assembled, the stones chosen with care, all flat
    and set tight with the top row upright
and angled, has fallen, sprawled away. Only
    parts of it remain to exhibit
the original construction. Life has worn
    thin here, and mine as well. A cuckoo
calls, calls, calls, damned mad invariable sound,

over and over, telling the mad
impossible hours. *Lo cinc d'abrièu,*
lo cocut deu chantar, mòrt o vièu.
And who can ignore such meanings, messages,
intimations? A squawking magpie
staggers through the lower air, a jerk and a
joke. Time flies. But murkily and in
confusion, cock-eyed. Yet it's mid-morning, mid-
April, the Ardèche, one might do worse,
one might do almost immeasurably worse,
and the sun at last is strong after
our long shivering in the *mistral.* Jacket
and sweater are pillow now, I'm down
to my shirt, my companion already down
to practically nothing, lovely
to see, and although I am content to bake,
eating the sun (as the Italians
say) to put marrow in my bones while I make
lazy words run in a lazy song
about stones, she is all business and she knows
her business – oh, nothing could be more
plain, she in the lotus position, her board
propped on her knees. She draws. She is young,
she has a right to be serious. Finches
are serious in the oak-bushes,
chittering, chattering, gathering gray grass
and gray lichen for their nests. Finches?
They look more or less like finches. Ignorance –
how it invades a petulant mind
aging in laziness and lust. And the sun,
higher now, stronger, a radiance
in the sky and a blaze in the valley's faint
blue mist, burning on the stone, turning
our Ibie white, our river so greenly fresh
three weeks ago, now a slow seepage,
is hot, hot, blessedly hot, stirring my blood,
warming me through, and also moving
the summer savory to even greater

fragrance, the plant called *sariette,* known
as an aphrodisiac. Do I need that?
   Not after last night. Strange, the seed still
sprouting in hot sun from the hill of stone. Strange,
   the old spirit and old body still
flouting time and murk and confusion in lust.
   The young woman in her sunhat and
underwear peers off at the distance, then down
   at her page, so certain of her work,
its newness, its autonomy – her art there
   darkening the paper. But my song
is old, my stone song; I patch it up from shreds
   of Latin grandeur and trobar rhyme,
old, conventional, wrong – who knows it better? –
   though all conventions are old as soon
as they occur. They are always occurring.
   The song is all in my head. Shreds of
culture. Confusions of time. It is noon now,
   my shirt goes to the pillow, I look
at my own white skin, almost parched it seems, creased
   with age-lines. And it gleams! Suddenly
the republic of misery is blazing,
   the old stone is glowing, and as if
at a stroke of some cosmic tone everything
   falls silent, the finches, the tractor,
the cuckoo, the litho-pencil squeaking, yes,
   the small wind in the grass, but nothing
has stopped. Am I deaf now too? Or is silence
   the indispensable analogue
of brilliance? And stone is silent. Ancient stone,
   glowing stone. Song in its confusions
is all extraneous, it dies away. Shreds
   of time. In April when the seed sprouts,
in the Ardèche huge with silence where life is
   thin, an old man and a girl are held
in stillness, in radiance, in flames of stone,
   for the moment of eternity.

❭ *Song of the Two Crows*

I sing of Morrisville
(if you call this cry
    a song). I
(if you call this painful

voice by that great name)
sing the poverty of my
    region and of
the wrong end of Morrisville.

You summer people will say
that all its ends are wrong,
    but there, right there,
the very end of the wrong end –

a house with windows sagging,
leaning roadward as in defense
    or maybe defiance
next to the granite ledge,

our cliff of broken stone
that shoulders our dilapidated
    one-lane iron bridge.
Who lives here? I don't know.

But they (Hermes reward them)
made this extraordinary garden,
    geraniums,
petunias and nasturtiums

planted in every crevice and all
the footholds of the cliff.
    And then
they painted the cliff-face,

painted the old stone; no design,
just swatches of color, bold

rough splashes
irregularly, garish orange

and livid blue. Is it
fluorescent, do these stones
    glow in the dark?
Maybe. I only know

they glow in the day, so
vivid I stopped my car,
    whereupon two others
came inquiring also, two

crows in the broken spars
of the white pine tree, cawing
    above the house.
Why had those who inhabited

this corner of poverty
painted the stones? Was it
    that the flowers
in living bravery nevertheless

made too meager a show
for the ruined cliff? Or did they
    think to bring art
to nature, somehow to improve

this corner of ugliness?
For my part I thought how
    these colors
were beautiful and yet strange

in their beauty, ugly colors,
garish orange, livid blue;
    they reminded me
of those Spanish cemeteries

I saw in New Mexico, tin
mirrors and plastic flowers
　　　in the desert. Then
I knew why the stones

had been painted: to make
reparation, such as the poor
　　　might make, whose sorrow
had been done here, this

desecration. Is not this
the burden of all poor lands
　　　everywhere,
the basis of poverty?

A spoiled land makes spoiled
people. The poor know this.
　　　I guess
the crows know too, because off

they flew, cawing above
the bridge and the slashed hills
　　　surrounding Morrisville.
I started my car and drove

out on the iron bridge
which rumbled its sullen
　　　affirmation.
And I sang as I sing now

(if you care to call it song)
my people of Morrisville
　　　who live
where all the ends are wrong.

› Mild Winter

Mid-December but still the ground's unfrozen, taking
my impress receptively, as if it would pull me in.
The snowfall melts wherever it finds warm earth
but clings to everything aboveground, twigs, leaves, stems,
debris of the woods floor. It is a tracery
under the trees, a damask. Behind me my boot-tracks
are a clumsy soilure. Beside me little snow crystals
make arabesque on the bark scales of an old spruce,
filigree on the ear-like petals of lichen. Somewhere
in the trees ahead a raven rises and moves away
and at once in my mind dark wings labor. I peer
through gray air but the raven is not visible; only
a voice is there, guttural bad news penetrating
the thickness of spruce trees. No wonder cousin Edgar
chose a raven to be his metaphysical bird,
though he was wrong to give it no more than that silly
word to say; ravens are articulate, like the whole
race of pessimists, speaking in many tones. I too
have had my Ligeia, I have had my Annabel Lee.
A web of snowflakes brushes my forehead, I hear
the United Farmers milk truck gear down and rumble
on Schoolhouse Hill, but Edgar, cousin, you died
twelve years ago now when we were forty, and I've
outlived you, somehow I've left you, and I'm
changed, so sober in these damp northern woods.
I wonder will anybody remember to tell my wife
she can draw on my social security when the time
comes? The raven will. I hear him muttering far off,
his voice now, with the voices of the others, very soft
yet lucid across gray air. In my mind black shapes
settle and shift and rise and settle again, talking
in the spruces. Strange how their words, quiet and remote,
yet come distinct over the distance, like words in dreams.
Idiot ravens, take off – depart! You should have been long gone
to the valleys, the garbage-laden rivers! I always
said if the winter must come then let it be cold,
let it be bitter and pure and silent, not like this.

» *Who Cares, Long as It's B-Flat*

Floyd O'Brien, Teagardens Charlie & Jack
    where are the snowbirds of yesteryear?

Boyce Brown, Rod Cless, Floyd Bean
    Jimmy McPartland, Danny Polo
Hank Isaacs, Davy Tough, Jim Lannigan

    where are you, Jim Lannigan?

Jesus but you were awful musicians
    Pee Wee, Abby, and you Faz
awful awful. Can you please
    tell me the way to Friar's Point?

"Aw, Jess." "Shake it, Miss Chippie, but don't
    break it."
"Listen at that dirty Mezz!" Can you
    tell me please
the way to White City? Where
    can I find
the Wolverines, Teschemacher?

    Leon Rapollo?

Eubie, Punch, Darnell? "Cut him
    Mister Reefer Man." "I wisht
      I had a barrel of it."

Muggsy, Muggsy where art thou
    where is Pine Top
where are the Yanceys now?

35 years
    swish-swish of a velvet cymbal
    twinkling leaves
in the lilac tree

"When I die

    when I die

        please bury me

sweet mamo

    in a sardine can . . ."

Coda

    And these little cats think

        they discovered something

                (gawd

damm)

❯ Rummage

Growing old in shabby clothes
is a bewilderment for someone
who wanted all his life
to wear something handsome
under the handsome sun.

In darkness under the bent
moon I bend
to pick from the frozen road
a shred of birch bark
blowing in the wind.

❯ The Sorrow Song

Tata, Baba, Great Spirit –

    "O Sons of Cush
who feed upon suffering
    and quench your thirst in tears
your slavery will not endure
    much longer."

Retain the old festivals
    but not all/
these are the true festivals:
                Feast of the White Dog
                Strawberry Festival
                Corn Festival or Feast of Feathers
                Festival of the Green Corn/
thus Handsome Lake.

        The child
was lost, long long gone
                so that the woman became mad
and wandered away, searching in strange places,
        but found nothing
except thirst like dry thistledown
and the hunger of skeletons in the sand.
            She stumbled, near death
                and lost consciousness
stretched on her side on earth
                curved, a crescent
            beneath the crescent moon,
and her hands lay eastward, her feet westward,
                and she dreamed.
        A voice spoke, saying
the child is found, all will be well, only
            take the plant growing near your hand
                and eat of it.
        And she looked and it was there
                and when she ate of it
her strength returned, she rose intact and young
                from the ground
            and gave thanks east and west
and went back to her people, who called her
        the Peyote Woman.

Regeneration, redemption, earth and the moon
        and the plant growing
carrot-shaped and small
            a "button" on top.

In the Iroquois Confederation
the New Testament
was not well regarded
except by the Cayugas
who identified Jesus
with their own founding hero
called the Fatherless Boy.

Tecumseh:
               "The great spirit
gave this immense island
          to his red children, and placed
the whites on the other side
               of the big water/
but they were not contented
               with their own
and came to take ours from us/
               they have driven us
from the sea to the lakes
          we can go no farther."

Kanakuk:
               "My father
the great spirit
          holds all the world
               in his hands
and I pray to him
          that we may not be removed
from our lands.
               Take pity on us
and let us remain where we are,
          let us remain!"

Sitting Bull, Tenskwatawa, Smohalla,
Geronimo, John Rave/
               names
               in the void.

After the third day when Jesus ascended
he walked on the moonbeam –
        the Great Way
    through the thighs of the outstretched
       crescent
straight and high to the death-dwellers
      of the moon
    on the straight path from the longhouse floor
    on the white sand of the tipi mound –
     the Way of Peyote.

O lost children
in strange places wandering
     gather & look & see –
the moonbeam is rising and descending
    the moonpath going and returning
all night for thee,
       for thee.

❯ *Loneliness: An Outburst of Hexasyllables*

Stillness and moonlight, with
thick newfallen snow. I
go to the hollow field
beneath the little ridge
of spruces. The snow lies
on the trees, drapery
white and unmoving. I
cannot see any light
from here, no farmhouse, no
car moving through darkness.
A bird makes a sleepy
sound somewhere, probably
a pine grosbeak in the
trees. Often I visit
this place, here where no lights
show, only the cold moon
and the stars, for I have

so long a loneliness
(I think of all my time
compounded with all time)
that often it might cry
if it saw a lighted
window in the night. Now
a little breath of cold
air in the stillness sways
the white trees with a sigh.

·　　　·　　　·

Between two snow-heavy
boughs, a bright star. Perhaps
many stars combined in
one sparkling, perhaps a
galaxy. I look up
to incalculable
space, on which my two boughs
almost close. Somewhere there
a world like this exists,
as beautiful as this,
snow in moonlight gleaming,
yet with no mind. Nothing
on that world knows what is
beauty or loneliness.
Only the snow-draped trees.

·　　　·　　　·

Moonlight is "reflected
light reflected again
on snow." It seems – no, it
actually is from
everywhere. It casts no
shadow. It is pale and
what is called, with justice,
ethereal; and yet
its brightness is enough
to show up everything,
"as bright as day." But this

is not daylight; it is
the visible aspect
of stillness: the two are
one. See how the spruces
stand in moonlight as in
the silence, unmoving
and soundless, held like that
to be reflectors of
loneliness, the arras
hung in this empty room.
These spruces belong to
Marshall Washer, my friend
and neighbor, whose light I
can never see from here.

• • •

Cursed from childhood with
incapacity, with
the vision of the void.
Everyone now has thought
how it may be when soon
universal death comes
down the mountainsides, creeps
up from the seas, appears
out of the air like snow,
and how one lucky or
unlucky person might
escape the multitude
and survive alone. This
is the archetypal dream
or daydream of our years.
That man or woman will
be much more alone than
anyone ever was;
no look, no voice, no touch,
no *mind* in all the world.
It might be me. It might
be now, this moment, here.

• • •

The snow sculpts this object,
a snow-tree, and does it
neither by carving nor
by molding, for there is
a third way nature knows
and a few men besides
(who will not give themselves
to the controversies
of theorists). Rather
this sculpture is made by
the whole of motioning,
all in a concert, which
condenses out of air –
out of universal
substance – the exact form
this tree must take. Never
a flake too many or
too few: it is exact.
All growth is a kind of
condensation, like these
intense words gathering
here. Its exactness is
all that we understand
of perfection. Yet it
cannot last. That dream was
a folly, for the sun's
first minutest degree
of heat at dawn, the wind's
least pressure, will change it
irretrievably. This
snowy spruce is good for
these few hours only, in
a quiet winter's night.

                    •   •   •

This is being alone,
this learning with the years
how exactness fails, how
it must fail always, how

the momentary fit
of mood and circumstance
must necessarily
decay. One consciousness
in the night can never
find another to share
or even know this, this
particular felt hour.
O God, I know you don't
exist, or certainly
you would blast us or lift
us backward into that
simplicity they knew
long ago when people
had someone to talk to.

         •   •   •

But if it were only
the problem of a new
metaphysics! One could
invent something, almost
anything. Think what schemes
and dreams have served. But I
am here in this real life
that I was given, my life
of a withered tongue. I
brush through the trees, and snow
spills down on me, a chill
colder than the cold. Mad,
maddened, turning around,
I beat the tree with my
arms; unweighted branches
spring upward and snow flies,
a silent fury. Then
I fall back, winded, wet,
snow melting in my shirt;
I stumble in ruckled
snow, all exactness gone,
only the stillness left

in its indifferent
perfection on my ruin;
and I am limp, frightened
of myself, yet saddened
by such futility.
I go away, slogging
in my own tracks that make
an erratic passage
like a wounded bear's, scuffed
over the lovely snow.

. . .

At home the fire has died,
the stove is cold. I touch
the estranging metal.
I pour tea, cold and dark,
in a cup. The clock strikes,
but I forget, until
too late, to count the hours.
I sit by the cold stove
in a stillness broken
by the clock ticking there
in the other room, by
clapboards creaking, and I
begin to shiver, cold,
at home in my own house.

. . .

Down in the duckpen they
are stirring in the bright
white moonlight and they are
affected by it, they
gabble, and from time to
time – now – the hen ducks break
into quacking, raucous
in the still nighttime. I
cannot decide if it
is laughter. I cannot
decide if this laughter

is derisive or just
maniacal and sad.

＊　　＊　　＊

I do my work, all night
until the dawn comes, late
in this week of solstice.
Then pink, as I look up,
is the snow out in the
garden, pink is the snow
on the spruces, pink the
immense snowy mountain
across the valley. I
lean on the cold window.
A jay slips down and lights
on the birch, dislodging
drops of snow from his bough.
The moon is a pallid
disk on the horizon,
as if it had been washed
with snow. The world has turned
from night to day, and this
event is still touching
deep sources in me, though
I do not know what they
are. The cold weight of my
body pulls downward and
I feel it as if my
years were heavy, and I
feel a drop of moisture
sliding down my nose, cold
and weighted, until it
meets the glass. I know that
I am a fool and all
men are fools. I know it
and I know I know it.
What good is it to know?

❯ Of Brook and Stone

Bo, may you someday,
as I now you,
here by our brook in a yellow
August afternoon,

bless your son in his absence
from you, you then
standing as I stand, alone
on our big stone.

And may, though many changes
will have transmuted many
things, this rock still
hold you, and this old brook's

water still flow then
as now, murmuring
beneath your feet of why
and how and when.

❯ Moonset

The dark will come, I said,
soon now at moonset.

And I looked and looked to see
our night-lady

so grave and magnanimous
go away

over our hill, smiling
a moment, no more, through pointed

spruces; and the dark came,
the snow turned gray.

Yet then slowly the gray
was silver, the snow-clad

spruces began to sparkle,
and even the frost of the air

was illumined, a low
mazy

dance of light-specks. I
looked overhead

to the stars, suddenly
so present, so much a part

of the night. The night,
I said, is all grave

and all a dance and never
dark. And on my slow

snowshoes I danced and skipped
gravely down the meadow.

❯ *Afternoon of a Faun*

(Translated from the poem by Stéphane Mallarmé)

ECLOGUE

These nymphs, whom I itch to perpetuate —
                                            so clear
Their lightness, yet incarnate, flesh of this air
Made rosy by woodland slumber.

                            Was loving a dream?

Like a drift of ancient night my misgiving grows,
Numberless subtle ramifications, which merge
In these real branches – ah, proof that I wake alone
Who mistook for triumph the dreamt ideal of roses!
We must think again . . .

                    Or suppose these two you spell of
Are no more than desires of your own wondrous senses!
Faun, illusion trembles in those blue cool eyes
Of the one more chaste, seeping as from a pool.
And then this other, all sighs, will you say that she,
Contrasting, is the day's hot breeze in your fleeces?
But no. Through this swooning immobility and laziness,
Cool morning (if it resists) smothered in torpor,
No water murmurs except this from my flute
Wetting the verdure with harmony, and the only wind
Is from these two pipes which exhale quickly
Before it disperses their song in an arid rain –
This now on the far unrippling horizon,
Visible and serene, this artificial breath
Of inspiration remounting to the sky.

O calm banks of that pool I plundered in Sicily
With my self-love once to spite the jealous sun,
Silent beneath those spark-like flowers, RECALL
"How I here, cutting the hollow reeds that genius
Subjugates, see wavering, on the hazy, distant,
Golden greenery which consecrates its vine
To the springheads, an animal whiteness come to rest;
And how then in the low prelude when the pipes
Are born this flight of swans – ah, naiads! – runs
Or plunges . . ."

              In the hot hour the inert world burns,
Not revealing by what art that virginity,
Craved by him searching the *la*, vanished together:
So I shall rouse myself to my original fervor,
Upright and alone, under the sky's ageless flood
Of light, you lilies, and one with you for innocence.

Besides this nothingness, sweet hint from their lip,
This kiss all in its promise of betrayal,
Still my shoulder, unproven, exposes a mysterious
Wound – am I bitten truly, am I exalted?
Ah, enough! Something arcane chose to confide
Below the azure in this great twin reed we play on,
Which dreams in a long solo, taking to itself
The cheek's shamed blush, how we were amusing
To the beauty around us through false confusions
We conceived between her and our credulous song;
And how also in song's sublimity a purging
Might strike from our worn fantasy of a pure
Back or flank, pursued by my half-closed eyes,
One sonorous and vain and monotonous line.

Try therefore, o instrument of transports, cunning
Syrinx, to spring and flower again by the lakes
Where you await me! I, proud of my intoning,
Will speak at length of goddesses and strip off
With idolatrous images their sashes in the gloom.
Yet then, when I've sucked brightness from the grapes,
What of regret? And what of my scattered pretenses?
I laugh and raise the empty cluster and blow
On the translucent skins, crazy for drunkenness,
Gazing through them at the summer sky till evening.

O nymphs, let us renew our particular MEMORIES.
"My eye, piercing the reeds, darts to each
Immortal neck as it drowns its burning in the wave
With a cry of rage flung to the forest sky;
And the splendid liquescence of hair disappears
In brightness and shimmering, o jewels, jewels!
I run near; whereupon at my feet, entwined (tousled
In the languor sipped from this poison of duality)
They lie sleeping, tangled in their accidental arms,
Alone; I seize them, not untangling them, and run
To this bank abhorred by the frivolous shade
Where roses exhaust their perfume in the sun
And our frolic too may consume itself in a day."

Oh, I adore you, virginal anger, horrified
Delight of the holy naked burden that slips
Away from my flaming lips as they drink, quivering
Like lightning, the terror secret to the flesh:
Yes, from lascivious limbs, from the timid heart,
Two in one instant forgoing innocence, wet
With wild tears or with less sorrowful moistures.
"Happy in overcoming their traitorous fears,
My crime is to have parted the disheveled locks
For kisses that the gods kept so well mingled:
For hardly had I buried a fervent chuckle
In the willing coils of the one (while holding
The other, so little, naive, not even blushing,
By only a finger so that her feathery innocence
Might be tinged from her sister's arousing passion)
When from my arms, unclasped by death's shapelessness,
This prey sets herself free, ungrateful forever,
Unpitying, though I am drunk still on her tear."

Let them go. Others will lead me to happiness
With their tresses woven around my head's horns;
My lust, you know how each pomegranate bursts,
Crimson, ready and ripe, murmurous with bees,
And how our blood, in adoration of what will subdue it,
Pulses for passion, that swarming profusion, forever
So at the late hour when woods turn golden and ashen
A festival proclaims itself in the fading leaves –
Here, Etna! here where Venus herself visited you,
Treading on your lava, her bare pure feet,
In tremors of a wistful sleep or the flare dying.
I hold the queen!

O sure retribution...
No, yet my soul
Is empty of words now and this ponderous body
Succumbs sluggardly to fierce noon's quiescence:
No more, we must sleep now, forgetting blasphemy,
Fallen on thirsty sands, opening my mouth

For love to the powerful wine-giving sun!

Good-bye

You two; I go to see the shadow you have become.

❯ *They Accuse Me of Not Talking*

North people known for silence. Long
dark of winter. Norrland families go
months without talking, Eskimos also,
except bursts of sporadic eerie song.
South people different. Right and wrong
all crystal there and they squabble, no
fears, though they praise north silence. "Ho,"
they say, "look at them deep thinkers, them strong
philosophical types, men of peace."

But take

notice please of what happens. Winter on the brain.
You're literate, so words are what you feel.
Then you're struck dumb. To which love can you speak
the words that mean dying and going insane
and the relentless futility of the real?

❯ *The Cowshed Blues*

> *Exsurge, gloria mea;*
> *exsurge, psalterium et cithara*

INTRO

Intent in the
night in the
cone of light
writing

VAMP

Or what's called
writing
though words must come

throb by throb
through the membrane
of the great black drum

16 BAR THEME

It was a cowshed when he took it
a one-cow barn beside a brook
in a cove of alder and birch

floor of plank and rank urine, the wooden
stanchel worn in a cow's long wintertimes
heavy with animal woe

in the back wall
was a hole
with a board flap
hinged on a harness strap

where they shoveled through
the manure
onto the manure pile
once in a while

so he made a window where the hole was
a table and a stove, and sought the grace
words give for love in a writing place

PIANO SEGUE

Light on the page and all else
the raging dark

12 BAR THEME

And tonight the shed rides free and the cove
its alders and birches
falls downward among the stars

because intensity does this, a mind
out of time, out of place –
body a field of forgotten wars

and making does this, the breakthrough
to a great beat throbbing
in a place without place

o moment, moment pure
he is an undetermined existence
part of eternity, gone in inner space

STOP-TIME CHORUS, TROMBONE
Soaring
    on the modes
    of sound
the modulations

moving
    over and through
    the pulses
of his love

known by no name now
    although
    a muse of everlasting
voluptuousness is aware of him

and the particular
    tones follow
    one another
freely inexorably

SCAT CHORUS
Cow now . starflow . the slow
beat . over and over . flies .
ow . the cords . the blood
urine and dung . how
flying . chains in the neck of
Hathor . perpetual beating .
her womb . beating . hot eyes .
now . beating . a great flying .
and pain . and beating . now

TWO CHORUSES AD LIB, TRUMPET
What our people have never known
but always felt
in the mystery of the word

is a force
contained but not expressed
spoken and unexplained –

for meaning falls away
as the stars in their spirals
fall from the void of creation

how simple and how necessary
this discipline! which is the
moment added to moment of being

movement added to movement
notes in the throat of the horn
being and being and being

dying, born   and he
is alone, free
creator of what he cannot help but be

VAMP, GUITAR AND BASS
"Holiness," he says
hearing an unexpected
modulation:
at the point of flow
always this beat, this beat
repeated
instant of everything he knows
now   forever   existing   here
it must
be holiness

OUT-CHORUS
And blues is also

a crying in the night
exhaustion, constriction
in the cone of light

and he looks up sighing
to the dark glass
where looking back at him
is his father's face

STOP-TIME BRIDGE, CLARINET
All's fallen back
back
collapsing into time
time
the beat   of the great drum   is going
going
in the wind in the trees
in the wind in the trees

RIDE OUT, HALF-TIME
It is   his face now
his own   his
and old in a moment
miseries, histories

his and his father's
reflected   little things
among others of this earth
the alders and the birch

TAG, DRUMS
But the beat remains
the moment of purity somewhere
poised on its long
flow   far out, far in

TUTTI
or on this page fallen
notations   of remembered song.

« X »

from

ASPHALT GEORGICS
[1985]

❯ *Names*

I had said improbable. I
    always do, that being
who I am. Nevertheless it
    stopped pouring. We could bring

the defective electric per-
    colator back to where
we bought it, the K-Mart up in
    Seneca Mall. So there

we drove, past Hiawatha Pla-
    za, Wegman's, Bayberry
Mall, with all the other pieces
    of the strip strung in be-

tween. Friendly and Ponderosa
    looked o.k., but Carvel
was dilapidated and Mis-
    ter Donut had a hell

of a big jagged hole through both
    sides of its glass sign. I
saw the killdeer running that has
    her nest next to the high-

way on the gravel strip between
    Rite-Aid and Sunoco,
and I heard her cry in the gnash
    of heat at my window,

as once in cool March rain by the
    Hoh River. Once. *Non c'e*
stato nulla, assoluta-
    mente nulla die-

tro di noi, e nulla abbi-
    amo disperata-

mente amato piu di
quel nulla. Once. Tra la.

The main reason for putting that
in is it was written
by a guy well up in his eight-
ies. He knows. In one sen-

tence, the past is nothing and we
are in love with it. Prag-
matically speaking we are
in love with nothing. Shag

me some more of these fungoes, boys,
before we quit. His name
is Eugenio, mine is Sam –
I like that name, that game

too, though totally useless,
the animal in us
just sufficiently domesti-
cated, our venomous

American aggressiveness
confined to balls and bats.
O.k. Back to the beginning.
The saturated fats

of so-called living filled the so-
called air. The rain stopped. Zing –
the sun came down. Not out, down. Made
me think how earth might swing

out of orbit – what's to prevent it
now that reason fails? – too
near the sun: our sulphurous sky
a pot of fuming goo

from rim to rim. I found myself
    praying. It happens all
the time. Sam, you poor deracin-
    ated numbskull, you call

on the Tetragrammaton with
    no more conviction than
on Quetzalcoatl, no? Yes!
    O.k., but as a man

among men – I mean the billions –
    I'll tell you a secret.
I call with no less! Goddamn it,
    no less. You dig me, get

the point? And what you do with this
    amorphous faith, desire,
wanting, let someone else figure,
    why me? I was on fire,

so was Poll next to me, so was
    the whole world. To get through,
get to the K-Mart, probably
    was all I asked. So who

cares who I asked? Does it have to
    be Somebody? It's better
not. The asking is what counts. Poll
    says the same. She says her

mind is always praying these days.
    We talked about it. What
else is there to do, she says. And
    getting through all the hot

traffic to the K-Mart is good
    enough for a prayer, be-
lieve me. Aren't they all the same? I
    tell you that's exactly

what it means: nothing. Just a hope,
  like a rabbit frozen
under a bush when the hounds come,
  no sense in it. So when

we got to the parking lot, shim-
  mering like fire, some fly-
weight crunched our fender, but Poll said,
  "Can you turn the wheel?" I

tried it and it worked. "So what's the
  diff?" she said, and I said,
"Yeah, what's the diff?" She laughed, the fly-
  weight laughed. Cracked in the head,

all of us. We slugged our way to
  the K-Mart where we gasped
from the air-conditioning. Poll
  sneezed. Gesundheit. We clasped

hands and went to the customer
  service, and the lady
said, "You didn't buy that here." We
  showed her the slip, the re-

ceipt from the cash register. "Why,"
  she smiled, "that's dated more
than a month ago. And besides,
  this is a different store."

Well, o.k. We went outside, wilt-
  ing right off, and looked back
up, and sure enough, the sign said
  Ames, though we could see black

letters on the wall, sort of scorched
  there, that still said K-Mart.
I'm Arthur. I always liked that
  name. Molly calls me Art.

·   ·   ·

Ray Latourneau calls me Had. Al-
        ways reminds me of my
buon maestro, Mr. Bechet, him
        sort of say-singing, "I

had it but it's all gone now." I
        still hit fungoes for the
boys, pop flies, nothing balls. "Me! Hit
        one to me, why don'tcha!"

·   ·   ·

Direct statement, many say, is
        best, such being the vain
way of judgmental classify-
        ing minds, the might and main

of intellect. But tell me, how
        can any manner of
wording in itself prevail? Language
        not urged and crammed with love

is nothing, while that which is is
        everything (at least in
art). Let plain statement be terse, not
        too eager to begin,

and above all reticent to claim
        special virtue. Many
paths in the forest have chosen
        me. I go on any.

·   ·   ·

Mindy's rose at last became too
        forlorn, the pink petals
faded almost to white except
        at the curled edges, pals-

ied by every passing truck, the
    color of dried blood. I
stuck it stem-down in the dispos-
    al, which whirled it. Good-bye,

Mindy's rose. But as it vanished
    the petals flew, hundreds
falling everywhere like limp rev-
    enants. Ah, empty beds,

love betrayed. Tragedy (read life)
    has its comic aspects,
granted, usually produced
    by genius, the effects

of machines malfunctioning; but
    tragedy still dissents.
Comedy is the somehow need-
    ed poet's misfeasance.

      •   •   •

I was talking about the heat.
    My name is really Ted,
which I really like. Dolly likes
    it too. The heat is said

to be pollution mostly. Don't
    ask me. What the hell do
I know? But you see, we've got this
    lake, in its way a beau-

ty, called Onondaga – now that's
    a name! – runs down to Syr-
acuse on the south end, Solvay
    to the west – on a clear

day you can see the factories
    and chemical plants – and

over here we're Liverpool. Just
         up from us on the land-

ward side the highway (57)
         cuts John Glenn Blvd.,
which leads into Buckley Rd., then
         into Henry Clay – hard

right – which takes you to Electron-
         ics Parkway, and you're al-
most back where you started. A big
         circle. You might just call

it the Action Circle, because
         that's where most of it
is around here, the lake being
         what you could call a bit

dead, over there behind the strip.
         Dead, hell – it's the oldest
dead lake in North America.
         Well, if you can't be best

you might as well be worst, that's how
         we look at it. Any
how it's dead. Last live fish was caught
         in 1870

according to the records, which
         is a pretty good while
back. Onondaga. It looks great,
         all shiny and cool, smil-

ing in the summer sun, until
         you look closer. Then you
see how there's no green plants, not ev-
         en scum, and the gulls mew-

ing and circling overhead don't
    ever sit on the wat-
er, won't touch it, not like any
    gulls you've ever seen before. What

makes it worse is how that brine heats
    up, filling the air full
of particles that catch all the
    guck those smokestacks in Sol-

vay are putting out night and day
    the year round. That's what makes
this slimy air. Cut it with a
    knife? Hell, no. What it takes

is a goddamn chainsaw. Then you
    can chunk it and stack it
and truck it down to Albany
    to be analyzed. Lit-

tle bits of protein all through it,
    they say. You could refine
it and sell it to the Ay-rabs
    for caviar – a min-

or retribution. As for the
    Action Circle, well, there's
everything from the Ramada
    to Smoky Joe's. Where's

the Pancake House? Why in the North-
    ern Lights Shopping Center,
where else? That's out next to Hancock
    Airport. They got eight syr-

ups on each table, all marked "im-
    itation." Of course you
can get flapjacks most anywhere
    and just as tasty too,

like right over there at Bill's Bo-
    nanza. I recommend
it. You can have the salad bar
    with your buckwheats and end

up with frozen strawberry short-
    cake, all for six-ninety-
nine. And get your oil changed next door
    while you drink your coffee.

Plus 7% sales tax, of
    course. My name is Jake the
Dope, which I don't like at all, and
    neither does Holly, a

true blue friend if there ever was
    one. Her real name is Round-
heels Jane, but everyone calls her
    Jackie. There may be ground

for thinking I'm not smart, I be-
    lieve there is, but I know
this: the system around here can't
    be fixed or beaten. No

way. You don't have to be an i-
    deologist to see
what's wrong. It's too big. It's so big
    nobody can agree

what it really is, much less con-
    trol it, not even that
Reagan and his gang – they're in it
    thick as thieves. Swing a cat,

you run into a tax; swing it
    again, you run into
a business that's tax-busted. Look
    at the Apex Laundro-

mat over there, all dust and cob-
        webs since J. D. Smith went
broke paying percentages to
        this or that government,

poor old bastard. Why right here where
        we're standing was J. D.'s
farm only a shake more than ten
        years ago. He had bees

toward the end, trying to make a
        go of honey after
he lost his cattle, but he was
        done from the start. No sir,

you can't beat it. J. D. had to
        rent the space for his store
from the same development com-
        pany that bought it. Sore?

You might say he was. That store stood
        just where his milkhouse used
to stand. Maybe that's partly why
        it failed. Of course he boozed

himself pretty good too. Jackie's
        his daughter. She sees him
once a week or so down South War-
        ren way. She says he's sim-

ple now, but not so simple he'll
        tell her where he lives. She
says it was great here when he had
        the cows. It's flat, easy

to hay, and watered good, just right
        for dairying. She says
they had at least one-third fair weath-
        er then, not like now, hes-

itating all the time between
    rain and haze, haze and rain,
not one clear day in ten. That's the
    sign. Oh some can explain

it half a hundred other ways,
    I know. Well, o.k. But
to me the climate's basic. Change
    that and you're done for. What

could do it but the system? Turn-
    ing women into whores,
our women. You recall what hap-
    pened to the dinosaurs,

no doubt? Hell, change won't stop, but by
    Jesus, it came slower
once, so a man could handle it.
    Now it's about over.

        •   •   •

No fish, weedless, sunk deep in the
    earth. Waste. Barren. No wind
would lift these waves. My name is Sea-
    mus, it really is, twinned

with Poldy. "Grey sunken cunt of
    the world," he murmured. Poor
dear man, what does it mean he did
    his best for women? Sure

now, nothing at all, at all. They
    scream that the time grows sim-
pler because so completely near-
    er their distant maxim,

history's finishment. Oh, look
    at their lovely lake, dead.

Onondaga. And what more? Dead
is dead (as Poldy said).

     •   •   •

To draw the line between something
to say and self-indul-
gence is easy with someone else –
Ammons, say – but awful

hard with yourself. You just cannot
get outside or arrest
the flow. So you go plowing a-
long and hope for the best.

     •   •   •

My name was Julio. But now
by enormous effort
I have transformed my consciousness
to the gleam of consort-

ed light that scintillates round the
dome of gold on the ca-
thedral all day at the top of
the capital plaza.

My name is Santa Julia.
It was necessary,
this change of gender, to make such
an extraordinary

transition, as was the change from
mortality to sub-
limity, which I know now is
not the angelic club

I once believed but a state of
mind at least theoret-
ically attainable by
all those who must forget

themselves completely and abso-
        lutely in order to
pass through and beyond the pain that
        surpasses knowing. Do

you see there beyond the city,
        beyond the plain, that wisp
of smoke at the foot of the moun-
        tain? Do you hear the whisp-

ering moan? But no. You have not
        my transperception. That
is where Julio is in a box,
        unable to lie flat

or sit, the box being one cub-
        ic meter with a small
barred opening. He wears his shit.
        He is moaning like all

the others in their boxes, an
        almost lost minor note
in the great chorale you cannot
        hear. But I am devot-

ed to that music, it is my
        existence, the under-
song. Oh, is not this world beauti-
        ful, the one unimper-

fection, mountains, plains, the river
        glittering there, the sky,
the sun! I am aware. But not
        for this I sanctify

myself. Rather the univers-
        al song that silently
rises from the splendid façade
        and that has no form, be-

ing only history. I hear
    it. I cannot have pit-
y for Julio. They call him
    Communist. What is it

but another name? We have known
    so many, meaningless,
always changing. Julio knows
    nothing now. He, digress-

ing in his box for seven months
    and fourteen days toward death,
is the merest grasshopper. Nor
    do I feel much sympath-

y for myself, though I, Santa
    Julia, will go when
Julio goes – that is the way
    with souls. But I have man-

y sorrows for the living who
    do not know, who somehow
keep ignorant, for ignorance
    is forever the pow-

er of evil. Oh, song, song, the
    song! Blades cutting, acids
burning, guts torn out, penises
    wrenched off with pincers. Lids

closing continually on
    cages. That whisper of
intended screaming defiance
    dying beneath the cov-

er of mighty sun and sea and
    wind and land. This I serve
as priestess, this song known to me,
    for no end but a nerve-

less adoration, a point of
	light, a witness, a hom-
ing never home. O sorrow! Round
	and round the golden dome.

   • • •

Hi. I'm Jackie. Glad to know you.
	Maybe we'll fall in love.
Why not? What else? It's easy. I'll
	give a push for a shove.

What the hell? Rotten times. Who knows?
	It's nothing you can buck.
Give me a buzz. Drop me a line.
	Send a dollar for luck.

   • • •

My name is Johan, which is both
	John and Joan, but mostly
in my case the former, which is
	appropriate, I be-

ing masculine both in nature
	and in history. I
died young and lived to a great age.
	I knew peace and war, i-

dentity and depersonal-
	ization, love and hate,
poverty and affluence, all
	of course proportionate

to the continuum of mis-
	ery. I was sane or
insane depending on the weath-
	er, incidence of bore-

dom, and sexual circumstanc-
es. I lived in a man-
ner entirely determined by
society, yet fan-

atically insisted on
my individual-
ity. I was fascinated
by sex, games, cars, mortal-

ity, my parents and children,
and many other things,
but above all by names. Names were
my food, and christenings

my epiphanies. However
I was never quite dunce
enough to think my own name
could bear the least importance.

·   ·   ·

Well, for now that seems to be the
sum of it. You ask, "What
then?" Who knows? No finish, just a
stop.

› *How To*

Aw right then. Chillens, I know you
thinking it be too tough,
now ain't that so? I know every-
thing about you. That's rough

on you too, I understand, but
fact's fact, and it could be
worse. Suppose the principles were
hard to see and the rea-

sons difficult to comprehend.
    But they ain't. They almost
too simple. That's what's hard. It will
    make you moan and, yes, boast

too before much longer. The main
    element of technique
is verve, movement, energy, what
    musicians also seek

under the rubric *attack*. You
    have to *hit* and keep on
hitting, sharp, hard, make it crackle,
    make it brilliant; maun-

dering ain't allowed. Hit each note
    unmitigatedly
and just a hair off the beat. Lis-
    ten to Little Jazz, see

how he snaps it, or the Hawk, how
    he whops it – not much le-
gato there, chillens. And here's the
    clincher: this do not de-

siderate loudness, not never.
    Think of Sweets or Pee-Wee
or Mr. Webster. (Man, what chops!
    Do you realize he

blew on a cast-iron reed? And yet
    he could carry that axe
in his mouth all night and then still
    eat steak for breakfast.) Max-

imum energy is sometimes
    obtained by restraining
the inner violence of force,
    though always with the swing-

ing propulsion that comes from clar-
   ity of phrasing a-
gainst the beat. What you've been told is
   too easy. Listen. The

ear is more important than the
   eye. Dass de trooth! So next
week let's have 30 lines, allit-
   erating *m* and *k*.

> *Lost*

Many paths in the woods have chos-
   en me, many a time,
and I wonder often what this
   choosing is: a sublime

intimation from far outside
   my consciousness (or for
that matter from far inside) or
   maybe some train of mor-

tality set in motion at
   my birth (if our instru-
ments of observation were fine
   and precise enough to

trace it) or maybe only dis-
   parate appeal, pure chance,
the distant drumming of a par-
   tridge in spring, the advanc-

ing maple-color along a
   lane in fall, or only
that the mud was less thick one way
   than another was. Free

or determined? Again and a-
    gain I went the one way
and not the other, who knows why?
    I wish I could know. May-

be it would explain the other
    things that worry me. But
I have no compulsive need now,
    not any longer. What

I know is that whether I walked
    freely or trudged exhaust-
ed I chose one way each time and
    ended by being lost.

I think I sought it. I think I
    could not know myself un-
til I did not know where I was.
    Then my self-knowledge con-

tinued for a while while I found
    my way again in fear
and reluctance, lost truly at
    last. I changed the appear-

ance of myself to myself
    continually and
losing and finding were the same,
    as now I understand.

❯ Lana

Last night I dropped in at the Con-
    cord – out on Erie? You
know it, like all the other joints
    along the strip there, glu-

cose and styrofoam, but it's Greek
    and they got baklava
that Lana likes – that's Lana Schom-
    bauer – so I'm there a

good many times already. God
    knows I've looked at that same
painting on the wall enough, in
    that shiny fake-gold frame,

only of course it's not a painting
    but one of those repro-
ductions they do now with the raised
    up surfaces, like so,

to make it look like brushstrokes. Made
    me think of '52
when the wife drug me all over
    half of Paris to scru-

tinize all those pictures. Should have
    done it years earlier
when we were young enough to learn
    something. Well, you don't per-

fect your sensibilities in
    law school, I can vouch for
that. Yuh, I'm a lawyer. Or I
    was. Got what they call tor-

pedoed, being a bit too close
    to the politics of
the business. Busted and disbarred.
    Sure, it was undercov-

er, so to speak, but I had to
    take the fall. I didn't
deserve it, but who does? – and may-
    be it's not important –

I did my time down in Ossin-
     ing, and whatever you've
heard about life in the joint you
     can double it and move

it on up to the fifth power –
     in spades. So get through and
out, o.k.? I did it. Survived.
     I give myself a hand

for that, though that wasn't the worst.
     You know what it's like be-
ing disbarred? It's like they threw you
     out of everything, de-

clared you persona non grata
     in the whole world. I get
by, the boys take care of me, a
     clean check each week, it's bet-

ter than social security,
     and sure, they know I took
a bum rap, but that's not the
     only reason they look

out for me. They do it because
     they *like* me, they can talk
to me, and we're all scared togeth-
     er. So there I am gawk-

ing at this picture out at the
     Concord, and it's flashy,
cheap, I know enough to know that,
     too bright, colors like ne-

on signs. You know? You've seen the same
     in half the feeding joints
in America. It's a scene
     with a buck, fourteen points,

standing next to a frozen stream
        with snow everywhere, some
white birches, a mountain in the
        background, a platinum

sky with a trace of pink like a
        real winter sunset. Aw-
ful, nobody would hang it on
        their wall, even a law-

yer. But then all of a sudden
        I saw it for real, out
of its frame, just like I saw it
        once hunting, up about

five, six miles above Old Forge, beau-
        tiful, so beautiful
I couldn't move and the buck broke
        and jumped off, gone double-

time through the birches and firs, puffs
        of snow drifting down, and
I didn't even mind, I just
        looked and kept looking, stand-

ing until it was near dark and
        my feet near frozen. But
if that was beautiful, how come
        the picture is so ut-

terly ugly? They're the same, I
        tell you. Well, the picture
lacks something, don't ask me what. Then
        Lana. I looked at her

gray hair and wrinkled face, and all
        of a sudden I saw
like an aura around her she
        was so beautiful, claw-

ing her napkin to wipe the hon-
    ey off her mouth, she was
beautiful, she was – but I can't
    describe her now because

already I can't remember,
    like something I read long
ago when I was a kid, or
    maybe dreamed, or a song

I heard once. Who, Lana? No, not
    her, I don't have a wife
any more. She's a steno down
    at the courthouse. Her life –

well, it's not exactly great ei-
    ther. Schombauer, Lana.
We go Dutch. The movies, then the
    Concord for baklava.

> *Marge*

   (1896-1981)

Look, friend, you got troubles? Like it's
    damn hard figuring what
it all means, right? Right. So let me
    tell you. The Pizza Hut

won't throw out a couple old guys
    like us, it's a slow night,
we had our supper, now we're just
    gabbing, eh, with a mite

more coffee if you can call this
    coffee, and what would you
give for a real old-time mug
    right now instead of who

knows what this cup is, pressed glue – why
    hell, a lunger like me
even could blow it out the door.
    So let me tell you. We

were close like that, Margery and
    me, close as two fingers
until she died last night. And no
    funny stuff, what was hers

was hers, and mine was mine, and be-
    sides she was 25
years older than me, though sometimes
    you couldn't tell. A live

wire she was. M-A-R-G-E-
    R-Y, that's how she spelled
her name, she said it was English,
    from England, and her eld-

er brother got killed in Flanders.
    Could be. But for sure she
was born in Orange, N.J., I
    saw it written out le-

gal on her death certificate
    this afternoon. Well, I'm
the only one left to handle
    her affairs at a time

like this. But now you got to go
    back maybe 15 years
when I was near 45 and
    she was 70. Here's

how it was. I had me a nice
    little business going,
o.k.? – contracting, out around
    Camillus, the phone ring-

ing all the time, money coming
    in pretty good. The wife
did the bookwork, I did the rest,
    and I don't know, but life

seemed to be humping along with-
    out too much trouble. Plen-
ty of work in those days. Usu-
    ally had 5 to 10

hands on the job, with all the tax-
    es, codes, insurance, and
that stuff, red tape like you wouldn't
    believe, but the wife hand-

led it, she even liked it, all
    that figuring. Jesus!
Then we got divorced. No use ex-
    plaining, the both of us

were nuts, I think, bored crazy, but
    if you haven't been through
it you can't really understand,
    though like as not you do,

these days practically every-
    one knows how it is. Well,
I tried to keep going. But the
    truth is I had one hell

of a time with hired accountants,
    and I was boozing too,
half skunked by 10:30 every
    morning. So what else? You

know as well as I do. Sure, the
    business went, then I went
too. Ended up selling the Olds
    to eat with and to rent

me a basement room here in Liv-
        erpool, down in the vil-
lage on Aspen Street. Been living
        there ever since. What'll

happen now? I'll have to get out,
        that's obvious. But damned
if I know where to. No picnic,
        being 60, chest crammed

with rock wool and a million cig-
        arettes, what's left of it.
So Marge was the landlady, she
        had this 5-room cape sit-

ting on a 150-
        foot lot with half the base-
ment fixed up for a roomer, kitch-
        en privileges, place

for a car. I'd bought an old heap
        by then. So I moved in,
and soon we were friends, shared our meals,
        maybe went out for din-

ner once a week, the movies, et
        cetera. But mostly
we sat and talked. Why? What did she
        want with a lush? Well, she

figured she could save me, see, and
        she was the saving kind,
but a good one, you know? – no lec-
        tures, no getting me lined

up to be converted, nothing
        like that. She was solid
gold all through, no plated stuff.
        Booze wasn't quite forbid-

den in her house, she'd nibble a
    sherry herself once in
a while, but she made it clear; no
    scotch, no vodka nor gin,

and the first time I got smashed I'd
    be out – out on my ear,
you understand? But of course I
    did it, that was damn near

inevitable, I got juiced
    but good, boiled like a cab-
bage, three days in the pressure cook-
    er, crocked, and next day rab-

bity as an ice-cube in a
    skillet while I packed my
gear. But she come in. She come and
    leaned on my bedpost, sigh-

ing a bit, and she said, "Neut —" that's
    what she called me because
you see my name is Spaid, Charlie
    Spaid, I know it ain't plaus-

ible but it's true, S-P-A-
    I-D, and when I told
her I'm Mr. Spaid she gave a
    shiver like she was cold

and said you must mean Mr. Neu-
    tered, don't you? – so now she
said, "Neut, I changed my mind. You can
    stay if you swear off, tee-

total off, and join the AA.
    And if it'll help
I won't take no more myself." I bust
    out bawling then. And by

Jesus, Joseph, and Mary too,
    I did it. I quit. Not
one sip from then till now, you know
    what I'm saying? The bot-

tom line is death, and I'm still liv-
    ing. I went to AA
three times a week at first. Don't knock
    it, plenty guys from way

down in the hole have come back up
    alive because of it,
and plenty dames too. It's great to
    see. One friend of mine, lit-

tle guy named Cheever, came in the
    same time I did, and he
was already 65. "How
    come?" I said. "You ask me,"

I said, "at your age I'd go on
    out sozzled." But he said,
"Yeah, that's one way of looking. And
    then there's another. Dead

I can take, but who wants to die
    puking all over some-
one else's furniture?" By God,
    that hit me. I won't come

to disremember that in a
    hurry, no sir. But back
to Marge. She taught me how to play
    cribbage. You got a knack

for cards? Not me, but I learned good
    enough to beat her may-
be one out of six, and the game
    wasn't much anyway,

not for either of us, because
　　the main thing was just re-
laxing like, you know, talking, laugh-
　　ing hard enough to bust

our crankcases, and drinking iced
　　tea, oceans of it, sum-
mer, winter, spring, fall, it didn't
　　matter. We loved it. From

then on I was o.k. Marge got
　　me a job on the grounds
out at General Electric
　　through a cousin. It sounds

goofy, I guess. But I was fed
　　up to here with being
a boss, husband, lover, father,
　　the whole schmeer. A damn ding-

bat, that's what a man is in this
　　world today. I resigned.
I was single, but I had a
　　real friend. Never could find

anything like that in the young-
　　er broads that got into
my bed. So at night Marge and me
　　played cribbage or made do

with whatever was on the tube.
　　Fridays we went to the
bank and the Price-Chopper. Weekends
　　out of town, like to a

state park, Beaver Lake or the falls
　　up the Salmon River.
It went that way for ten years. Then
　　Marge got cirrhosis – her,

not me! – then shingles in her mouth
and nose, phlebitis, faint-
ing spells. She'd keel over right off
her chair, then wake up paint-

ed head to toe with her own vom-
it. Her teeth got loose, eye-
sight not so good. In the hospit-
al, then out. What could I

do? In and out, in and out. She
lost 40 pounds. Final-
ly she had a stroke, but not quite
good enough, she lost all

feeling from the neck down, no con-
trol, she was blind, para-
lyzed, couldn't talk right, she was help-
less. But she knew wherea-

bouts she was, and why. Two and a
half years she lay there, clear
enough to know what's coming down
but not enough to gear

herself up for it, so to speak.
Two and a half years, that's
a hell of a long time to be
in the line of fire. Rats

have it better, you know that? "Neut,
take me home, take me home."
She'd wail it out like that. Ho-o-o-m-me!
My lungs turning to foam,

no money, what could I do? It
killed me. Two and half
years. Nobody should have to die
that way, nobody. Af-

ter a while she just cried, all her
        strength gone. Then finally
she had another one, massive,
        and five days later she

went under for the last time, just
        a few minutes before
I came for my daily visit.
        When I went through the door

to her room I knew she was gone
        even though she looked the
same, all shrunk up. Well, you got to
        say for her it was a

break, there's no one should be tortured
        like that, but for me – what
am I going to do now, with
        old Marge gone? Not much but-

ter on my bread these days, no two
        ways about it, I ache
for her something awful. You know
        that? It begun to take

quite some time back too. So now I'll
        have to move, and the dis-
ability don't pay much rent
        either, so I'll get this

spongy chest down to the old ho-
        tel, I reckon, where all
the other old guys are rooming,
        where I can watch the crawl-

ing traffic on the main drag and
        catch the sun when it shines
once every ten days, a second-
        floor window, creeper vines,

an outside sill where I can put
    seed for the sparrows. That's
not too much to ask, is it? Once
    I had a dog, two cats,

and Marge. Why don't I go to the
    Senior Citizens? Have
you ever tried it? I did, but
    just once. Sat on a dav-

enport and watched the tube. Played cards,
    and one guy forgot his
turn, he didn't put down a card,
    staring at some invis-

ible something, like we all do,
    and the rest of us wait-
ed without saying anything,
    not waiting for the eight

of clubs or the jack of hearts or
    whatever, just waiting –
you understand? Not like AA
    at all. Marge always ding-

ed it into me how you got
    to keep fighting, other-
wise you lose yourself and turn in-
    to a thing, like a burr

in a dog's ass, that's how she put
    it, something to be got
rid of. But look at her. Was she
    fighting at the end? Not

likely. And me? Emphysema
    is slow, gradual, yet
you wind up on your back, crazy
    for one more cigarette,

concentrating every bit of
    energy and thought on
getting one more breath. Is that fight-
    ing? Or is it more hon-

orable to take things into
    your own hands. I remem-
ber my friend Alf years ago who
    shot himself with a Rem-

ington .22 up in the
    woods. He looked so peaceful
laying there with his head resting
    on a mossy stone. Null

and void, that's for sure, but at least
    he looked like himself. Marge
looked like old, like rotten. So I
    won't be getting much charge

out of the good old days while I'm
    sitting in my window,
no sir. Once I heard a guy say
    on some kind of talk show,

"Nostalgia is the poison of
    old age." I never for-
got that. No, I'll be thinking a-
    bout Marge and me, or more

about what we really are, her
    dead now, me in this mess,
and what it really means. Things or
    people. Well, I don't guess

my thinking will amount to much,
    but that's what I have to
do. No choice, is there? So take
    care. I'll be seeing you.

> *Cave Painting*

FOR CLAYTON ESHLEMAN

"Might he [Cro-Magnon] have drawn bi-
        son to induct a mys-
tery far more distant than the
        [vanished] animal is

from us today? Where do the ex-
        tinct species go?" Yes. Pre-
cisely. And don't we draw the same
        so poignant imagery

on the walls of our skulls, on the
        insides of our eyelids?
Where are the extinguishing spe-
        cies going? Homonids

we call our fathers, watching them
        watching themselves as they
draw and draw away from the an-
        imals, hearing them say,

as we ourselves say, No, it's the
        animals who are go-
ing, the great recession that nev-
        er ceases, fading to-

tality, for Mammoth and Sa-
        ber Tooth are not "species"
but our own others, our somehow
        better egos, like trees,

like savannahs of moving grass
        that speak no names, since on-
ly we speak their names, but not to
        them, to ourselves, our own

fixed and impoverished being. They
    are going away. See
this tetched and tabescent quad-
    ruped in his cage. De-

code his sign. "Wild Mongolian
    Ass, extinct in its na-
tive habitat; seventy-one
    known survivors today

were bred in captivity." See
    into his unreflect-
ing eyes. The species go and go,
    leaving behind these wrecked

pieces of junk. They vanish deep
    into themselves, sink
into mystery, into ourselves, dis-
    tant beyond chance of think-

ing, imaging, defining, where
    essence was encoded
and knowing was not knowing and
    existence only bred

existence and mystery was
    the wondrous warmth of sun-
light, then when all things began the
    journey to extinction.

We were with them. They went away.
    And now every bell in
every tower in every vil-
    lage could toll the tocsin

of our sorrow forever and
    still not tell how across
all time our origin always
    is this knowledge of loss.

≫ *New Hartford*

Let me tell you, Mac, it's sure great
    seeing you again, I
kid you not. Like old times. You're look-
    ing good. The reason why

I ain't been around is I moved
    out. That's right. After that
by-pass I had down to Upstate
    Medical. Nothing flat

is how long it took me to get
    down the pike from Liver-
pool, soon as they handed me my
    pension. Sure looked like cur-

tains there for a while though. Thanks be
    the old ticker took hold
finally. Like the guy said, a
    quart of oil in the old

Caddy and there you go, she'll run
    another ten thousand
mile. I'm over in New Hartford
    now. A breeze. Like the fund

pays me two thou a month, right? Then
    cash some bonds and sell the
old shack here in Liverpool for
    enough to pay down a

good two-thirds on the new one, a
    nice five-room split ranch, which
ain't bad, a seventy-five foot
    lot. I ain't talking rich,

you understand, I'm talking nice,
    real nice, with no plastic,

real wood veneer panels and a-
    luminum siding, pic-

ture windows like real doors, they slide
    open onto the ter-
race, outside shutters, a chimney,
    a real one, and a fair

spread of stone façade, real stone, the
    whole bit, I'm telling you,
real nice. And it's a real nice town,
    too, it don't matter who

you talk to, everyone says the
    same. Makes Liverpool look
like after the war, you ask me.
    Sure we got a strip. Took

right off the tube, you could say, Ha-
    waii, Vegas, some spot
like that, real nice, McDonald's, Sam-
    bo's, the Ground Round, we got

it all, plus real nice wop joints, fish
    joints, nice, nothing junky
or half falling down like here, it's
    clean, right? You ought to see,

like these real little old shingle-
    type houses with roses
all over still right there on the
    strip, and a schoolhouse says

1821 on the stone
    lintel sandwiched between
a clam joint and a Midas Muf-
    fler, restored. Well, it's lean-

ing some, not too bad. They made it
    into a museum
now. Couple more years, then the old
    ticker busts, I ain't dumb,

that's all I ask, sitting out there in
    my lawn chair watching the
charcoal do my steak and onions,
    what more do you think a

retread like me is going to get?
    Whop! Then out I go. No
tomorrow. O.k. You know why
    I come back here? Just so

I can take a look and be glad,
    that's all. It's like I say,
New Hartford's real nice. So take care.
    Have a real nice day.

❯ Phone

Ruthie? That you? Well, how's it go-
    ing back there, good? Yeah. Look,
the reason I'm calling, you got
    your ma and me all shook

with that last letter, see? I mean
    it's great to get a let-
ter from your own daughter a
    couple times a year, set

us up real good, that stuff about
    Jim and the kids fishing
out to Willowdale and all, but
    why did you have to ring

in that clipping from the *Chroni-*
    cle? Yeah, that one. You think
maybe we don't know you folks got
    enough whammy to sink

the whole goddamn planet back there
    in Rome and Utica,
all that nuclear junk stockpiled
    out to Griffiss like a

goddamn soup factory, you think
    we got nothing to do
except sit around talking all
    day about the way you

and Jim and the kids will be the
    first to get it when them
button-pushers down to Washing-
    ton——Yeah, well, I'm a mem-

ber in good standing of the V.-
    F.W. too, you can tell
Jim that if he don't know, and I
    ain't saying——How the hell

can he come home at night and look
    at you and the kids, af-
ter messing all day with them bombs?
    Yeah, I know it's a half-

assed world, you don't have to tell me,
    we're sitting just thirty
miles downwind from that Diablo
    Canyon thing. That's right. Me

and your ma went out and demon-
    strated with all the oth-
ers, you bet, thousands of us, and
    pretty damn hot and both-

ered about it too, and we got
　　　it stopped, you see it on
the tube? We was right there. And you
　　　better believe we con-

centrated on the beer and lob-
　　　ster after that one, that's
for sure. But ain't nobody fool
　　　enough to think one rat's-

nest out of action is going
　　　to stop the rats. No way.
So, baby, we're grateful, but please
　　　from now on can you lay

off the pieces from the newspap-
　　　er? I mean the whole bit,
disaster, pollution. You think
　　　we don't know? Who needs it?

❯ *Septic Tanck*

Well, everyone wants to know, of course, that's
only natural. If I was Ignatz
or Polyphemus it'd be the same,
you'd be hinting at me, like I was fam-
ous or something, you'd be insinuat-
ing this or that, and so on. So I'm grate-
ful I got something you can really get
a hold on. Yes, by God, you hear me bet-
ter than most, and that's a fact. O.k., my
grandpa, my father's dad, he was known by
the name of Friedrich Tanck, come from the Ruhr,
and far as I know that's our moniker
from way back. Pronounced Tank here, of course. No-
body's got no records, but hell, who'd go
fake a name like that? So that's it. Only
grandpa become humorous, I guess, see-

ing he was American now and all,
and when his son came, that's my dad, he call-
ed him Watering – wouldn't that kind of
grab you? Just what you might say was a lov-
ing father's best shot, right? Yet my dad kept
it up. Yes, sir. You got him pegged. Except-
ing you don't know it all yet. I got one
sister Acetylene, ain't that a hon-
ey? – she's Acey-Deucey for short – and a
second by the name of Gas. The fami-
ly calls her Gassy of course, but she won't
take it from no one else. "Jesus, I'm ruint
by my name," she used to say, but she nev-
er done nothing to change it. "Could be Bev
or Barb or Clytie," she'd say. "I guess I'm
just as glad." Well, in fact most of the time
it ain't so bad, and even kind of sight-
ly when you look at me, an old guy writ-
ing poetry in the waiting room at
Hancock Airport, all these eyeballers that
think I'm wigged or something. The way I look
at it, Septic Tanck is a real good shook-
down name for a poet nowadays, the
ending-up place for everything, don't you
know, everything that comes down. And once in
a while maybe we even make something
useful out of it, I mean us poet-
ry writers. Hell, it's what I do, just set-
ing here, an old guy's hobby like, the same
as some that go out fishing with the name
of Tom or Dick or Harry, day in, day
out, even if they don't catch nothing. Say,
you wouldn't pony up four bits for cof-
fee, would you, seeing as you're taking off?
I got this here piece xeroxed, you might be
interested. "Demolition Derby,"
it's called. Thanks mister. Have I got a kid?
Two. Two kids. One's Martha and one's David.

> *Capper Kaplinski at the North Side Cue Club*

What's it like? You take it from me,
    kid, the old dinger don't
raise up like he used to for a
    squint at every nice grownt-

up piece moseying down the main,
    not no more – no, sir. But
it ain't so bad. Wasn't nothing
    but a pain in your nut

anyways when he used to pop
    up all the time with no-
where to put him, nothing but grief,
    the same old crazy go-

round, don't think I don't remember.
    By the Jesus, boy, it
ain't so bad at all without all
    that, specially since a tit

still gives me a real good feeling,
    but like it's mental, not
in the gut, you understand? So
    I see some young broad trot-

ting along the asphalt hurry-
    ing somewheres, her boobs jig-
ging a little under her sweat-
    er, nice and not too big,

now ain't that a good sight to see?
    No question. You bet your
ass. Why, it makes me feel warm like,
    like sunshine all over

and me up setting on a bench
    in Hillside Park just watch-

ing the kids skim them saucers, or
 the girls doing hopscotch,

or anything, it don't matter,
 just so it's spring and a
sunny afternoon. What I mean
 I can still glom onto

the things that make life worth living
 and sex still has something
to do with it, and always will,
 even if I ain't been

too sharp at explaining. Life's a
 doozy, that's how I see
it. Well, this here's called nine-ball. Is
 we playing or ain't we?

❯ *Sam and Poll Go Back to the City*

Look, friend, you don't know the half. Me
 and Poll come up in the
world some since the last time I seen
 you. Oh, no big deal, you

understand. I'm not talking rich,
 it ain't anything like
that, but Poll's uncle croaked last fall,
 hit by a motorcyc-

le when he was taking his eve-
 ning stroll in the parking
lot up at the Northlight Plaza –
 made him look like a string

of spaghetti, with sauce on, the
 way it wrapped him around

one of them sky-high utili-
        ty poles. You know it. Ground-

ed the kid on the bike too, and
        a couple of seagulls
into the bargain, like it's a
        limited war or Dulls-

ville on a Sunday in the ear-
        ly bright. Right? So Poll's unk,
he never had no kids, nor no
        wife neither, so he sunk

his all in a nice little dis-
        tributorship up in
Oneida County, and lo and
        behold, he was skin-

ning beaver up there same as the
        old days, you get what I
mean, and he checked out with a stash
        of chips a half-mile high,

I wouldn't kid you. Left Poll three
        big ones plus. You bet. So
Poll and me bought this two-bedroom
        Caper back of Abe's dough-

nut shack out there in the old neigh-
        borhood, just like we al-
ways wanted. Funny how life comes
        downfield with the long ball

right to you sometimes, ain't it? So
        we're back in town again.
No more pizza huts and hamburg
        joints out on the strip. When

we want excitement now we get
  a couple of Abe's new-
fried sinkers, a hunk of java,
  heavy on the moo-moo,

and we sit there talking and watch-
  ing the lottery num-
bers on Abe's terminal, and you
  know, that ain't such a dumb

way to plug along, you get to
  our time of life, eh? You're
wondering about the niggers.
  Well, so did we. For sure

the old neighborhood's a shade or
  two darker than it used
to be, ain't no two ways about
  that, and some of them boozed

or zonky half the time too. But
  we don't call them niggers
no more. I tell you what, once you
  hear the way a cat purrs

you get to like the sound. That's the
  bottom line. Them folk talk
like poetry, once you learn the
  lingo, and when they walk

it's dancing, and that's a fact. Eve-
  rything they do is like
music is always running through
  their heads, but nothing psych-

o, nothing weird, it's more like some
  good old tune with a ex-
tra kind of a beat in it, or
  as if everything's sex-

y for them, but nice sexy – hell,
    I can't explain. You got
to hand it to them though, their way
    of life makes a whole lot

more sense to me than getting blind-
    sided like Poll's uncle
in the Northlight. You use good sense,
    like with anyone, you'll

never have no trouble. And by
    God, they laugh, they're always
laughing, joking around. Hang out
    for a month of Sundays

up at the Northlight, you won't hear
    anything like that. Well,
it means something to me and Poll,
    a whole lot, muscatel

for your ears like. Then say when you
    need a hand, like Poll's bat-
tery that pooped out the other
    night, here's where help is at,

right here in the old neighborhood.
    Hell, the truth is somehow
it wasn't ever what it claimed
    to be, gemütlich, pow-

dered all over with sweetness like
    a goddamn cake. No, sir –
Krauts, Harps, Hunkies, Wops going at
    each other with no mer-

cy every weekend, take my word,
    them old days don't compare.
It's fine now here. Look, I got to
    haul it. Right. You take care.

❯ *Shake, Well Before Using*

That guy three lots down on the oth-
    er side? Name of Crawford,
but I don't know him. Now ain't that
    a bomb, eight years we ord-

er our *Herald* from the same pap-
    erboy and ain't even
shook hands, but like I say he's got
    this smokebush, see, a ten-

footer, maybe more, it's what I
    mean big, right there in his
front yard, a beaut, take a dekko
    next time your business

brings you round here by daylight, it
    looks real fancy and high-
tone, like this bozo Crawford's pour-
    ing dollars on it, ni-

trogen and potash and all that,
    which he no doubt is, you
know what I mean, but the only
    bitch I got is long a-

bout this time every year, the last
    week in August, them
things, whatever they are, them bunch-
    es, like they say resem-

ble smoke, see, them little smokers,
    they bust off and the wind
blows them every whichway over
    the whole street like some thinned-

down leftovers from the sixty-
    nine drought, they make me

think of five years ago I was
doing maybe thirty-

five down Rt. 54 in New
Mexico hauling the
old Winnebago into a
headwind like standing a-

bout twenty yards behind a B-
52 when she lets
loose, you know what I mean, pedal
to the floor and it gets

you thirty-five per, and then these
big tumbleweeds coming
at me from two o'clock like boul-
ders spinning and looping,

and when the first one hit I sure
ducked down, believe me, on-
ly of course they don't weigh nothing
and it just bounced off, moan-

ing like as it went by. Well, these
little smokers, they can't
compare for size, but when they come
fast at you, hundreds, slant-

wise across the street, dry-sounding,
you'll take note. No question,
believe me. O.k., I wouldn't
tell it to everyone,

but days like this, windy, it sort
of feels like the end of
the world, all them stiff dead gray things
blowing loose just above

the asphalt, drifting like some kind
    of ghosts with that scratchy
sound. Can't you hear it right now ev-
    en at night? You ask me,

it's one hell of a scary sound.
    Ora pro nobis, that's
what we used to say. *Ave Ma-*
    ria. Hissing like rats'

feet, like them smokers – that's the sound.
    Didn't mean much then, what's
it now? Who's Mary? Priests whisper-
    ing and me with the hots

for Mary two blocks down, but I
    sure didn't want her pray-
ing for me, no sir, you said it.
    And now I'm too old. May-

be the world's too old, we're all go-
    ing over the hill, you
think that's it, like together? Well,
    I pray, damned right I do,

what else with all them smokers tum-
    bling like New Mexico,
reminding me. Soon it'll be
    the dead leaves. Then the snow.

What a mishmash – the suburbs! You
    know it. So I pray for
Crawford, the street, the smokebush, the
    works. I pray for no more

Reagan. Well, you got to keep your
    wig on, you can't give in
to the dead. So what if it don't
    mean much? It means something.

from

THE OLDEST KILLED LAKE IN NORTH AMERICA [1985]

To answer transcendent questions in language made for immanent
knowledge is bound to lead to contradictions.

— ARTHUR SCHOPENHAUER

Yet still the emotion that beckons me on is indubitably the pursuit of an
ideal social self, of a self that is at least *worthy* of approving recognition by
the highest *possible* judging companion, if such companion there be.

— WILLIAM JAMES

❯ The Oldest Killed Lake in North America

One night the water lay so deathly still
that the factories' constellated lights on the other shore,
the mills and refineries, made gleaming wires
across the surface, a great fallen and silent
harp; and the moon, huge and orange,
shuddered behind the trembling many-petaled efflorescence
on the stalks of the chimneys, white mortuary flowers.
Really, from the nearer shore on the highway to Liverpool,
one saw the kind of splendor that lasts forever.

❯ Unnatural Unselection

It's true. When a crazy woman
        howls in the night
her hair rises and writhes like snakes
and she is inhuman
        by moondark or moonlight.

Then, lover, be you ware,
        for of the possible dozen
this one alone will throw you out
in your trouble and care
        whom you have ill-chosen.

❯ Eternity Blues

I just had the old Dodge in the shop
with that same damned front-end problem,
and I was out, so to speak, for a test run,

loafing along, maybe 35 m.p.h.,
down the old Corvallis road,
holding her out of the ruts and potholes.

That's out in Montana, the Bitterroot Valley.
Long ways from home is how they say it.
Long ways from home, boys, long long ways from home.

Might as well not put this clunker in the shop
and keep my hard-earned in my pocket,
she wobbles and humps like a scared rabbit.

But it's a real fine summer day in Corvallis,
and I'm loafing along watching the sprayers
do their slow drag on the fields of alfalfa,

and I come to a side road with a little green sign
says "Kurtz Lane" and I said to myself out loud,
"Mistah Kurtz – he alive. Him doing just fine,"

because of the sign, you see, and because I'm lonesome
and maybe kind of bitter in spite of the sunshine.
It's still a goddamn long ways from home.

That's one thing, though, that *Heart of Darkness,*
I read that story every year, I never forget
that crazy old son-of-a-bitch, that Kurtz.

And the next thing I see about a quarter-mile
down the road is somebody small on the shoulder,
a kid looking for a ride home, I figure.

And he's a kid all right, maybe ten or eleven,
but no Montana boy, he's an Oriental,
one of those Laotians that got resettled.

Can't figure why they brought them to Montana.
He's got those big eyes and caved-in cheeks
like the pictures on the TV during Vietnam,

and his mouth is open a little. I say to myself,
I'll give him a ride if he wants, and I even
begin to slow down, but he didn't

put up his thumb. Just when I went by, he waved,
real quick and shy, but still like he was trying
to reach me. I drove on. Then I bust out crying.

❯ *Fragment*

Who can know more deeply than I your loneliness there?
I saw you, I spoke, sometimes you answered.
It was, dear mother, so very clear
that we touched only what we both knew has no words.
Three years you lay there. Truth, why did you
do this to us? No answer. Never. Futility.
And your aphasia seems to me like a little Lydian
song, a tree-song among the gleaming instruments.
Insurmountable the uselessness of words.

❯ *For Papa*

So long ago that was called Jimmy Yancey,
that played the piano blues, that like his eyes
heavy-lidded searching the cocaine haze
laconically drew as it were a necromancy
from very ancient melody where no fancy
thing was heard, but a lingering, falling phrase
or a slow trill touched over the limping bass
in reticence, in almost silence, the chancy

lines of the song held in informing purity,
the bitterness of his love, the soul of *sonetto,*
as once with him that was called Dante, for so –
and only quietly so – might simple clarity
flow in the antsy moan of the crowd, a tone
of primordial sorrow, the deepest and so long gone.

❯ The Language of Flowers, Etc.

My last fringed gentians
twenty-two years ago
    exactly; and I remember my heart-clench
    and wonderment for that blue so

intensified by the darkness
in it, near Falls Village
    by the roadside, a brook
    flowing along, and for that courage

as well, most rare and beautiful
(having a darkness in it)
    among coarse grasses and tall
    reeds. But yet —

flowers can't have a character!
O.k. Hooray for you.
    Only sometimes a mind brims over
    remembering such blue.

❯ When I Wrote a Little

poem in the ancient mode for you
that was musical and had old words

in it such as would never do in
the academies you loved it and you

said you did not know how to thank
me and in truth this is a problem

for who can ever be grateful enough
for poetry but I said you thank me

every day and every night wordlessly
which you really do although again

in truth it is a problem for how can
life ever be consonant with spirit

yet we are human and are naturally
hungry for gratitude yes we need it

and never have enough oh my dear i
think these problems are always with

us and in reality have no solutions
except when we wash them away on

salty tides of loving as we rock in
the dark sure sea of our existence.

> *All Things*

The music of October
is the wild geese in the night
that bring me to rediscover
above the citylight

how all things are a song
unmeaning but profound
and fundamental to the tongue
we speak here on the ground.

St. Harmonie, let me sing
the music of October
in my loquacious stammering
till all hell freezes over.

Chicory

IN MEM. PAUL GOODMAN

Paul, did you mention chicory?
Maybe, but I think not.
    It also has no easy
    life on the hot

wayside. Yet it is the good news
I read in the salty gravel
    and monoxide residues
    of our mad travel.

In July the loosestrife too
and the cow vetch flower,
    but chicory is more blue.
    It is Mary's color

because it is beautiful and because
like the whole few of living
    things it suffers and gives praise.
    And it is forgiving.

An Excursus of Reassurance in Begonia Time

For surely the flower, as Williams
    believed, the plant itself,
        is as good a measure as one

may hope for, this one, this
    begonia I rescued from
        withering in the supermarket

that now thrusts from beneath
    its brown leaves these sprays,
        these gushes, these fountains,

the rich red blossoms
    in three-quarter rhythm –
        and what does the poet make?

Not the poem, though of course
    he does, because the poem
        is a thing of words and so

of limits, not worth much,
    nor is it experience brought
        conformably to some rule

of our desire, because that
    also is limited, is
        sometimes mean. I think

from experience, and I feel
    from experience, but I
        imagine from I don't know

what – call it the darkness
    hidden within the leaves.
        And what I imagine comes

true, though granted it
    takes a hell of a long
        time. The power of sun

on this June day at five
    o'clock in my west window
        falls from high above

the city upon the begonia
    like a glory. Yes, like a
        glory. Let us give praise

to Dante, who in the light
    imagined from his darkness
        the woman Beatrice, and to

Turner, who saw glory
fall from the sky upon
a rag and a stone. My

vision from dark experience
for years and years projected
itself outward above poems

until it became true, a glory
upon my life falling
now in the light of you.

I come to the point where
I must say I am a flower,
which is embarrassing,

but no! what is old age if not
a shaking off of darkness
finally before the plunge

and a recognition, although
never final, of what
the poem has done, the real

thing made real. You have become.
And I am in the full flood
of light at last, a flower.

Indeed a flower.

> ## *Carnations*

Carnality, the organic ruffles of
opening pink and white and red,
still folded as if quicker to respond
to a touch, flesh-petals, the bond
therefore for this that we are said
to have invented, to have abstracted,

what inadequately we call love,
a kind of validation exacted
from the uncaring world, a bouquet
for you, saying what I cannot say.

❯ *Song: The Old, Old Man*

Everywhere reality offers
    the old, old man
its misery and tawdriness, which
is why he is so tired and why
    the weathers have become
tedious for him, but then what's this,
this instant – a cardinal in May
    in a lilac tree –

this deepness and darkness
of inner foliage, the gleam
    on the upper leaves,
the pendulous fresh clusters
of lavender blossom, the red
    bird? Not beauty,
nor truth in any useful way.
    It's the instant,
it's the cardinal in May
    in the lilac tree.

    The old, old man is weary
of instants, so heavy the score,
    and weary of weariness;
it's true, he has come very far.
    He pauses to see
how the springtime has returned
    invariable again,
    and how he notices
this instant, this cardinal in May
    in the lilac tree.

Song: The Famous Vision of America

A long sweep
of prairie to the mountains,
        distance made clear
in green grasses colored
        with yellow, with blue,
        the wide sky over all,
and at night somewhere out
        there in the wind
        moving gently
the lynched man hanging from his tree.

Distance. And somewhere out there
        at night in the darkness
a coyote sits in animal wonder
        unmoving under the lynched
        man who turns unseeing
this way and that, hanging from his tree.

Song: Luxury

Even to think
of installing an air-conditioner
        in his car is
to the old man a
        shame and hurt,
who throve on hardship.

On a day once
        the thermometer
had stood at 103 degrees
        when he and his partner
labored the afternoon
        in the hayfield
        until they were limp
and lay in thirst and exhaustion,
yet he throve on that hardship.

The climate has changed,
humidity and pollution
are greater, and the city is no
place for a farming man,
but still he is hurt and shamed
and self-reproachful,
who throve on hardship.

He feels himself slipping, he
believes eventually
he will order the luxurious
machine, and he thinks
how he in his own strange self
stands for the species now
that strove in the wilderness –
how sorrowful, how dis-grace-ful,
bitterly he thinks the
syllables separately and in his
olden speche saith, "Alas!"
who throve on hardship.

❯ *Song: The Young Man with the Guitar, Testing*

The young man with the guitar, testing new riffs
with harmonic variations, sat in the maroon
wingback chair in front of the Christmas tree,
a very good tree this year, shapely and full,
and beyond the window, its glass set in a zinc
lattice, I saw a mockingbird perched in the snow
that clung to the yew tree. The bluesy tune,
the bird, and the two trees were like ifs and buts
in a fiercely complicated discourse in my head.
The young man was Dave, my son, whom I call the Bo.

And I said nothing. What words were there to say?
Mutability, you are the existing of all things
in this actual world, and without you every day
would be today, fixed and intolerable – so

my friends tell me over and over. They take
grace and joy from the existing that I do not
easily find or respond to, for a great sorrow
holds my mind. Then let me change! – for the sake
of the trees, symbolic and natural, the bird that sings,
and a young man, Dave, my son, whom I call the Bo.

That was the year's last afternoon. Now midnight
strikes. The young man, who likes to be called Dave,
has gone out with his friends. The firelight
flickers and dwindles, the bird sleeps in the snow.
Should I also call him Dave? The new year
has come, I'm foolish and old, I think I am
vanishing, and he is the wise one now and true
in himself – as I was once long years ago.
Turn off the tree. But how strong is this dark love,
young man, my Dave, my son, whom I call the Bo!

› *Song: So Why Does This Dead Carnation*

So why does this dead carnation hold
particular charm? Ten days ago
it was fresh, a bright, vibrant red,
but now has lost its gleam, and the fold
of its petals has loosened. It's like a flower
in a painting, or an ordinary imitation
in paper or cloth. One would have said
it is useless, yet I feel a kind of power.

Were they right, the Egyptians, to mummify
cadavers? I've pinned the carnation
upside down to my bulletin board
the way Kazuko used to pin roses, to let it
dry completely, I'm not sure why.
But I know my frightened mind can cower
to see my brown-spotted hand moving toward
uselessness, though it still has a kind of power.

From moment to moment the world becomes
memory, a still life, what the French
call *nature morte*. No embalmer
could make my hand lifelike for an hour
after its gone. But I'll keep the dry
carnation anyway, the best I can do
to abstract our existence and wrench
from the useless past a kind of present power.

« XII »

from

SONNETS
[1989]

> Sonnets

1

In the mind of the kiss occurs a thought so rich
that it exonerates the astonished philosophers.
Ah well, we say, something beyond converse
of systems is working after all, in which
nothing is absolute, never that, but pitch
by tone by timbre (or every his by hers)
includes all musics, all visions, and so refers
both ways deep and deep to the farthest niche
of being. The kiss is one and is egoless,
free and undetermined; the two exist
in its intelligence, original and new,
knowing more than they know in their access
of single subjectivity. Van Gogh once kissed
a cypress tree, and I have once kissed you.

2

How is it, tell me, that this new self can be –
and so quickly? God knows, none is the lord
of his own face or ever was. So what accord
of rearranging nuclei changes me
into this alien now so familiarly
staring from the bathroom mirror? What word
reforms my mind and all its wretched hoard
of worn-out feelings suddenly fresh and free?
Woman, I'm not sure of much. Are you?
More and more I believe the age demands
incertitude. I am no one. Yet your hands,
touching, word-like, can make a person. Who
is the strange new myself? Woman, do we know
the I of love that you in love bestow?

3

Last night, I don't know if from habit or intent,
when we lay together you left the door ajar,
a small light in which to see how you are
very beautiful. I saw. And so we spent
ourselves in this private light; the hours went
in a kind of wisdom, the night in a love far
inward drawn to the hot center of our
compassion, which was a wonderment
to me.
      But today in a cold snow-light,
so public and glaring, I have seen a wrong,
a brutal human wrong, done in my sight
to you, and the world I have tried to put in song
is more ugly to me now than I can say.
Love, we must keep our own light through the day.

4

While you stood talking at the counter, cutting
leftover meat for a casserole, out came
a cruelty done you – yes, almost the same
as others, but of such evil I think nothing
could enter my mind like this and be shut in
forever, black and awful. No tears of shame
secreted from all humanity's self-blame
will ever leach it or cover it. What in
this world or out of it, Christ, you horrid
cadaver, permitted you to permit this
to happen to her? Silly to think a kiss
or a sonnet or anything might help: that coward
did what he did. Evil is more than love.
It is consciousness, whatever we're conscious of.

5

From our very high window at the Sheraton
in Montreal, amazed I stood a long time
gazing at Cosmopolis outward and down

in all its million glitterings, I who am
a countryman temerarious and lost
like our planet in the great galaxy,
one spark, one speck, one instant, yet the most
part of my thought was not displeasing to me,
but rather an excitement, a dare that could
still raise my pulse-rate after these sixty years
to exult in humanity so variable and odd
and burgeoning, so that bewildered tears
stood briefly in my eyes when we went to bed.
For hours we made love and the night sped.

6

Dearest, I never knew such loving. There
in that glass tower in the alien city, alone,
we found what somewhere I had always known
exists and must exist, this fervent care,
this lust of tenderness. Two were aware
how in hot seizure, bone pressed to bone
and liquid flesh to flesh, each separate moan
was pleasure, yes, but most in the other's share.
Companions and discoverers, equal and free,
so deep in love we adventured and so far
that we became perhaps more than we are,
and now being home is hardship. Therefore are we
diminished? No. We are of the world again
but still augmented, more than we've ever been.

7

Fear of falling is why the old men walk
with their eyes on the ground, fear of stumbling
into some empty grave or other. Thus bumbling
downstairs this morning, with a great block
of sleep still in my head and my eyes peering
into the shady recesses to find what toys
and books lay under my tread, with the low noise
of eternity in my ears, unsteadily, fearing

the worst and blind as usual, I passed right by
the sign that Kate had taped inside the front
door saying, "I love you, Hayden," in blunt
bright lettering as if I would never die.
Never's too long a time, dear little Kate,
but if you forgive me, today won't be too late.

8

Yes. After all my arguments with myself
and having repeatedly said No and Never
Again, – for I don't like that bookshelf
full of sex without love and passionless endeavor
whose titles gleam like phosphorescent bones
in the dark, this huge pornography by the punk
youngsters of our epoch of rolling moans
and stoned gangfucks, – nevertheless, sunk
in your loving, my most hot beautiful woman,
I must now publish the amazement of my flesh
inside your flesh. We are beasts, we are human.
By love refined we touch, we intermesh,
we make this sense exceeding all sensation.
Feel, feel and feel and feel, our exaltation!

9

To see a woman long oppressed by fear
come free at last is joyous and a wonder.
As a poet I don't care for the stale remainder
of conventional sonnetry, yet just to savor
my own outpouring pleasure in this affair
I must lean backward lazily, as it were,
in the old romantic bed, an absconder
and apostate in my era. Today I wonder
where love's ideas lead me, and I don't care.

Well, she is like a *flower*. Let's say a Turk's-cap
lily. Somehow the nodding horn has lifted
and its complex hazel smile has opened

to the light. More, more, it has *wafted*
a clear high tone like a trumpet from the steppe
of home to heaven, that there has never happened.

10

You rose from our embrace and the small light spread
like an aureole around you. The long parabola
of neck and shoulder, flank and thigh I saw
permute itself through unfolding and unlimited
minuteness in the movement of your tall tread,
the spine-root swaying, the Picasso-like éclat
of scissoring slender legs. I knew some law
of Being was at work. At one time I had said
that love bestows such values, and so it does,
but the old man in his canto was right and wise:
ubi amor ibi ocullus est.
Always I wanted to give and in wanting was
the poet. A man now, aging, I know the best
of love is not to bestow, but to recognize.

11

Was Yahweh chosen by the chosen people?
I think so. Was their Covenant with themselves?
Of course. Did, as an animal kind evolves,
the god-idea begin with some apish couple
not risen yet to intellectual scruple
fucking in dark desperation? How the wolves
howled in the night! How the flimsy valves
of the lovers' hearts gave way!
                                    I'm an old cripple
dragging my mind like a clubfoot, but nothing comes
from nothing. Dearest, search as I will, age-proven,
back, back in imagination, still some given
is there, some glory in pandemonium's
gloom. Is it thus the great mind-light derives?
Cindy, in that god-glimmer we live our lives.

14

Why extremely do we observe more of
outrageousness now? Just yesterday
at the barbershop the door let in this guy
with an open red hole in his throat and a half-
bent tube coming out. He looked forty-five
and thin and shy. His footsteps were very slow.
A huge blue sunken scar was where his jaw
had been carved away. Everyone there gave
a gasp. You couldn't hear it. It was as if
a mind-shock had passed among us. Why
had he come? What was happening? How?
The barber shook out his cloth as usual. Love
did not soften his eye. He took up his scissors. But
really the guy didn't even need a haircut.

15

O Jesus, thou who sittest up there on the right
side of the fence, help if you can (which I doubt)
this poor bastard who sits here in the night
on this spavined sofa, smoking. He is knocked out
and galley west because he knows he knows
nothing but love and death, which the useless
philosophers for millennia in their useless throes
of uselessness have transfabulated into the mess
of good and evil. Jesus, what in the name of God
good does that do? No reciprocity, no
circularity is evident in the straight rod
of time, no method at all, at all, although
the philosophers pat their jowls with aftershave.
Two things exist. They are Cindy and the grave.

16

If I die today, which statistically speaking
is a greater likelihood than this man-child's
mind can readily grasp, please cart the leaking
bag of bones to the incineratorium that yields

a handful of dust, which scatter in the woods.
Not much humus will accrue, but at least a little.
No ceremonials. No specious interludes
in the public and private drinking. Pour a bottle
of brook-water for form's sake if some criticaster
demands libation. For monument, quite enough
to mount a stuffed crow on a rock, his posture
to indicate either alighting or taking off.
Then, Cindy, I don't know what you'll do.
I can't imagine. My heart goes out to you.

18

The loving mind in this death-haunted body
finds no accommodation. Let who will
admonish me of spirit and the study
that loving gives to kindredness of soul
or any other comfort imaged up
from human consciousness, I say the pain
of fleshy systems slopping to a stop
blows them all out and liquifies the brain
Mercy, mercy, I cry, not knowing whom
or what I cry to. Dogs struck on the street
cry so in shock, in woe, the rotten shame
of reeling, drunken death that steals their feet
We are such animals. We live to love,
yet practice death because we love to live.

19

At the hospital where I had the echocardiagram
I saw the shuffling troop rescued from death.
Let one suffice, the old man (my age) with his pajamas
open (on purpose) to show his wound, his torn chest –
frightful. I thought of the field of Troy. Not charming,
not at all. And laboring to catch my breath,
I of course asked what's the use, this rescuing. Lamb
or ram, the flock cares nothing. Must we be the shepherds?

No. Nor do I wish any longer to be accused
of humanism, that delusion, having in these threescore
years seen evil, hatred, ugliness, and perhaps more
than my share.
              Yet, Cindy, have not these rescued
a sterner meaning? Maybe that desperate guy
was Eros grown old and hurt, who cannot die.

     2 1

The Recollected Actual Voices of Romanticism

Ah now great brothers, you two centuries past,
that awful thing, that dread mysterious thing,
Despondency! – it doth play hell with sing-
ing. You who told us how the mind at last
could only split us off from earth and cast
us deep in fear, in loneliness, you ring
your words through history like soft gongs that bring
me down and down and down. You were steadfast
in pain and fantasy. Wouldst then that I
were strong as you! But no one now can cry
so valiantly, for you stood at the brink
and still could see the sunny hills behind,
hills lost in the chasm's depth to us who find
no vision here of what our minds must think.

     2 2

Cindy, I've used my writing all my life
as the one inoffensive yet functional way
to escape what we agree no longer to try
describing, the System, and it's not enough;
my poems too are incorporated, taken off
to system-land, and everything they say
is co-opted. I hate to admit that that French boy,
Rimbaud, was right, but he was. And so I scoff,
mostly at myself, because weeping gets nowhere,
like writing, and there's not much else to do,

and anyway I'm too old. Let's let these few
poems left in me, long or short, "out there"
or "confessional," be just for us – not much
like writing, no, but more like a glance or touch.

   2 3

It's said by the thoughtful masters that to know death
is what returns us to "essential solitude,"
to absolute singleness, killing the good
of the world, hard work, purpose, habit, and so forth,
and this is true, for I too am a man of the north,
as gloomy as Heidegger or Hamlet, and I have had
what may be properly called my first interlude –
sure not the last – of pained and faltering breath
in my old age; I can speak now with a certain
fervor about solitude and how self stares at self
in eternity's mirror. Yet I know something else.
As long as I breathe, however my breath may shorten
and aloneness seize me, your love will make my song
of death still richen and in its weakness strong.

   2 4

What if the psychologians, those grand old frauds,
were reconciled for once, taken altogether?
And what then if Eros and the Will to Power
were one in people as they had been in gods?
What-what?! The language burps; its words are suds.
And animal man still goes out wild to cover
animal woman who thought she had a lover,
and they are one, *one*, ONE, the bads and the goods.

Friedrich! Brother in madness! Have I not seen
the beautiful vacancy you left us shrivel
into a nest of serpents squirming? Evil
is Being. The actual ganglions of the brain,
the genetic tangle. I live, I love, I eat.
So what if absurdity is all my meat?

25

Freedom in love? It has been questioned. Think
of the unconscious as no longer a great power
of lust or murderousness as Freud and Adler
told us; no longer determinative; not a hunk
of a monkey; but more like a kind of mutual bank
of all our imaged emotive funds, withdrawals
unlimited. How's that strike you? Bourgeois?
Mechanistic? But money and love are freedom, blink
as you will, and Eros is not Libido. Eros
is Self, the transcendent subjectivity,
undetermined, Cindy, or one aspect of it.
It's to *find* love offerings that Eros goes
to unconsciousness, to *choose* the sane or loony,
and to *learn* to tell the real ones from the phoney.

27

Most brainy woman, the sexuality of your thought
has put me, some good time since, in this momentum
carrying me now, whether I ought or not,
forward, headlong forward, a plunging plenum
of sonnetness and everything going with it,
such as these acrobatics of 2:00 a.m.
that amaze the universe peering in, those outright
scandalized, bless their small souls, the seraphim
so cheery, who should, but for their good reason
seldom do, remind me soberly of my duty

to the bugeyed kangaroos in designer jeans
over there at the desolate unifarcity
who hate sonnets and would be dismayed by my body
and can't stand thoughts that come the least bit bloody!!!

28

Like the magnificent stationary animal it is,
its pelage tipped with color, our cutleaf maple
has already in two months become companionable

as it begins to turn, a flush of rose
over the filigree of green. No doubt now, this
is autumn, the equinox is past. Night is sable,
silky, and the gray sky of daytime opal,
my favorite season and, you have told me, yours.

We fell in love in winter, in spring we planted,
in summer we made our home, our family, keeping
the grand tradition, which may thus be augmented
minutely in nature's way. What are we reaping?
Someday we'll know. Now see the silvery rain
that falls in the blush of the maple leaves like grain.

2 9

I want to do a complaint now. Which is to say
simply that a hypertrophied prostate,
whatever women and other such novices may
choose to believe, is quite precisely not
my idea of a *baba au rhum* at the Chez
Paul or a Sunday outing with the laureate
or a grandiluminarious sunset display
over the park, etc. Also it is somewhat
not like strawberry shortcake.
                              On the contrary
it is that insidious, invidious last drip
which always waits, the inner adversary,
till I'm upzipped, helpless, and heading out, to slip
down my thigh like a seed of dying ice,
leaving a streak on my pants, which is not nice.

3 2

This is our perfect silver maple's day
of fullness. Carnelian in the sun and not
one leaf departed, a maximum of why
this species is. Yet who now can without
great sorrow recognize it? The millions of years
of beauty, known to be perpetual

and always becoming, now no more than a star's
streaked falling in the mind's sky, and all
with it of the finite world, gone. A puff
of air stirs the branches, with still no speck
of color descending, the tree near bursting, leaf
clinging to leaf, waiting. Will beauty make
no leniency in the mind's moral holocaust?
A burning brightness brightens and is lost.

33 SIN

Sin is not so much knowing (if it were,
everybody would be innocent) as wanting to know.
— ALBERT CAMUS

This is the sonnet I wanted to write yesterday.
It didn't work. I wanted to know just how,
in spite of authentic evil, I still know
my lack of an urge to kill. I threw away
the worksheets. What's left is literalness: to say
I am innocent. Innocent. I recall my overflow
of grief in boyhood when the newfangled radio
clubbed down an African man with a brute cliché,
how the boy I was then knew he would never dance
with the others in the streets where the great "will
to power" (for they never say "urge to kill")
wastes all embraces; I loved, but at a distance.
End of sonnet. Except, Cindy, that the proof
of love is grief, and grief is never enough.

34

Women in anger, it seems, become theatrical.
They perform. In pose, gesture, tone of voice,
even the masks their faces wear, they choose
fury self-consciously, and sob and wail
glancing over their shoulders at the spectacle
in the hall mirror, so to speak, turned-on Medeas

practicing for their dénouements. What's the use?
If I were a woman I wouldn't do that at all.

A man will roar and stomp and threaten and spew out
vile verbosity all over the neighborhood
and punch holes in the paneling and plasterboard
as a primate should, without caring a hoot.
But hell,
> Aint nary woman couldnt win her fight
> jest settin still & lookin out at the night.

35

for James McCartin

Well, Jim says that the couplet at the end
is a mistake. Funny, I always liked it
even when in Shakespeare it's only a trinket
sort of tacked on, a rhinestone on a blonde,
a parfait when you're already overstrained
from the tournedos, etc., but Jim's instinct
is often right, I know, rightly antipoetic
and favoring clarity over mere pretty sound.
If Jim thinks the couplet is usually clackety
and meaningless, I have to take his objection
seriously. What else, knowing I've done it
not by intelligence but by esthetic election
most of the time, and that both I and the sonnet
are getting up in years and doubtless yackety?

36

The Word for Today is "panoptic," which the goddamn
logocide defines as "permitting the viewing
of all parts." Jesus, I wish I never knew
the language, had never learned it, were deaf & dumb
& blind from birth, instead of what I am –
your anxious nephew, John Lyly. Who

would know the difference, of those that spew
foul dead words at me? None. Then like some
beautiful flower I would have grown, trembling
only for the breeze, never afraid, never
conscious of the power-mad, mercenary, clever
fools knifing me with words, never dissembling,
never anything but a pure sprout of this
indifferent nothing, happy as a kiss.

3 8

"All revolutions in modern times have led
to a reinforcement of the power of the State."
Cindy, this is the stunner. Granted, what
we, being rebels, must do is easy (fed
to our ears): decline, disacquiesce. Our head
is straight. But our life? An aimless fate
has brought us to live in a system more absolute
than any kingdom, for now the State is god,
total annihilation being its sign and power,
and when all heads, past, present, and to come,
have been smithereened will it matter that some
were straight? Will it help in life's final hour?
No, it will not help. Then only love
will help, and the suffering it is made of.

3 9

Poor little book, *The Sleeping Beauty* died.
I mind one fall up on the mountainside
I found a cow, strayed – or perhaps denied,
I thought – a Guernsey with a scurfy hide
and bleeding feet, sharp-boned and rheumy-eyed,
who stood as if she half thought to confide
in men when I came near, although her pride
held her to herself. What would you do? I tried
to lead her home, and for a halter tied
my jacket-arms around her, but she shied
and would not. Next day the world seemed wide

with new snow and I found no trace of her
until, in June, white bones and scattered fur –
lost but for me, who would have been her guide.

4 1

Why complain, brothers, to you, my writing
a futility, my teaching impossible? We know.
We know our country has no use for how
value survives, you in your labor shooting
staples in walls planned to fall down, computing
new means by which your bosses may disemploy
intelligence – do you complain? You do.
We all complain. That also is corrupting.
Transfiguration! What a marvelous word.
We dream it, that style of an older life,
yet accelerate unchanging toward our grief.
Small useless rodents rush upon the fjord.
"Waste!" I cry out. "Waste! Waste!" you answer back,
running, running, carrying what we lack.

4 2

The only coherent attitude based on non-signification would
be silence – if silence, in its turn, were not significant.
— ALBERT CAMUS

The hubbub of the Hall of Languages, our Babel
in Syracuse, is distracting to say the least,
or to say the most. Our clamorous deceased
proclaiming their mortality. Yet behind the gabble
of voices we hear the silence, we are unable
not to hear it. Radio astronomy has released
the noise of the universe, the howling beast
who prowls the stars, but still we have this trouble,
that silence is *always* heard. It caterwauls
in our blood, in the spiderweb in the corner of

the bedroom, in the wordlessness of love
bursting within us, in the void of sleep, the walls
of an empty room . . . but really is it anywhere?
Knowing no place is what we know of fear.

4 4

Persistent is the thought for me of that
midnight at Minton's, eerie and eternal, when
Dizzy at last was dominant and cut down
Little Jazz in their great black magnificat.
I hear it in other ears. Was Buddy Tate
the one who sat sideways smiling with a frown,
chuckling through his tears? It was someone,
I know it was someone. Removed, I celebrate
the moment as Pindar did, the dreadful passage,
one champion to another – ah, what glory!
And what sorrow. The Canto of Mutabilitie
will never be completed, nor the message
delivered to tell us what we need to know.
I always was not there, yet am also.

4 5

To rebel is suitable philosophical tactics
for the young. In fact, it served me well
and forced me to find myself and to excel
who had small wit and even smaller praxis.
It's true. In the world I made meager way
by failing intelligently, which will not last
forever or even for a lifetime. I amassed
anthologies of denials, good for a day
and now used up; rebellion works no longer.
Do I dream transcendence? Is it a dream
unglimpsed among the droves of academe?
May mechanics also rise and be the stronger
because their means (their words) are nuts & bolts?
Doctori, measure my lines in amps & volts.

46

To rebel. So I have saved my life, not once
but over and over these sixty years, and I'm
grateful to myself, of course. Epidemic time,
the bomb, gives any health a special importance.
Yet can it mean survival? This puppet dance
of outraged dignity, so theatrical, this mime
of Being? How futile. It asks more than rhyme,
not a changed self only, but changed existence,
and there is none. I don't know why rebellion
doesn't suffice. Maybe after all some given
in humanness, the "natural" dream of heaven,
drives us to hope, the one chance in a million.
But I give up. Comrades, you can have my books.
No longer will I throw poems at the fat archdukes.

47

*Certain kinds of foolishness are such that a greater
foolishness would be better.*

— MONTESQUIEU

To have been Diogenes. Why not? Or de Sade.
Mighty cynics in the world of probationary
All-out and desolate with the outcast curs
of the Pripet Marshes. Or to have found God
divulgated like a black pea in a green pod,
a shriveling prophecy for you, my Sirs,
from the heart of being, howling like one of yours
in bloated British, the era's Supersod.
Or contrarily to have married young
and raised a round half-dozen roundly squalling
over the Sunday comics in a round appalling
suburban house that sighs like an iron lung.
Oh, various are the ways more cracked than rhyming!
Obsession is only a matter of bad timing.

48

Cindy, the secret's out. Yes, you're addict-
ed! All these years, and now — well, who'd've thunk
you'd fall, though there it is. As a grand drunk
from the grand era of grim-visaged strict
American ginheadery, let me say,
"I know, my dear, I know." When you sneak out
to Woolworth's every other day, no doubt
you hope you won't be seen, you tremble, pray,
and hunch yourself (don't think I don't recall!)
and nothing works. Addiction will not keep,
but slips from you like words said in your sleep
and flits from ear to ear throughout the mall,
"See how she scurries past all unawares!
See how her purse is stuffed with Gummy Bears!"

51

You in a tallness slenderly, as a lone
white birch I knew once swaying in a small
wind, walk
              away from our bed to the window,
and in the light from the old streetlamp I am shown
the glisten of the line of the curve of the fall
from shoulder to flank, breast to knee,
                                        in shadow
the gleam of the inner edges of your long legs
so that a wilderness in me, rising, begs
silently,
         and you turn, a calculus of bright
changes, glyphs in the dimness, and you walk
silently back, delicately, as the egrets stalk.
Truly, all things most good happen at night.
We know. Later with our last energy we talk
and fall asleep,
                embers of abeyant light.

53

Thy sting sufficeth, Death. If Heidegger first
saw through the human consequence of Darwin's
dread, the ingenious flight from Thee, his daring
nevertheless was only everyone's coarsest
intuition. Sufficiently, Death, thou partest
lovers – Cindy, how then I shall be abhorrent! –
as sufficiently hath thine oppression driven
all history in a flat-out surge from "durst not"
to "civilization," to thwarted Being. Death,
shall we thank Thee? Cindy and I can love,
love more than sufficiently, driven by Thee
to extremest sexual refinement in our wrath
and anguish. We do give thanks, we do. Reprove
us not if we give lamely and philosophically.

54

Must genius always struggle, always exaggerate,
in order to reach a simpler, humbler, clearer
vision? John Coltrane, you were the bearer
of our lives. True, we've Picasso's lovely late
eroticism, and the aging Yeats's last great
rage, but not what you might have done! Our era
needed you. A calm in the rising terror
was in your horn had not an insane fate
zonked you in mid-flight. Yet you lost us, Trane,
before we lost you. You systematized, caught
in the ambition of a middle-aged, middle-class culture
to rationalize your music in an accountable brain.
And now you hover above us, a black vulture
squawking forever, as after all you ought.

55

If you see a child that shivers when it hears
a diminished fifth, nurture and protect him,
for he only in the schoolyard's fierce abstraction
will know the cry of the lynx, the cry of the hare,

and that of the old man and the young woman.
Shivering is his genius. If he have speech,
he will utter it greatly. If not, he will search
in other ways beyond the ordinarily human,
the hating and angered. He will hear the light,
he will sing the light and the darkness, or will sound
the ideas of them in the concrete nothingness
of tones vibrating in the air that sight
cannot conceive, yet they touch each one of us.
He will hear love where we would behold a wound.

56

The Bo was three when we slugged through Arizona
in exhaustion and wonderment, unkempt, unshorn,
our boots scuffed, our hats stained, and in torn
shirts and jeans, and I said by God we'd done a
good month's work and it weren't unfittin', somewhat,
to acclaim ourselves ragamuffins. The Bo did not scorn
my suggestion, but two days later, with a forlorn
smile, "Papa, I am not a rag of a doughnut,"

he said. Good St. Chance, thanks be for him!
And also thanks now for Cindy. In this weather
so deupholstered by the winds of time,
I am much torn and scarcely able to cover
my elderness, but she is a good true lover
and thinks me not a rag of a doughnut either.

57

To the aged, trembling, illiterate woman yesterday
killed in some unpronounceable town in Lebanon
by a Christian rocket supplied by the Pentagon,
it's not enough for me in my comfort to say
I had nothing to do with it and that anyway
religious war is a silly anachronism; fun
and games, that's what the generals call it, let it con-
tinue, they with their implacable faith in the sway

of murder; it's not enough to assert the contrary
while watching the TV or to pay the usual price
of concerned Americans, so prompt and voluntary,
this Euripidean, musical, significant sacrifice
of metaphysical self-dismissal. Old woman, will you
please never forgive me? I'll never forgive you too.

58

I think continually of the differences.
Foolish ever to have believed that change
is not absolute. Suddenly, peeling an orange
becomes utterly futile like these days that seize
in time, like this particular day, which is
the end of the world, disgusting, truly strange,
and we long to cross the differences and plunge
into nostalgia, that "acceptable disease."
Life is setting; but not behind the hill
where the bob white called at evening. It falls
in Solvay behind the refineries. Nothing calls.
The argon-lighted billowing gasses fill
the western sky all night across the lake.
The sterile water flashes, *Mistake, mistake.*

61

Key-reist, I am fed and sick unto death with this
mumblin' poetry all around me, my own
included. "I'm aware of her earlobe – " dronedronedrone,
etc. What possible apotheosis
of speech can be if our speech no longer is
a folk-thing but from that fraud, Mr. Microphone,
the ad-gal's smarm, the anchorman's cornpone,
the politico's gobble-gobble and periphrasis?
I ask you. For my part I purpose now
throwing my own yawp into it, this so aged
and disreputable and petulant and enraged

wordiness. And if it seems more like an old sow
roaring in heat, clamoring, than like high
talk, well, all right. At least it won't stupefy.

6 2

Honey, darling, baby . . . but no endearments
suffice us now. We say we have surpassed
the forms of love. Even these words, like garments
worn through the ages, lovers' rags, at last
how stripped and threadbare is the mediating
our mutual storm! The hot wind blows. We're left
like tailors without thread in our own mating,
our forms strewn round us, useless, worn, and reft.
Such is love's maturation. Such these sonnets,
wordings reduced to babble. Think. The master
gave this convention his hot rounding minutes,
but not a year. Gauds are for the imposter.
Cindy, I need more difficulty now,
more wilderness than these quick rhymes allow.

6 3

But still, still . . .
                    In stillness mystery calls,
though calling no one, being simply there,
somewhere I cannot tell, singing, not near,
not far, but song always, an ayre that falls
on my silence as if heard in the long halls
of eternity, of existence, this that I hear
in the incomprehensibility we share
and cannot speak, a touch, a glance that forestalls
the foreignness we felt before we came
into our knowing one another, yet no touch
nor glance in fact, nothing definable, no name
in materiality, only this singing, such
that together silently we hear and we belong
at last,
        always this sonetto, this little song . . .

« XIII »

from

TELL ME AGAIN HOW THE WHITE HERON RISES AND FLIES ACROSS THE NACREOUS RIVER AT TWILIGHT TOWARD THE DISTANT ISLANDS

[1989]

The Incorrigible Dirigible

Never in any circumstances think you can tell the men from the boys. (Or the
    sheep from the goats.)
Nevertheless unavoidably and interminably – up to a point! – one observes
    tendencies, the calculus
Of discriminative factors in human affairs. Alcoholism, for instance, is the
    "occupational disease of writers"
(And a good fat multitone in the vox populi too, that sad song), and I cannot but
    approve
My friends Ray Carver and John Cheever, who conquered it in themselves;
I cannot help, for that matter and to the extent I am friendly with myself at all,
Approving my own reformation, which began 30 years ago today, the 3rd
    September 1953.
Well, your genuine lush never forgets the date of his last one, believe me, whether
    yesterday or yesteryear,
And one time I asked John, who had quit at 65, why he bothered. "At your age I
    think I'd have gone on out loaded," I said.
"Puking all over someone else's furniture?" he answered, and much can be derived
From his typical compression of judgment. We were men as men go, drinking
    coffee and squinting through cigarette smoke
Where we sat at a zinc-topped table at 7 o'clock in the morning.
We were men buoyant in cynicism.
Now I remember Lucinda de Ciella who drank a pony of Strega every morning
    before breakfast
And was sober and beautiful for ninety years, I remember her saying how peaceful
Were the Atlantic crossings by dirigible in the 1930's when her husband was
    Ecuadorian ambassador to Brussels.
Such a magnificent, polychronogeneous idea, flight by craft that are lighter than
    air!
I am sure it will be revived.

Not Transhistorical Death, or at Least Not Quite

Jim Wright, who was a good poet and my friend, died two or three years ago.
I was told at the time that we did not lose him.
I was told that memories of him would keep him in this world.

I don't remember who told me this, just that it was in the air, like the usual fall- out
from funerals.
I knew it was wrong.

Now I have begun to think how it was wrong.
I have begun to see that it was not only sentimental but simplistic.
I have examined Jim in my mind.
I remember him, but the memories are as dead as he is.
What is more important is how I see him now.
There, there in that extreme wide place, that emptiness.
He is near enough to be recognizable, but too far away to be reached by a cry or a
gesture.
He is wearing a light-weight, brightly colored shirt.
His trousers belong to a suit, but the coat has been discarded.
His belt is narrow and somehow stays straightly on his pot belly.
His shoes are thin and shiny.
I think he bought those shoes on his last journey to Europe.
He is walking away, slowly.
He is wandering, meandering.
Sometimes he makes a little circle.
Sometimes he pauses and looks to one side or the other.
Sometimes he looks down.
Occasionally he looks up.
He never looks back, at least not directly.
Although he recedes very gradually and becomes very gradually smaller, I
continue to see all the aspects of his face and figure clearly.
He is thinking about something and I know what.
It is not the place he now occupies in my life.
He cannot imagine that, only I can.
He is neither what he was (obviously), nor what he is (for I am quite sure I am
inventing that).
Is he Jim Wright? Is he not someone else?
Yes, he is Jim Wright. No, he is not someone else. Who else could he possibly be?
When I die, he will arrive at where he is going. And I will set out after him.

An Expatiation on the Combining of Weathers at Thirty-Seventh and Indiana Where the Southern More or Less Crosses the Dog

Oh, Ammons rolled the octaves slow
And the piano softened like butter in his hands,
And underward Catlett caught the beat
One sixteenth before the measure with a snip-snap touch on the snare
And a feathery brush on the cymbal, and Shapiro
Bowed the bass, half-glissing down past E-flat to A, to D,
And after a while
Berigan tested a limping figure low
In the cornet's baritone and raised it a third and then another
Until he was poised
On the always falling fulcrum of the blues,
And Bechet came in just as the phrase expired
And doubled it and inverted it
In a growl descending, the voice of the reed
Almost protesting, then to be made explicit
On the trombone as O'Brien took it
And raised it again, while Berigan stroked a high tone
Until it quavered and cried,
And Carruth came achingly on, the clarinet's most pure
High C-sharp, and he held it
Over the turn of the twelfth measure
And into the next verse with Bechet a fifth below rumbling
Upward on the back beat powerfully,
And O'Brien downward,
And Catlett press-rolling the slow beat now,
The old, old pattern of call and response unending,
And they felt the stir of the animal's soul in the cave,
And heard the animal's song, indefinable utterance,
And saw
A hot flowing of the eternal, many-colored, essential plasm
As they leaned outward together, away from place, from time,
In one only person, which was the blues.

Sometimes When Lovers Lie Quietly Together, Unexpectedly One of Them Will Feel the Other's Pulse

'Tis just beyond mid-August. The summer has run mockingly away, as usual.
The first equinoctial storm has killed a certain paltry number of innocents in
      Galveston, who will be hardly missed,
And now its remnant brings a wind to Syracuse, a zephyrous wind that clears the
      air a little.
Not much. Haze lingers over the Bradford Hills.
What the Preacher said about retribution is true, true in the very nature of things,
      and therefore we Middle Americans must pay now
For our sins. Standing by the kitchen window, I escaped into my woodland soul
Where I saw our willow, the great eastern Maenad, Salix babylonica, toss her wild
      hair in sexual frenzy.
Then I went to my chair in the living room. I drank coffee and smoked, the
      relentless daily struggle to awaken.
Above the street at heavy opalescent noontime two electrical cables, strung from
      pole to pole,
Hung in relationship to one another such that the lower swung in and out of the
      shadow of the one above it,
And as it did so the sunlight reflected from it was sprung gleaming outward and
      inward along its length,
A steady expansion and contraction. And for a while I was taken away from my
      discontents
By this rhythm of the truth of the world, so fundamental, so simple, so clear.

The Impossible Indispensability of the Ars Poetica

But of course the poem is not an assertion. Do you see? When I wrote
That all my poems over the long years before I met you made you come true,
And that the poems for you since then have made you in yourself become more
      true,
I did not mean that the poems created or invented you. How many have foundered
In that sargasso! No, what I have been trying to say
Is that neither of the quaint immemorial views of poetry is adequate for us.
A poem is not an expression, nor is it an object. Yet it somewhat partakes of both.
      What a poem is

Is never to be known, for which I have learned to be grateful. But the aspect in
        which I see my own
Is as the act of love. The poem is a gift, a bestowal.
The poem is for us what instinct is for animals, a continuing and chiefly unthought
        corroboration of essence
(Though thought, ours and the animals', is still useful).
Why otherwise is the earliest always the most important, the formative? The Iliad,
        the Odyssey, the Book of Genesis,
These were acts of love, I mean deeply felt gestures, which continuously bestow
        upon us
What we are. And if I do not know which poem of mine
Was my earliest gift to you,
Except that it had to have been written about someone else,
Nevertheless it was the gesture accruing value to you, your essence, while you were
        still a child, and thereafter
Across all these years. And see how much
Has come from that first sonnet after our loving began, the one
That was a kiss, a gift, a bestowal. This is the paradigm of fecundity. I think the
        poem is not
Transparent, as some have said, nor a looking-glass, as some have also said,
Yet it has almost the quality of disappearance
In its cage of visibility. It disperses among the words. It is a fluidity, a vapor, of
        love.
This, the instinctual, is what caused me to write "Do you see?" instead of "Don't
        you see?" in the first line
Of this poem, this loving treatise, which is what gives away the poem
And gives it all to you.

❯ *Of Distress Being Humiliated by the Classical Chinese Poets*

Masters, the mock orange is blooming in Syracuse without scent, having been bred
        by patient horticulturists
To make this greater display at the expense of fragrance.
But I miss the jasmine of my back-country home.
Your language has no tenses, which is why your poems can never be translated
        whole into English;
Your minds are the minds of men who feel and imagine without time.

The serenity of the present, the repose of my eyes in the cool whiteness of sterile
  flowers.
Even now the headsman with his great curved blade and rank odor is stalking the
  byways for some of you.
When everything happens at once, no conflicts can occur.
Reality is an impasse. Tell me again
How the white heron rises from the reeds and flies forever across the nacreous river
  at twilight
Toward the distant islands.

❯ Survival as Tao, Beginning at 5:00 A.M.

Shadows in the room. Strange objects. The gladiolas on the coffee table, for
  instance,
The pink, deep red, yellow, and tangerine, these are all now more or less tropical
  and black,
Somehow menacing in the huge earthenware pitcher, which resembles a sea
  anemone.
Three small mantas swim through. Insomnia, the *demonstratus* of the ground of
  despair,
Mixed with several kinds of tranquilizers: the mantas are not unexpected,
Nor is this atavistic sense of elsewhere. What is unexpected
Is this sentence by Leibnitz: "Music is an exercise in metaphysics while the mind
  does not know it is philosophizing."
I ought to look up the original, I do not care for
The word *exercise,* I suspect an infelicitous translation.
L. himself was seldom infelicitous. But never mind the words for once, the
  statement catches at something
True and important. Music is the attempt to survive the unbearable through
  freedom from objectivity
Bestowed from outside, i.e., by the variable frequencies of sound waves.
Loving, on the other hand, is an exercise, so-called, in metaphysics while the mind
  is perfectly aware,
For sex would be merely an objective conduct, an addiction, without the intellect
  to discover the meanings
Implicitly always in it. Loving is to survive the unbearable through freedom
  bestowed

From the inside, mutually. It is the only functional exercise in metaphysics still
    enduring, still
Enjoining our otherwise denatured sensibilities to perceive and understand the
    positive aspects of Being,
As the dawnlight indicates. The mantas swim away. The gladiolas, smiling
    lugubriously,
Deposit the unbearable upon the day, that is, their lower blossoms, withered
    overnight.
Coffee and cigarettes in my Chinese bathrobe. The day, Sunday, will be hotter
    than yesterday, Saturday, which was
Hotter than the day before, Friday, etc. Now the child's television emits the most
    incredible
Noises I have ever heard. Where's the music? ("*Wo ist die musik?*" the Bo said, so
    many years ago.) No one
Remembers how it was made, except I – *ego, scriptor.*
Yet in the freedom of orgasm my thought of the woman
Is indeed a song, a metaphysical song, soaring in the inconceivable, brought to the
    fullness of harmony
By her thought of me.

» *Ovid, Old Buddy, I Would Discourse with You a While*

upon mutability – if it were possible. But you don't
know me. Already you cannot conceive my making the second line
of a poem so much longer than the first.
No matter, mutability is the topic, and I see you there exiled on the Thracian shore
among those hairy mariners speaking an improbable tongue,
a location of you damnably similar to Syracuse, N.Y., and I see
you addressing your first letter to the new emperor, Tiberius,
looking blankly out to the rocks and the gray ocean
as you search for rhythms and awesome words to make this
the greatest verse-epistle ever written and obtain your pardon, your freedom to
    return
to Rome, so long denied by Augustus.
Do you know me, after all? But of course, how could you not when my words are
    your very bones?
You speak to me of two thousand years of solitude.
Yes, you are writing that letter forever.

You tell me how you cannot name your crime because you only suspect what it is
 and to name it would make it true.
You are innocent. Tiberius will not grant you pardon. He cannot.
But he can fling those victims, stopped forever wild-eyed in mid-air, off the
 precipice at Capri!
Some powers are always powerless.
The change from Augustus to Tiberius, what does it mean,
that instant of mutability continuing forever
between a death and an investiture?
You whisper to me, No pardon, no pardon, no pardon,
and the three sprigs of white lilac in the glass pitcher on my table
that are slightly, but only slightly, wilted –
the stems weakened, the heavy blossom-clusters depending –
tremble as if a wind even from Olympus were meandering through the room.

❯ *The Sociology of Toyotas and Jade Chrysanthemums*

Listen here, sistren and brethren, I am goddamn tired
of hearing you tell me how them poor folk, especially
black, have always got a Cadillac parked in the front
yard, along with the flux of faded plastic and tin.
I just blew fourteen thou, which make no mistake is
the bankroll, on a Toyota Celica. "The poor man's
sports car," the salesman said, which is the truth.
(I'll write about the wrongs done to car salesmen
another time.) She do look mighty good there in my
front yard too, all shiny red and sleek as a seal.
It means a lot to me, like something near or almost
near what I've always wanted, and it reminds me of
the Emperor Tlu whose twenty-first wife asked him what
he wanted for his birthday, and he being a modest man
said the simplest thing he could think of off-hand,
a jade chrysanthemum, and thirty years later he got it,
because you see that's how long it took the master
jade-carver and his apprentices to make it, and when
he got it – Tlu, that is – he keeled over on the instant
in sheer possessive bliss. Why not? Professor Dilthey

once said history is the science of inexactly recording
human inexact passions, thereby giving birth to sociologists,
as every schoolperson knows. Well, let them have a look
at all these four-wheeled jade chrysanthemums around here.

❯ *"The World as Will and Representation"*

When I consider the children of the middle class
as representatives of phenomena to my subject sense
I can hardly see them at all, they fade
into the shrubbery, of which a superabundance
is *sui generis* their world. I am likely to be overwhelmed,
or distracted, leaning my mind on some green bosom.
But then they are things-in-themselves, these children,
and their glee is a thing-in-itself, their exuberance
as they terrorize one another, wiping themselves out
in a continuum of destruction, themselves
as surrogates of parents. But the parents remain
representations, never things-in-themselves, but only
shadow-figures taking out the garbage; and thus
the Will of Schopenhauer's essay leaps out at me
in children-in-themselves, starker than stones or stars,
so that I cower; for the future is theirs, day by day
they remove it from the plastic wrap of non-being,
and leave it on the death-strewn lawns. Yes, if will
is all we know of ourselves as things, and thence
of all things, how can I not infer a radical divergence
of degree between everything else and children? The spirea
dies, the little nebulae of viburnum wink out in willing
whatness, but the children's shrieks of bliss and triumph
are merciless, raging from another world, another time,
so that all understanding is blocked and thrust back
as mere knowledge, odious data, nauseating demonstrations,
these relentless present children of the middle class.

To Know in Reverie the Only Phenomenology of the Absolute

Why was it Bavaria? The house in the forest
was modest, a cabin, though rather substantial
with latticework on the porch, a window in the gable.
Each afternoon I walked to the village
down a woodland path among great dark trees,
across a bridge made of cedar poles. Patches
of violets and forget-me-nots. At the café
I smoked a cigar, drank coffee or lemonade,
read a newspaper, wrote postcards, an occasional
letter. I talked with the proprietor.
I walked home at twilight and rested
on the bridge, looking down into the stream,
the weeds oscillating in clear water. I carried a stout
walkingstick, a staff really, cut from a straight
ash sapling. I did this for many years in my
old age, and in the gable room wrote a number
of better-than-average books. But I have never been
in Bavaria.

Meditation in the Presence of "Ostrich Walk"

Of the two cardinals the female is both bolder and more "beautiful." She comes
To the railing, crest raised high, snapping her eyes this way and that,
Uttering the nasal ech-ech of fear and belligerence,
Then down to the lower travis, then finally to the flagstones, where she feeds.
Now comes the male, seeing the way is safe, and begins to hull seeds and feed them
To her. The mind performs its wearisome gyrationing. The female accepts
These token mouthfuls, but eats on her own between them. She is very obviously
Able to take care of herself. Although most people say otherwise, and say so
    vehemently,
The difference between Floyd Bean and Joe Sullivan is distinct, crucial,
And unique. I move my hand to rewind the tape and the cardinals
Are gone forever. *Ora pro nobis*, my good St. Chance, my darling.

No Supervening Thought of Grace

for GALWAY

My true friend's poems about aging and death held my mind as in a sea-surge
this afternoon, for they are true poems, and good ones,
and I myself feel weakened much of the time now from the nights of death-laden
     insomnia,
which no weakness cures.
Almost equinox. A cold March day in Saratoga with hesitating rain in the pines.
Beyond the woods, rushing cars and trucks on the interstate
make a sound of continual rising and falling, almost like the seething sea,
which is almost like the sound of my friend's poems.
But he is five or six years younger than I, what does he know?
What does anyone know? Here, here is where it is, here in my own skull.
Well soon enough he will learn. And so will everyone.
I went out walking in the woods with my hands in my pockets,
thinking and brooding, because like the sea trees are important, and rain is
     important,
and the important wet brown needles were springy beneath my feet
that nevertheless went falteringly, cautious for the litter of downed limbs,
the boneyard of the pines.
I found a half-buried old wax-paper Dixie cup
almost like a fungus, stained softly gray in a flocky pattern edged with coral and
     orange. Sometimes one doesn't care
any longer about oneself, but for a true five-or-six-year-younger friend
one would dash into the sea, if that would help,
one would beseech the gods.

No Matter What, After All, and That Beautiful Word So

This was the time of their heaviest migration,
And the wild geese for hours sounded their song
In the night over Syracuse, near and far,
As they circled toward Beaver Lake up beyond
Baldwinsville. We heard them while we lay in bed
Making love and talking, and often we lay still
Just to listen. "What is it about that sound?"

You said, and because I was in my customary
Umbrage with reality I answered, "Everything
Uncivilized," but knew right away I was wrong.
I examined my mind. In spite of our loving
I felt the pressure of the house enclosing me,
And the pressure of the neighboring houses
That seemed to move against me in the darkness,
And the pressure of the whole city, and then
The whole continent, which I saw
As the wild geese must see it, a system
Of colored lights creeping everywhere in the night.
Oh the McDonald's on the strip outside Casper,
Wyoming (which I could indistinctly remember),
Was pressing against me. "Why permit it?"
I asked myself. " It's a dreadful civilization,
Of course, but the pressure is yours." It was true.
I listened to the sound in the sky, and I had no
Argument against myself. The sound was unlike
Any other, indefinable, unnameable – certainly
Not a song, as I had called it. A kind of discourse,
The ornithologists say, in a language unknown
To us; a complex discourse about something
Altogether mysterious. Yet so is the cricketing
Of the crickets in the grass, and it is not the same.
In the caves of Lascaux, I've heard, the Aurignacian
Men and women took leave of the other animals, a trauma
They tried to lessen by painting the animal spirits
Upon the stone. And the geese are above our window.
Christ, what is it about that sound? Talking in the sky,
Bell-like words, but only remotely bell-like,
A language of many and strange tones above us
In the night at the change of seasons, talking unseen,
An expressiveness – is that it? Expressiveness
Intact and with no meaning? Yet we respond,
Our minds make an answering, though we cannot
Articulate it. How great the unintelligible
Meaning! Our lost souls flying over. The talk
Of the wild geese in the sky. It is there. It is so.

"Sure," said Benny Goodman,

"We rode out the depression on technique." How gratifying, how rare,
Such expressions of a proper modesty. Notice it was not said
By T. Dorsey, who could not play a respectable "Honeysuckle Rose" on a kazoo,
But by the man who turned the first jazz concert in Carnegie Hall
Into an artistic event and put black musicians on the stand with white ones
    equally,
The man who called himself Barefoot Jackson, or some such,
In order to be a sideman with Mel Powell on a small label
And made good music on "Blue Skies," etc. He knew exactly who he was, no more,
    no less.
It was rare and gratifying, as I've said. Do you remember the Incan priestling,
    Xtlgg, who said,
"O Lord Sun, we are probably not good enough to exalt thee," and got himself
Flung over the wall at Machu Picchu for his candor?
I honor him for that, but I like him because his statement implies
That if he had foreseen the outcome he might not have said it.
But he did say it. *Candor seeks its own unforeseeable occasions.*
Once in America in a dark time the existentialist flatfoot floogie stomped across the
    land
Accompanied by a small floy floy. I think we shall not see their like in our people's
    art again.

A Post-Impressionist Susurration for the First of November, 1983

Does anything get more tangled and higgledy-piggledy than the days as they drop
    all jumbled and
One by one on the historical heap? Not likely. And so we are all, in spite of
    ourselves, jackstraw diarists.
This afternoon we went walking on the towpath of the Erie Canal, which was
    strangely
Straight and narrow for our devious New England feet. Yet it was beautiful, a long
    earthen avenue
Reaching far and straight ahead of us into the shifting veils that hung everywhere
    in folds, oaks clinging to their dry leaves,

Bare maples in many shades of gray, the field of goldenrod gone to seed and burnt-
out asters,
Sumac with dark cones, the brown grasses, and at the far edge, away from the
canal,
A line of trees above which towered three white pines in their singular shapes.
I have never seen a white pine growing naturally that was not unique and
sculpturesque.
Why should one not devote one's life to photographing white pines, as Bentley of
Jericho
Spent his photographing snowflakes? But it's too late, of course. At all events the
colors,
Not forgetting cattails and milkweed, dock and sorbaria, ferns and willows and
barberries,
Were a nearly infinite variety of the soft tones, the subtle tones, made even more
indistinct
In their reflections on the greenish water of the canal. And a light breeze was
blowing.
For once I will risk the word *zephyr,* which is right and which reminds me of
sapphire,
And I realize that beneath all these colors lay an undertone of blue, the gentle sky
as it curls
Below the penumbra of vision. A small yellow butterfly tricked its way across the
brown field beside us,
And I thought to myself, Where in hell did you come from? Last night was a hard
frost.
And then I knew it had been born this day, perhaps a moment ago, and its life was
fluttering, flickering, trickling out in our presence
As we walked with our hands in a lovers' clasp on the straight towpath beside the
canal that made us think
Of France, of tumbling autumn days, of hundreds and hundreds and hundreds of
loves and visions.
Sometimes my woman is half ill, sometimes more than half, because she doesn't
know as much
As people she envies. She writes poems about not knowing, about her anguish over
knowledge,
And when I was her age I felt the same way. Ah I know that anguish. I used to be
pained especially
Because I could not name the colors I saw, and I envied painters their knowledge
of pigments,

I studied the charts of colors and I looked up the names – mallow, cerise – in the
    dictionary,

I examined the meanings of *hue, shade, tone, tint, density, saturation, brilliance,* and so
    on,

But it did no good. The eye has knowledge the mind cannot share, which is why
    painters

So often are inarticulate. Is the eye ignorant, uneducated? How absurd. That
    would be impossible.

Hence I became eventually, gradually, unashamed of my mind's incapacity, just
    as I had once written

Poems to be read many times, but what was the use of that? Now I write poems to
    be read once and forgotten,

Or not to be read at all.

❯ *"I've Never Seen Such a Real Hard Time Before": Three-Part Invention*

Having planted our little Northern Spy at the wrong season,
Having pruned it in trepidation and ignorance, having watched it
Do nothing at all for a month in the drought-burned, weedy wasteland
Of the front yard – that prefiguring desolation! – now I am
Uplifted truly and in glory
By the sapling's big new leaves and its stems lengthening,
And my mind carries everywhere I go this image of a pale green upsprouting
In the form of a fountain, a small, natural, simple fountain:

And having learned at last, from an intelligent and willing young man
Behind the counter at Superior Sound, Inc., on East Erie Boulevard,
The conclusive difference between a ceramic and a magnetic
Cartridge for my stereo turntable,
Having placed this sparkle of knowledge in my mind like a jewel on a dark
    velvet ground,
I glance at it hundreds of times in passing, so to speak,
With a little thrill of gratification for its novelty, its actuality,
And especially for its purity, its unfailing, useless betokening of what is:

And every day these twinges of pain in my heart, that muscle unenvisionable,
Draining me downward like the "flow of atoms" into cool organic earth,

The quicksand,
Downward in this strange new fluidity, this impersonal dissolution,
Drawn by an energy somehow inside me and yet not mine –
How stunning the methodical magnitudes of force! –
Make me wonder, abstractedly, about the pulverization of the soul,
About vast windy scattering wastes of crumbled joys and drifting knowledge, about what becomes
Of all the disjuncted dregs of consciousness:

This song is a wave rolling forever among the stars.

Letter to Maxine Sullivan

Just when I imagined I had conquered nostalgia so odious,
had conquered Vermont and the half-dozen good years there,
here you come singing "A Cottage for Sale," which is a better than average song as
a matter of fact, though that's
not saying much and it's been lost to my memory for years and years,
but you always had good taste, the same as mine.
Oh Maxine, my dear, how screwed up everything is now.
Your voice in 1983 is not altogether what it was in 1943,
nor are the Swedish All Stars up to the standard of John Kirby, Russ Procope,
Buster Bailey, Charlie Shavers, Billy Kyle, and – but who was on drums?
Ben Thigpen? Shadow Wilson? – I don't remember but oh
the names, names, lovely old names calling to me always through echoing dark;
no, nostalgia will never be conquered –
yet your singing is as as ever, a passion evinced in these exact little accents and
slurs and hesitations, the marvelous stop-time measures, the languets of
song,
so that I am overcome, I am almost devastated, by your musical excellence and
also by anger and sorrow because everyone
hoo-hahs so outrageously over Ella Fitzgerald, the eternal bobby-soxer (and
millionaire).
You, a black woman singing a white Tin Pan Alley tune in Sweden about my home
back in the sticks of Vermont,
and I in Syracuse, where the jasmine has no scent –
feelings and values scattering as the death-colored leaves scatter on this windy
day.

Maxine, I cling to you, I am your spectral lover, both of us crumbling now, but our
      soul-dust mingling nevertheless
in the endless communion of song, and I hope, I believe, that you have striven, as I
      have,
beyond the brute moments of nostalgia,
into the timelessness of music,
and that you have your people with you, as I have mine.

› *Une Présence Absolue*

Not aware of it much of the time, but of course we are
Heedless folk, under the distracting stars, among the great cedars,
And so we give to ourselves casual pardon. It is there, though, always,
The continuum of what really is, what only is.
The rest is babble and furiosity. Imagination, let me pay more attention to you,
You alone have this letting power; give me your one gift, which is the one
      absolution.
I am this poor stupid bastard half-asleep here under this bridge.

› *How Lewisburg, Pa., Escaped the Avenging Angel*

"Dust," she said. "What is it? Where does it come from?"
"What do you mean dust?" I said
"Dust," she said. "That stuff that comes back on top of the refrigerator three days
      after you've wiped it off."
"Lint," I said. "Bits of soil. Danders. Carbon. Vegetable matter."
"Oh," she said.
"Generalized metaphysical fall-out," I said. "Dust to dust, etc."
"How do you know?" she said.
"I don't," I said.
"Then kindly refrain from being so fucking authoritative," she said.

❯ Underground the Darkness Is the Light

When I first started out to make what later became known as Hayden's Runaway
    Pond, I borrowed
Baldy Langdell's little Cat that he used mostly for sap-gathering in his hillside
    sugar orchard
Over in Waterville, but he had a blade on it, and once I got the hose connections
    tight
It worked well. I had a good spot, and Pop Foster, the county agricultural agent,
Agreed. "Ideal," he said. It was a gentle downslope sort of folded in the middle,
    where a brook
Ran straight down from a spring in the woods behind, a good spring, never known
To run less than nine quarts a minute in the driest season. I went to work.
"Now watch you don't scrape too deep in the hardpan," Pop said, and I nodded.
I pushed dirt to all sides, but mostly to the front, where the embankment would be
    highest,
Like a dam. Pop showed me how to set up the standpipe with a wing valve at the
    bottom, the outlet pipe
Headed straight forward under the bank and into the brookbed again. It didn't
    take long,
A day and a half with the dozer. Then I set the valve just a mite open
So some of the water would continue flowing out into the brook and on
    downstream,
But enough would catch in the pond to fill it. I watched. Slow, very slow, only a
    puddle
After the first two days. But I expected that. I sowed the banks to rye, clover, and
    orchard grass.
Of course that summer, after the pond filled and water spilled into the standpipe so
    I could close the bottom valve,
It was a sterile pond. But the next spring I had frogs, big ones and little ones, and
    that summer
What I call the purple water flower seeded in and some bulrushes on the far side.
    Then the following spring
The stoneflies hatched, and the mosquitoes, so I stocked some minnows and brim.
    By the end of July
I had a muskrat hole on the upper back just over the water-line. Next spring I
    stocked brookies,
A couple of dozen, and they took to it, and I used to go at twilight with my part-
    shepherd bitch Locky

To feed those trout bits of hamburger. How they rose to it! Locky would stand
  downbank
With her front paws extended and bark at them, and sometimes I thought maybe
  the trout
Were barking back. It was a fine pond, alive, a going concern. Swallows from
  Marshall's barn
Skimming the surface. Once I saw a heron. Then two summers later I saw the
  water
Was sinking. "Must have scratched the bottom a mite hard," Pop said. It went
  down slowly
The same way it had filled, but after six weeks it was all gone, nothing left
But mud and the brook trickling across the bottom and down into a hole I could see
  plain enough,
Jagged, about eight inches across. No fish, no frogs. They must have gone down
  too.
Down into the earth, a live pond flowing into all those channels and chambers
  down there.
Strange to think of. Locky went trotting and sniffing here and there on the sun-
  dried mud,
Looking half scared. "Don't that beat all?" Marshall said. And I said, "Yes, it
  does."

> Cross My Heart and Hope to Die, It Was the Very Same Song Exactly

Where does the sadness come from? The great Seychellesan tortoise that heaved its
  quarter-ton of body up onto legs
Plainly misengineered to support it and tottered a few yards uncertainly across the
  grass and gravel
Seemed old enough to know, so wrinkled and outcast. Out of the air then? Some
  distillation of the color green?
This was at Clyde Peeling's Reptileland south of Williamsport on Rt. 15 in
  Pennsylvania,
Which is not a mere tourist trap. Mr. Peeling knows his animals and studies them.
  He treats them well.
But on the subject of sadness he only turned his gaze eastward, like the tortoise,
  toward the Muncy Hills.

The eyes of the tortoise are as beautiful as any I've ever seen, perfectly almond-
shaped, brown and deeply lustrous,
And they are filmed with tears. My companion was on the verge of tears herself, I
knew this in the same way that she
Knew the animal's sorrow. If women ruled the world – real women, not the blurry
rag dolls cast up by the sea of history
Like any detritus – it would be a sadder, saner place. Old age accedes, which is not
wisdom precisely but the best we can do.
Yet where does the sadness come from, this saturation of everything, this seepage
into the world?
Women are the true pragmatists, and William James is their best friend, if they
only knew it. They are also sentimentalists, which is not
The paradox it may seem, for what should the end of the universe, this "heap,"
elicit if not love? The end is what
Women have been talking about since before the last ice age. Hence they are
passionate as well as pragmatic.
Balzac wrote: "All passions are essentially Jesuitical," and indeed this is almost a
truth – as close as we are likely to get
In our promiscuous knowing called language – but is passion therefore somehow
inferior? It sees all things
And insists on distinctions, and it never gives up, but this does not mean fury, it
does not necessarily mean pride.
Are not we, in what is left of our own vestigial and unselfconscious instinct, seeking
the cognitive mode of the animals
And of women, we with our programmed thinking machines? The sadness is the
mystery of beginning, a parchment map with terra incognita
Inscribed on the northeastern sector. The sun shone brilliantly over Pennsylvania
in late May.
Now it is August and hazy, and we are elsewhere, remembering that the great
Seychellesan tortoise with its tearful eyes was not looking at us.

from

NEW POEMS
[1986 – 1991]

❯ Living Alone

For John Cheever, from whose writing this epigraph is taken:

A few minutes later a miscalculation of the helmsman sent a wall of water up the side of the ship and filled the stern deck with a boiling sea. Up swam the Ping-Pong table and, as I watched, it glided overboard and could be seen bobbing astern in the wake, a reminder of how mysterious the world must seem to a man lost overboard.

Mystery. Seed of every motion.
See out there beyond the thermal-
pane that last chrysanthemum
in the frozen bed by the concrete wall
swing wildly its lavender
and shattered head. How fast
the wind rises. How the mud
elaborates in patterns of ice.
A gull, hovering, shudders and cries.

   •   •   •

And what if as often does
this epiglottis fail to close
    once for all
    and need is final,

comfort me who will then?
Or otherwise that time soon when
    writhing in wayside clover
    I shall be like the snake run over?

   •   •   •

Jettisoned in one night
from her house by my
successor I was as if
falling as a parachutist might
in vacant air, shocked
in the silence, nowhere.

   •   •   •

No more than a bad
cold in a strange town? Suppose
    really it might be

pneumonia? No one
to call; phone useless; fever
    smoldering. I see

the winter sunset
behind my curtain casting
    its thin light on me.

      •   •   •

No. Experience is unique and equivalent.
I have always asserted it, I won't
look for similitudes on other gallows.

O Villon! O Spartacus! Yes,
I know. And also I know this other,
a cruel, stupid, and bat-sighted lover.

      •   •   •

Flu, bronchitis, pneumonia
("a touch of") – as I thought
timid to seek help. Being right
justifies me some. Euphonia –

but I am done with you! Weak
as a kitten. My Song, you alone
not faithless and more or less at one
with me, let us not be to seek

timid any more, but tough
in our own melodiousness
toward everyone. The hell with her madness,
you and I in each other being enough.

      •   •   •

Peculiar now I have come among
all these so laboring and academic young
my own language is to me (although
intermittent, it's true) easy, strong,
and flowing in natural cadences of song.

.   .   .

These walls are I think well insulated,
not much sound comes through, except
the American ubiquity of flushing water,
yet down in one corner voices float
as if telephoned from Hell. "Shut up!
Shut up, you little bitch!" I hear.
A woman screaming at her wailing daughter.

.   .   .

Housekeeping an endless joy.
Endless and a joy, maybe
because. No use for the coy
poets who say they've finished
something. So this baby
spider (small anyway) has made
his web conveniently in my
bath tub and has already waylaid
two flies – in December! There
in his solitude he sits. And burnished
are his eyes in the small night light,
complete his aloneness, complete his care
for his bundled deaths to left and right.

.   .   .

Rachel, your name won't rhyme, the language itself
has given up on you. Zilch. You and your great fat
stuffed bulging shapeless antique ego that
you lug around like your grandmother's satchel.

.   .   .

I feared death and I sought it
        like other men

and doubtless like women too
        though I disclaim

whatever knowledge I thought once
        to have of them,
but that was in the mid-years
        of anguish and pain.

Weariness at last
        overcomes all,
six decades. Who cares
        if I fall

sick unto acceptance
        in this small bed
indifferent now? Either I am
        alive or I am dead.

              •   •   •

Nevertheless one rebels. "I dis-
acquiesce!" The funerary stars
burn relentless over the dying
earth that drops through silence –
emptiness as the order of reality.
"What barbarism!" So slight the words
they cannot flutter up in the darkness
on their shredding wings. Nevertheless.

              •   •   •

Matter? Does it? Anything
in this world of equivalence
("my only"), the one comprehensible
in all incomprehensibility? No.
Bare-ass in radiant fever, I
shiver from window to window,
twitch the drapes apart, look
out to red-neon Pizza Hut
in the rain, while the radio
plays "The New World Symphony"

all night long. Matter if it's
Vermont, a squalid farm, or here
this two-bathroom squalor, this
suburb? Don't be fooled
by "w/w carpeting" in the ads,
what it means is wall-to-
wall pins; also tacks; also glass.
I put on slippers. All equal,
all the same, and boredom
no longer stylish, just necessary.
Who, who could have foreknown
the best of thought would come
to this inevitable meaningless?
Lord God, you who are not, we
who are imploring go down
on our meaningless knees to you.

     •   •   •

"All one can do is to achieve nakedness."

    And do you –
You, Friend, Foe, Unknown –
see me here in this garden apartment complex
that is otherwise called forsakenness
(no different, of course, than anyone)
    bare-ass in woe?

     •   •   •

The notion of an austere measure
and speech once more purged
of vulgar inconcinnity
seems by solitude not only urged
but offered as a negative pleasure.
So I'll go back to it someday. Maybe.

     •   •   •

When the studio
musician remarked
that Russell had

no technique, there
in that dark room,

Pee Wee picked up
his horn and blew
a mistake so lovely
I saw a tear
even in the eye of
the idiot.
                    O Monte-
verdi. O Mahler.
In the dark room.

              •   •   •

Sleeping, the lovers. In the wet dark of morning
these millions, the young and fair who still outnumber
the old and ugly, the abandoned and sorrowing.
And insomnia's streetlights shine on the black
peaceful windows of their slumber.
It is four-thirty, hour of weeping or not weeping,
hour of rhyme.
                    And the neon is gone. And the rain
falls on the end of time.

❯ *Pa McCabe*

You tell these young spratasses around here
you got a ram down in the brook, they'll look
at you like you was talking the Mongolian
jabberfizzy, they ain't never heard of any such
a thing. Even if you say it's a *hydraulic*
ram, it don't mean nothing to them. Maybe
it don't to you. Well, a ram is a kind of a pump,
see? It works without any power except the force
of the water itself. How? You're thinking I'm
off my rocker? Ok. You got an inlet pipe
that's four to five times the diameter of the
outlet, and you set that inlet far enough up

the brook so it makes a fall of maybe two to
three feet, so the incoming water will hit
with force. What happens is it hits a little
weighted valve and pushes it upwards so most
of the water sprays out and goes back to the brook.
But then the valve falls closed again from its
own weight, and that pushes a little water up
into the dome, and of course that creates pressure
same as you got in any pump, and the pressure
will drive some of the water into the outlet.
Ingenious, ain't it? Of course it ain't what you
guys would call efficient; you only get out
about 10 to 15 percent of the incoming water. But
it don't cost nothing! Nothing! No electricity,
no gasoline. Once you got that pump going, it'll
run forever.

    I had a small one once, borrowed
off Marshall, and I set it up in the brook on a rock
so it would pump a stream of water about the size
of a pencil up to the garden. It worked fine. All
night long I could hear that little valve going
tap, tap, tap down there in the brook, working
away for nothing but the pure joy of working,
and that's something, if you take my meaning. Still
a pencil of water don't spread itself around much,
so I figured I needed a reservoir to catch it. Then
I could fill my bucket from the reservoir instead
of climbing down to the brook and back again,
and spread that water even, where I needed it. I
went up the road to see Pa McCabe. "You got any
kind of a drum," I said, "maybe forty gallon
or so." Pa looked sidewise and pulled his ear.
"Why," he says, "I got a old paint barrel holds
60 gallon. Trouble is it's still coated with
paint on the inside." "I can burn it off with my
torch," I said. "Yes, you could do that," he says.
"What do you want for it?" I says. He turned his
gaze up toward the mountaintop. "Why," he says,
"how about three dollars?" I damn near exploded.

Three dollars? I wouldn't have give three whole
dollars for a copper dog that laid brass turds.
But I seen that wan't the right approach, so to
speak. "Done," I says. And I handed him three
frogskins.
      So I had that barrel in the back
of my pickup just outside the barn door, and I
begin to put her in gear, when Pa hollers at me,
"Hold on a minute, hold on," and he runs in the
house – the kind of running you do when you're
seventy-nine and three-and-a-half feet wide –
and in a couple of owlblinks he comes out
waving a half-gallon of syrup, worth a good
six-fifty at the going rate in them years.
"Here," he says, "take this home to your wife
and tell her it's from her hot old honey up in
the hill section."
      It were the onliest time I ever
seen old Pa so downright ashamed of himself.
I'm using that barrel yet. But of course
we drunk up the syrup. Syrup don't last long.

❯ *What a Wonder Among the Instruments*
Is the Walloping Tramboone!

That elephantine bray in the upper register, that sagacious rumbling down below,
    that glissing whoop,
A human glory, a nobility – but ach, the good words for goodness have been
    bollixed in our degradation.
Recall then from the darkness of your adolescence, my still empowering spirit, the
    names of gladness,
J. C. Higgenbotham, Jim Harrison, Wilbur de Paris, Kid Ory, George Lugg,
    Dickie Wells, Trummy Young, Honore Dutry, Jimmy Archey,
And although in retrospection Teagarden was overrated, the white names too,
    Miff Mole, Floyd O'Brien, Brad Gowans, Lou McGarity, Vernon Brown,
May all their persons be never forgotten and their music continue in the ears of the
    chosen forever!

When the ancients first raised up the ram's horn to the heavens, it was in this loud
register.
When mountaineers in their isolation laid down an alpenhorn to sound across the
chasms, it was also the same.
And when the medieval genius of orchestra found itself in the voice of the sackbut,
it discovered resonance, which is to say, sensuality unlimited.
Let me, spirit, assert no equalness beyond the insanity that is the built-in tragedy
of homo sapiens,
But let me nevertheless, a pipping pallid clarinetist, say to the darker masters that
although
The tenor sax has seemed the proper instrument for your sensibility, and much
sound has come from it,
It is at best a facile machine lately devised by the engineering and anti-musical
European intelligence,
Whereas the trombone, known fitly and affectionately as the sliphorn, is truly
more near your *virtu*.
Spirit, let me revere and celebrate in poetry the life of Vic Dickenson, and let me
mourn his death.
As for you, pipsqueak literati, for whom all writing is a conspiracy of rhetoric, draw
yourselves far off yonder, for here is none of such intention.
Dickenson, no other could sing as you, your blasts, burbles, and bellowings, those
upward leaps, those staccato descensions,
Your smears, blurs, coughs, your tone veering from muted to stentorian, your
confidences, your insults,
All made in music, musically. Never was such range of feeling so integrated in one
man or instrument.
How you made farts in the white mob's face at the Belgian International
Exposition and Mr. Bechet laughed out loud.
You were the Wagner of tonal comedy, you were the all-time King of the Zulus,
you were jazz.
Thanks be to St. Harmonie for the others, yet next to you they are extraneous to the
essence, a throng milling outside.
I learned it all from you (and from a few dozen others), evinced so incompletely in
these poems, yet in my mind
A bliss for fifty years, my resource, my constancy in loneliness or loving. Now you
are dead.
You grew old, you lost your teeth, you who had seemed indestructible have been
destroyed, and somehow I survive.

Not long, however. Hence from aged humility I dare to speak. May these words
    point to you and your recorded masterwork forever,
Which means as long as our kind can endure. Longer than that, who cares?
    Thereafter will be only noise and silence.

❯ *Continuo*

At Galway's, such
    is the presence of the snows
even in summer and the touch
    of wind on the drifts

of green gleaming to white,
    that all this world's gifts
mean death in a cold light
    whilever the wind blows.

❯ *A Backyard in California*

Someone is actually playing a dulcimer
Not far from here,
Cool tones on the hot noon air.

And sunlight on the palm leaves in the sky
Is slenderly
Divided, a tango for the eye.

All is languorous. Old age
Is slow, the edge
Of shadow creeps, and lust and rage

Are the privilege only of the sun,
Which will go down
After the sufficient afternoon.

❯ Sonnet

"Whut do you spose thet thing is," Oi said. "Whut?"
she said. "Whoi, thet there annymule on thet
yaller diamon-shape soign back there set
boi the soid of the rouad," Oi said. "Whoi, Oi thut
it were a horse," she says. "Thet?" Oi says. "But
no horse look laik thet." "No. But don't you bet
on it. A horse look laik thet iffn you let
them daowncountry folk draw it," she says. "Cut
it aout," Oi says, "you doan meen it." "Whoi, yass,"
she says. "Waul, haow can ennybuddy tell?" Oi says.
"They tooken a sir-vay," she says. "A horse is
part Belgian, part ox, and it's got a moose's ass
with a mite of grizzly thrun in." "You doan say,"
Oi says. Thin Oi shut up the rest of the way.

❯ Sonnet

Well, she told me I had an aura. "What?" I said.
"An aura," she said. "I heered you," I said, "but
you ain't significating." "What I mean, you got
this fuzzy light like, all around your head,
same as Nell the epelectric when she's nigh read-
y to have a fit, only you ain't having no fit."
"Why, that's a fact," I said, "and I ain't about
to neither. I reckon it's more like that dead
rotten fir stump by the edge of the swamp on misty
nights long about cucumber-blossoming time
when the foxfire's flickering round." "I be goddamn
if that's it," she said. "Why, you ain't but sixty-
nine, you ain't a-rotting yet. What I say
is you got a goddamn naura." "Ok," I said. "Ok."

Homage to John Lyly and Frankie Newton

Not great, not
        among the acerbic
downtowners, the Dizzies
        & Bens, & too

late perhaps (or
        early) for
those terrific sessions;
        yet

you were perfection nearly
        when you were. So
good, so good – "Campaspe"
        & "The Bad Ass

Blues." St. Harmonie, let
        the great go
their frightening ways.
        Praise to thee

for these littler (Zuk!
        don't forget
him!) & these almost
        lost.

Mix the Ingredients

Coiled in the azimuth, Vipère
super-coifed shed down her
glitzy foil
throughout the whole prairie,
oy, her spoiling deliberations,

on falcon, who squawked like a chicken,
a sudden skeleton,
scanned and gone.

Mama snake, here's the hoe.
Till sundown shall your tail continue.

Paisley non-being, the gluey sands
sucked inward. Moon chips fall.
Hey, no phase.
This tomb has a narch. You
done now, crazy man? Yah. Boo. Shut (shut).

❯ *The Bearer*

Like all his people he felt at home in the forest.
The silence beneath great trees, the dimness there,
The distant high rustling of foliage, the clumps
Of fern like little green fountains, patches of sunlight,
Patches of moss and lichen, the occasional
Undergrowth of hazel and holly, was he aware
Of all this? On the contrary his unawareness
Was a kind of gratification, a sense of comfort
And repose even in the strain of running day
After day. He had been aware of the prairies.
He had known he hated the sky so vast, the wind
Roaring in the grasses, and the brightness that
Hurt his eyes. Now he hated nothing; nor could he
Feel anything but the urgency that compelled him
Onward continually. "May I not forget, may I
Not forget," he said to himself over and over.
When he saw three ravens rise on their awkward
Wings from the forest floor perhaps seventy-five
Ells ahead of him, he said, "Three ravens,"
And immediately forgot them. "May I not forget,"
He said, and repeated again in his mind the exact
Words he had memorized, the message that was
Important and depressing, which made him feel
Worry and happiness at the same time, a peculiar
Elation. At last he came to his people far
In the darkness. He smiled and spoke his words,
And he looked intently into their eyes gleaming

In firelight. He cried when they cried. No rest
For his lungs. He flinched and lay down while they
Began to kill him with clubs and heavy stones.

❯ *Essay on Death*

I

The prisoner ran forward. First his head
was lopped off by one sergeant swinging
    a scimitar, and secondly his neck-
        stump was seared

by another sergeant with a glowing iron plate.
Then the next prisoner ran. And the next. How far
    can a man run after he has been
        decapitated? The Emir

and the Sultan had a wager and were pleased to see
one prisoner run almost to the courtyard gate,
    to freedom. Then the Potentates
        lost interest and the

wager lapsed. But now think of those runners! Did
their bodies really strive for freedom without
    their heads? Did the severed heads
        cry out in shame?

Our horror takes us only to the instant
when they ran in front of the first of the two
    sergeants. Then ignorance begins.
        And yet I see that

courtyard, I see those bodies running atilt
with neck-stumps spraying blood (in spite
    of cauterization), I see the twitching
        corpses. Here in this

apartment complex in Syracuse where I live
I look out on our courtyard where the Christmas
    lights are shining in every window
        and strung in the little

trees, lighting the snow. Might this be another
carnage? Are the two courtyards connected
    by anything more than their pro-
        pinquity in

my mind? I have offered one candle, which I
believe is enough for an old man. But truly these
    gleamings here are peaceful, they
        are quiet, they

are no violence. Beyond the corruptions of faith
and of every kind of faith, which make us still
    eager for the bright impossible rationality
        which the people of the caves

thought they had glimpsed when they knew that they
had minds, are all these lights of love. The stars
    have come down to earth. When I walked out
        to the mailbox, carrying

a letter for my daughter, who lives three thousand
miles away in a country of desiccated, smoldering
    grass, though Christmas lights are shining
        in her town too,

I walked with my stick on the crusted snow, and I
looked back up at my window, my one candle
    in this extraordinary festival
        of renewing light,

and I was touched by it. Through a narrow
passage between these buildings, up the shallow
    flagged steps, out by the swimming
        pool I walked,

and saw there in the mulberry tree a spray
of little lights as if flung from Saint Lucy's
    little hand, lights set there
        however

by the management, whose revenues will not
thereby increase one penny. And so various
    they were! – all these glitterings,
        these scintillations,

like stars, or like minerals rather, risen from earth,
ruby, emerald, diamond, sapphire, gold, and silver,
    a splendor in the shabby suburban
        winter, created

by us all for the sake of beauty and to praise
our knowledge of the turning season. Then this
    is what we know? Not what those cut-off
        grimacing heads

were thinking, nor how those Potentates in easy evil
could command those men to run the murderous
    gauntlet; but rather that I walked
        through lights of love

to send my loving father-message to a woman
far away. And what we do not know is precisely
    death. In the heart of the light
        is darkness and Christmas

is a mystery. Trudging back down the shallow
steps, down through the shimmering lights, I feel
    an "irresistible gravitation,"
        as Proust called it,

drawing me downward always, down the steps,
down into the ground, so that my feet become shadowy
    in earth, downward through loam and grit
        as if I were wading

in earth-flesh. My tread becomes slow and urgent,
and my window, as I approach, shining its small light
    in the multitude, seems to reveal
        behind my candle

shapes I do not recognize that remind me
of things I cannot remember, things that occur
    and withdraw in the windowframe as if
        at the edge of knowledge.

       2

Once my friend Ray Carver spoke of the "relentless
logic" of waiting, waiting. Is time then
    logical? At all events it resists
        refutation. When

the terrorist exploded his bomb by the ticket counter
in the air terminal, who was terrorized? Those broken
    and wistful corpses lying there
        in death and dismantlement,

or all of us who are looking at them? Carl Jung
told us that the first time he died he went zooming
    off into space where he saw a castle
        floating, warmly

lighted and full of comfort, which he presumed
was his destination. Romantic boy! Let him
    look at the airport on Christmas
        Eve. Beyond that,

could enough castles exist for all the dead,
even in space? In fact the brain cells of the
    severed heads do continue
        to dream a little.

And the grimaces (that Mme. Defarge noted with such
satisfaction)? They may be only those of the violinist,

Allen Tate, whose mouth uncontrollably
　　　twists in sensual

concentration. In the graduate student's story
an adolescent buried a kitten up to its neck
　　　in the ground and ran over it with a
　　　　　lawnmower.

When? In 1930 a boy shot his BB gun
from an attic window at a chickadee in the maple,
　　　not thinking he could hit it, and the bird
　　　　　closed its eyes

and leaned forward slowly and fell to the ground.
The boy ran down two flights of stairs and took
　　　the bird in his hands, but it was dead,
　　　　　which was enough

death in his life, he decided. And in 1944
Polish farmers stood in their pastures watching
　　　the trainloads of Jews go by, and they
　　　　　shook their fists

and made the throat-slitting gesture and laughed.
They laughed. And long ago Alexander, who was also
　　　blond, ordered the city of Susia
　　　　　"put to the sword" –

and how did they do that? Did the Macedonian
soldiers post themselves on each streetcorner
　　　and line up the citizens and stick them
　　　　　in their bellies

with dull bronze sabers? The shrieking, the blood,
the long agonies. Why did the soldiers and boys and
　　　Polish farmers do these things?
　　　　　What did they think

about death? What of their own deaths to come?
Why do people gather at the site of an accident,
    looking down at the victim who oozes
        on the pavement? Are they

fascinated merely by the mystery? Are they
envious, recognizing the one who has passed beyond
    death, who no longer must face it?
        It's true, a joy

is in it, joy in the power of killing, even
on television. But nothing is known. Killer
    and killed whirl in a stupid vortex of
        ignorance. No

story any more, no tale, no adventure. The three
bears have gone to work for Disneyland
    and Goldilocks committed suicide
        in 1962.

Brains, bones, blood, synapses, little electrical
currents — but where do the souls go? Yes,
    when you say you love me, the tension
        and rapid heartbeat

and waves of my mind are measurable on the graph.
"Well, I'm a mighty tight woman," the night nurse
    sang, "oh I'm a real tight woman." And also
        in a dark abandoned

house I hear the intimations nearby, the rustlings,
the ghost-ideas. Basta! Only the blues remain.
    "I dreamed I was standing on 18th and Vine,
        yes, I dreamed

I was standing, baby, on 18th and Vine,
and I shook hands with Piney Brown and I
    could hardly keep from cryin'." That's
        the way it is.

Overhead now I hear the police helicopter –
arrumpt, arrumpt – and its powerful spotlight
 sweeps across our courtyard, obliterating
  our Christmas lights

in a greenish brilliance like an exploding nebula
whose relentless logic reaches us eventually,
 eventually. The terrorized are all
  who wait, everywhere.

   3
Age, the romanticists say, is vision and simpli-
city and brightened consciousness, but I say, Fraud,
 fraud, blinded by the light. Even
  the trees are reeling.

   4
Inside again, I switched on my lamp, and found
only my Japanese wind-carp and my Hindu
 cow-bells and the other strangely assorted
  objects I have

gathered over the years, which I know well.
No evil. And yet they are mysterious to me.
 I go to my chair. How often I have sat
  here in this cage

of light, reading, pretending to read, laboring
to read – sometimes to write, to make lines
 of language, glyphs on a page – but death
  has occupied me.

I imagine a pair of pudgy hands, like my little
grandson's hands but spotted with age, pushing
 against a huge gray leathery limp
  bag of nothing

that fills the room. Pushing. Sometimes in the last
year giddiness has taken me, but not giddiness,

nothing known or named, a moment
   of being alive so

altered, so abrupt in unexpectedness, that I have
moaned and fallen, the light has sunk down to
   dimness, and in a bewilderment of pain
     and humiliation and

despair, I have seen a stunned iguana sprawling
from my chair onto the carpet, vomiting black
   blood there. Even so I have read
     thousands of books,

a passionate searching, but have found nothing
not a part of knowledge. The iguana is dumb.
   So many pages of marvelous dying,
     but only gibberish

of death. And now from my neighbor's door
across the hall I hear music faintly, voices
   of women singing above deep tones
     of an organ-like wind

over the sea, not commonplace, a moment of great
beauty, and from the shopping plaza half a block
   away comes faintly the cry of a
     siren. Not

commonplace. My light blips. Someone has turned on
a television or perhaps the great grid of energy,
   civilization itself, has faltered far
     away. And my candle

grows a tall flame that flutters and dies and
leaves a rancid smell. In the courtyard
   lights still gleam, the headlights
     of a passing car

make tilting shadows that run along the opposite
wall, running away, and the Christmas lights
    are bright. But not as bright as they were
    a moment ago.

❯ *Songs About What Comes Down:*
The Complete Works of Mr. Septic Tanck

TANCK'S PROLEGOMENON

Five lines, not four. And keep the song
    not quite vulgar, people don't
want to hear themselves, why should they?
    One line unrhymed. That way
the singing will sound both right and wrong

together, like a flower with one petal
    cockeyed. Otherwise let
it be beautiful as it may but get
    at least a little meaning in,
this not-much for which we always settle.

TANCK'S SONG ABOUT HIS BIRTHDAY

Pains enough thou hast given me,
    Lord, to make me sixty-three,
which I am this day. Is that God's grace?
    I ask you. Here I sit
between a rock and a hard place

with my bad back, heart, eyes, gut, arthritis,
    and now this effing tooth, and Lord,
I am sore.
    Damned if I can understand what your right is.
Kindly just let me get to sixty-four.

TANCK'S SONG ABOUT SILENCE

Your silence against my shoulder,
    afterwards. My silence too.
Together in this becoming older,
    we who can trust the silence and who
at one time could only fear.

Yes, the great silence is out there,
    we know that always. But this
is different, this silence we share
    against that greater. So we rest in
gratitude. Give me a little kiss.

TANCK'S SONG ABOUT HIS UNICAMERAL MIND

In May, was it, Ophelia drowned?
    Today the watery breeze blurred
a clump of tulips, tight-set and orange,
    as though it were a wavering
face. I fell asleep then

in the chair of my old age
    as I looked out. I remember
wondering when springtime had left
    the world. Years ago, no doubt.
The truth is I knew the lady well.

TANCK'S SONG ABOUT WOMEN

"She had quickly learned to show
    unhappiness was to risk the loss
of love." I read that when I was laid low
    with my back at Gassy's place
from stumbling across

one of the kid's shoes dropped on the floor,
    read it in a book by a woman named P. D. James.
And it struck me and made me look

for more of the same, which I didn't find. The book
was mostly a bore.

That's how it is for women, though.
    The same for me, which is maybe why
I like women for company
    more than men, the jerks. But damned if I
really know what it means, for them or me.

TANCK'S SONG ABOUT EARL HINES

"Turn out all the lights
    and call the law
right now!" Right on. He had the raw
    animal spirits and he had
a hell of a good time all those nights

of his life, but you can't hear and not know
    how he studied to make his left hand do
those rhythmic inventions, how he began
    new musics again and again. "Father Hines, you
dirty old man."

TANCK'S SONG ABOUT NOVEMBER

So I'm antiquated. I still like to see
    the world decked out like this in its red
viburnum berries, blue ones of privet and yew,
    pokeweed's black and white, glossy, naked
death-seeds, pink waxy bells of the spindletree –

jewels they are at leaf-raking time,
    and look, the hills, the colors up there
now, birches gone lavender, beeches silver, the saffron
    tamaracks, and the grayish bare
maples varying as cloud-lights turn off and on.

Don't get revved up. Don't get on my case.
    I say I'm getting old because I am.

Maybe I will have twenty years more in this place.
   (Maybe I'll move to Herkimer or Amsterdam.)
But I'll never see enough of the world's bright seeds.

TANCK'S SONG ABOUT BRAINS

Damned ugly things,
   brains splattered across the hood
of your car
   or sauced at Chez Paul's or pickled in a jar.
Where is the part that sings?

Don't know. Don't even know if
   anyone knows. To me the brain
is a mess, that's all. Yet a great new riff
   can jump right out of there
somehow, as clean and bright as a pain.

TANCK'S SONG ABOUT THE JINX

Friend, call it bad karma if you're
   so inclined, but to me
that don't make much sense. Sure,
   you can do yourself harm,
you can shoot yourself, you can farm

your ground so it all blows away
   and ain't worth a curled-up peapod
to your kids. But nothing I ever done
   explains what old Sep's had to pay,
except the curse of God.

TANCK'S SONG ABOUT FEAR OF FALLING

Used to stumble, go down, bounce
   right back up,
no problem, like a wiggly goddamn pup
   that's slid off the hay wagon. It felt good
even, down in the dirt and weeds. What accounts

for the change is plain enough. I
    dream sometimes, me happening
to slip on the pavement and then falling
    not only down but through, the asphalt opening
to take me under, the passers-by

standing around. Don't
    need to be a shrinker or a reborn
to figure that. It's me, the runt
    of the world-litter now, like the lady
that found herself among the alien corn.

TANCK'S SONG ABOUT THE YOUNGER GENERATION

I know a guy, 63.5 years old
    exactly and none too agile,
you understand, with a trick heart and his back
    that you wouldn't wish on Leopold
or Loeb, what you might say *fragile,*

and him living in the same house with three
    other people, two of which
is young and healthy and strong
    as battery acid, yet wouldn't hitch
a finger to shovel, so along

about now, which is February, the outer door is
    jammed open in ice and snow
just right for the first likely
    northwest wind to blow
it clean off its hinges,

and the third is only a kid,
    but old enough to know better,
that throws everything on the floor,
    nevermind what, shirt, sweater,
underpants, toys, tools, books, records, more

paraphernalia than 99%
   of the world could imagine, all
to be picked up by you know who, plus a fair complement
   of spilled foodstuffs, and by the Jesus H. Jumping Godawful Fat
Christly Christ, can't the human animal

do any better than that?

TANCK'S SONG ABOUT SURVIVAL

"I can't make it, I won't survive,"
   the young woman said in bad
trouble. Old Sep, remembering friends he'd had,
   thought to himself, *Baby, ain't nobody
ever yet made it out of this mess alive.*

Which is a fact. But "survival" is in the air,
   maybe it's becoming kind of a myth
for this particular time, or almost a watchword.
   "You survived yet?" "I dunno. You?" Lately I swear
I don't understand half of what old Sep's ears have heard.

TANCK'S SONG ABOUT YOUTH AND AGE

Ach, mein Kurt, when we were young we sang,
   "Dance, laugh, drink the good wine, and above
all make love,
   tomorrow the atomic bomb will fall." But
we didn't believe it, the song was twiddly twang.

We believed in the compilation of books,
   for instance. In disease. The tide of events.
How a particular academic pineapple looks.
   Only now in old age and bad luck
do we see the importance of a good fuck.

TANCK'S SONG ABOUT PRIDE

I tried to help. Suffering catfish, I tried!
   And she just got more and more miserable.

Old Sep should not be so dumb. Yet
    if he'd done anything else the net
result would be the same. Pride

crept into my flat by the back
    window like a kitten on a rainy night,
frail and reasonable, but now it has grown
    into a fat cat, ugly, ready to attack
any man who thinks he can do anything right.

TANCK'S BRAG

My mother was a giant squaw, my father
    an unappreciated marine
animal who lived on whaleshit and sharkfarts,
    I was two when I killed my brother,
in kindergarten I was so mean

they elected me emperor, I eat
    coal mines for breakfast and rape
the ocean every night, for relief I escape
    to Butte, Montana, my pains
are in the world's ass, and when I cry it rains.

TANCK'S SONG ABOUT THE TRANSPORTATION BUSINESS

The cabby said: "Hey, what do you think that does
    to me when I pick up someone
I know is loaded and see that this is a man
    that mentally couldn't shine my shoes?
I say why? Something's wrong. The son

of a bitch, he knows nothing. He
    can't even speak. What did I do
wrong? It really bothers me.
    Then it wears off, and I continue on."
Tell me about it, friend. What else is new?

TANCK'S SONG ABOUT DYING YOUNG

I hear Robert offed himself
    in California. I hear it's the rage out there.
At twenty-nine his life closed like a book.
    Somebody put him on a shelf
after a quick look.

The realest library is the boneyard
    and that's a fact, subjects
all nicely catalogued. But read as hard
    as you can, you won't learn a thing.
So what if the dead were buried in winter or spring?

TANCK'S EPILOGUE

Enough is enough. If you got
    only one topic
you better not
    work it to death, eh?
Here in the Tropic

of Tenterhooks it's a fine
    winter's afternoon
with fresh snow and sunshine
    and a pale moon,
the barometer rising, the air

clear and cold,
    which is what old Sep likes best.
As for the rest
    I reckon it don't really matter.
Who cares if he's getting old?

› Silence

Sometimes we don't say anything. Sometimes
    we sit on the deck and stare at the masses of
goldenrod where the garden used to be
    and watch the color change from day to day,
the high yellow turning to mustard and at last
    to tarnish. Starlings flitter in the branches
of the dead hornbeam by the fence. And are these
    therefore the procedures of defeat? Why am I
saying all this to you anyway since you already
    know it? But of course we always tell
each other what we already know. What else?
    It's the way love is in a late stage of the world.

› Sex

On the first few nights of the new year, a week
    ago, we had a full moon or near it in central
New York and the air was cold, the snow frozen,
    metallic, and bright. On the steep field
reflected moonlight ran down from the crest
    of the hill to the little house. A frozen stream,
he thought—the man I am always writing about.
    But when he looked more closely he saw, or
thought he saw, the molecules of light flowing
    both ways in scarcely discernible swiftness,
down to him, up to the moon, minute glints
    in a flux of passionate intensity in a pure
and simple world, his peaceful valley. He was
    thinking about sex. He was thinking especially
of last night when he had been in bed with the
    young woman he called conventionally, as people
do, *his*, and he had been saddened. Aging men
    suffer two kinds of impotence, the ordinary
kind that everyone makes jokes about, and then
    the deeper psychic failure when they are full
of eros but it is hidden, too remote

to evoke the wonder of lust in their partners.
So it had been, and then afterward they lay
    looking out at the moontrack on the snow.
Now he is alone in his house with his gray
    neutered cat Pokey. In former times women
who would not heat up were made into slaves,
    and when too many slaves encumbered the
polity these women were lowered into
    wells until they drowned. Nor was this some
stewpot of Asian hillbillies in the *National*
    Geographic, but in Europe, a nation I do not care
to name. Pokey, on the table next to the Christmas
    cactus, was looking out the glass door, staring
at the moontrack with his yellow eyes immense,
    unmoving, until the spell was broken and he
glided down like a shadow and went to the kitchen
    where he fizzed the litter in his box. Is it
that aging people live in an assortment
    of remnants, impulses too worn, desires
too threadbare to function any more? The man
    felt all his love gathering outside him, a power
with no bodily counterpart, out there in the
    deathly cold, the ghostly light, as if
the beautiful young woman in her nakedness
    were a circumstance of the night, seen
in a time of unseeing. For many moments
    he looked out at the moon and the moonflow,
at the dark woods on either side, at the frozen
    snow, until finally he too went into the shabby
kitchen and opened the door of an upper cabinet
    and took down a jar of peanut butter. Death
may come in many forms, they say, but truly
    it comes in only one, which is the end of love.
The old clock on the bookcase struck two o'clock.
    A chunk of ice fell thunderously from the eaves.

> Pray You Young Woman

Pray you young woman come to my bed clean
And that your lover's dregs be drained away.
Come not quickly but leave time in between.
I'm old and waitful, I can stand delay
Better than that too clearly you'd betray
My doting. True. Sweetheart, you must be mean
A little, devious and deceitful, and not say
You come from him – I'll know. Just go, obscene
As ever you wish, play the long bright day
With his young body; then come, draw night's screen
Over me, pleasure me, let my decay
Be hidden. For your hands can touch gangrene
  And make it seem like my green springtime still
  In perjury and mercy if you will.

> Assignment

"Then write," she said. "By all means, if that's
  how you feel about it. Write poems.
Write about the recurved arcs of my breasts
  joined in an angle at my nipples, how
the upper curve tilts toward the sky and the lower
  reverses sharply back into my torso,
write about how my throat rises from the supple
  hinge of my collarbones proudly so to speak
with the coin-sized hollow at the center, write
  of the perfect arch of my jaw when I hold
my head back – these are the things in which I too
  take delight – write how my skin is
fine like a cover of snow but warm and soft and
  fitted to me perfectly, write the *volupté*
of soap frothing in my curling crotch-hair, write
  the tight parabola of my vulva that re-
sembles a braided loop swung from a point,
  write the two dapples of light on the backs

of my knees, write my ankles so neatly turning
    in their sockets to deploy all the sweet
bones of my feet, write how when I am aroused
    I sway like a cobra and make sounds
of sucking with my mouth and brush my nipples
    with the tips of my left-hand fingers, and then
write how all this is continually pre-existing in my
    thought and how I effect it in myself
by my will, which you are not permitted to under-
    stand. Do this. Do it in pleasure and with
devotion, and don't worry about time. I won't
    need what you've done until you finish."

❯ *Renaissance*

To him after long anguish
came, as when one returns
to grammatical speech after
intimidation by the language
of bureaucrats, a calm and certain
love. It brought him joy for his
place in the world again and his
kinship with the trees. So long he had
lived in the madwoman's bondage
that he could no longer explain his
own madness, but only that it
was over, his estrangement from
himself was finished. New love,
which nevertheless had grown
in the depths of consciousness
many years before its magni-
ficence blazed out, was so to speak
another island, a new stopping-
place in the odyssey – maybe
home, though in fact home had been
long ago in another direction
and could be remembered only
in images of pain, dreams of burning.

Here the oak leaves twisted in
the wind, and the fireweed at the far
end of the second pasture, visible
through the opening in the windbreak
as if seen in the window at the back
of a Renaissance painting,
was pale and cool and beautiful.
The spirit of the place was his
acknowledgment of it, without thought,
easy and natural. On the phone he
spoke as lovers do loquacious
gossip to reach the point of saying
"I love you" in the dark and hearing
it back again like a serious, simple,
repeated turn of phrasing before
the orchestra resumes its grandeur.
Soon the phone will be unnecessary.
The serious, simple phrase will be
in his touching her. The grandeur
will be the day and the night, the wind's
continual song in the trees, the slope
of the hill, the flight of brilliant gold-
finches across the crests of the grass.
The world will be transformed and
all its nature made like a home again,
serious, simple, and beautiful.

> *August*

He was a man of his time and of its distresses and he rode
pandemonium's engines shattering among the dying
    elms, through thickets of clematis, woodbine, sumac

with its medieval bright cones and serpent-headed leaves,
and he taught his love the way of the tractor, clutch and choke,
    acceleration lever, the brake lock, the gear lever that must rest

in neutral while the tractor is immobile, then how to insert
the cocky gearshift into second or third and go brandishing off
    like a croaking toad in the aura of the sodium-vapor lamp at twilight.

And Christ the great pluming elms! – the few remaining, and thickets
of mountain laurel, delicate enchanter's nightshade, Circe's flower
    that turned the warriors into swine, netted in the meadow grass,

alfalfa with its tight purple blossom, vetch with its promiscuity,
St. Johnswort and bladder campion in the repose of that hot isle.
    And away, away she drove with her skirts raised to the tops of her thighs,

and no inconsonant mechanisticism distressed the afternoon. Under
the apple trees, around the pears and cherries, skirting the grape arbor,
    and up, up the steep ridge of New York as if to spring, buzz, pop, spindle off

into heaven in its bluesy blues. He thought of her auburn hair
in its intricate coif so like a pelt, as dear as a pelt, her body in its
    leanness, her cunt as trim as a tigress's, this dear roving animal

of the hills who loved him, unaccountably. He thought and thought.
His cock rose and skizzled. Hah to the indignities of technology.
    Is a wolverine concerned? Yes, of course, always, naturally. Why

mess with electric fences? She in her perfect coordination
whirled the tractor around the inclined facets of the orchard,
    under the blue sky that is inexhaustible, pure, a function

of unalterable pigment in its jubilee, its birthday that is every day.
Smiling between her hollow cheeks, driving with thighs spread,
    her hands squealing in their rapidity, she darted to him, murderously,

for her love was in part a knowledge of his suicide, his loneliness.
She would have wiped him out of the universe gladly. But in ferocious
    candor and sympathy she spun the machine to a stop by his feet,

leapt off, kissed him, and in spite of everything the world shone as
it ever has in sexual grandeur, his cock came stiffer than in all its
    life, she wrenched him down in hot smoke and valve clatter and put him

into her, laughing the rightness forever of changing this,
of love, of the surprise of actual, intransigent things. Oh
wonderful and forever-goddamned-like-us things!

❯ *Fourth*

The townspeople, those Dr. Williams loved and despised
– as we too, we especially, love and despise them! –
say look at that old fool repeating himself, one failure
after another. My darling, what idiocy – this "common wisdom."
Here we are on our Thorn Hill, so green in its luxury
and with plenty of thorns to prick us if we need pricking,
here we are in the persistent summer always new, with
the amazement of nonbristly greenbriar, that carrion vine,
with asters and goldenrod and gentian and sunsets across
the Stockbridge Valley that awe us every time, each
single time, a glory ever new as we are new, two
young newlyweds with years of erotic pain behind us
sitting under our sycamore tree with good wine and good
books, with our hands straying toward each other, with musk,
with suffusions inexpressible, our eyes dulling to the page
but gleaming in the vision of beauty in our own bodies,
and the only question remaining is whether we shall
fling away our clothing and do it right here, or more
decorously like the townspeople go to our little house
and our big bed. Listen, traffic at the bottom of the valley
sounds like the mythology of an extinct civilization,
but here the hot little goldfinches tumble in the seedy
thistles like quick sexy intimations. Sweetheart, let's
get to the house if we can. Four is a holy and rational
number, the number of our good fortune and the luck
of our possible hereafters and our actual goldfinches.

❯ Listen

Cage's quartet no. 1 – really it's a
    thoughtful, engaging, and quite beautiful work
and not a bundle of clichés, as once was thought.
    So turn out the light. Listen. The storm outdoors
accompanies everything tonight, wind drones
    in the television antenna on the roof, sleet
crashes against the windows. The refrigerator
    kookilates as usual, and the furnace does its
booming and strutting below. Inside the man's
    head, along with incessant yearning for one more
beautiful poem and one more good look at a woman's
    nakedness, is the perpetual noise caused by
deteriorating aural nerves, high-pitched, a baby
    cicada wailing in its shell, "Let me out, you
fuckers! Let me out." And would anyone deny
    such a reasonable desire? Well, really all of us
would, and confinement is part of the deal,
    wailing is part of the deal. The cicada splits
and sings and dies, as every artist must go on
    always to dying, to what is new, repudiating
what has been done already, those remarkable
    and reasonable accomplishments, repudiating
us, but still one wishes that Cage had left
    Orientalism, which at best is a kind of rot
in the American mind, to the academic musicians
    and had continued to give us the confined, mellow
music of suffering. Listen. The wind makes its triads,
    the trilling nerve its E above high C, and the cello
        drones in the night.

❯ Æolian

The musician late at night in his little house
    on the hillside, working. His gray hair tousled,
wispy curls. He wears a gray sweatshirt.
    To make it from the immediate sounds, from

nature, as he had been taught, and he listens
    to the wind in the obsolete TV antenna
which he always means to take down. An
    æolian chord, the bent tines of the antenna
vibrating differently but in numbers, patterns
    of number. He writes them down for the
hundredth time. He gets up, lights a cheap cigar,
    sips his Metaxas from a shot glass. He looks
out at the first light, at the dead dark grass
    on the field littered with winter's branches,
the moon paling in the west. Upstairs his
    young woman, beautiful and enchanting, lies
asleep. It is Easter morning. They love the
    holidays, being sentimental, the ritual
occasions, and certainly in earlier
    incarnations their souls had been devout.
Last night they gave one another Easter
    baskets with eggs and candy and made love
and said it was a holy day indeed for them.
    Indeed. Is that the music? What's to be put
to use? Humming to himself, a rhythm, the slap
    of his car on the tar-ridges of the interstate,
so trite. The Æolian harp is on top of his house,
    sitting up there, a vulture randomly twanging.
Nothing beautiful. No meaning. Not even
    interesting. He scuffs his hand through his hair.
"In order to use it you have to put it in something,
    you have to invent something around it. What?
Only oneself, over and over." His cigar is
    bitter, he throws it in the cast-iron stove,
a puff of blue smoke emits from the firebox,
    his eyes water, he presses his palms against
his cheeks, forcing his mouth into the shape
    of a sucker's, his face looks like a mutilated
starfish, he falls on the sofa, that gray reef
    just under the water where the æolian
intervals are muted, distorted, but still
    audible, and he slides into his angry sleep.

❯ Gods

Sometimes it occurs to me in the moonlit
stillness of the summer night that Dionysus
will come and take you from me. He will
wrest your half-willing body away to fields
not far from here, disconsolingly close,
where you will gaspingly love the god of
passion and wine, thinking of me fleetly
in a minim of sorrow-song. What else may
the lover of someone as beautiful as you
expect? The gods are besotted with beauty.
In my reftness I cry, I bawl, a two-day calf
in the bitter Nevadan gale. I too am mytho-
logical. Dear woman, when you are bruised
and bleeding and shaken and indubitably
pregnant with holiness, will you come back
to me even so, to calm my fury that can have
no expression for fear of the fate of heaven
blasting me into nothing? – to soothe my hor-
ror with your bleeding, broken presence?
Maybe together, hand in hand, touching ex-
perimentally, we may find in our ghosthood
some shabby tissue of humanity, still brave
and somehow comely in our humiliation

❯ Opusthirteen

You lied to your mother, you told her you didn't do it,
and you thought she didn't know, but everyone knew it.
Mister, I'm an old man, and I ain't done nothing wrong.

And how did you treat your wife? You went after young cunt.
And what did you ever get from it? Nothing is what.
I'm an old man, listen, and I ain't done nothing wrong.

If you had a dog you'd kick it. And if you had a kid
you'd whop it upside its head. You know you did.
I'm an old man, sister, and I ain't done nothing wrong.

The only thing you was good at was cabbaging booze
and smiling when some black girl come up singing the blues.
Well, I'm an old man, okay, and I ain't done nothing wrong.

How do you like yourself, old rag tag and bob tail?
The only good thing about you is you ain't in jail.
I'm an old man, and I'm tired, and I ain't done nothing wrong.

❯ *Block*

Right up there this side the Five Chimneys Corners
    about a mile south the Oneida line, this goddamn
granddaddy sugar maple block I tell you it's
    what you might call a real out-size block a old-time
ball-busting son of a bitch of a block laying by the side
    the road where that house with the busted porch is
the worn-out gray asphalt siding? the lawn sale
    going April to November? you know where I
mean, this block if it was a redwood you could cut
    a hole in it for the tourists to drive through, a good
12 foot high just laying there by its stump, maybe about
    20 foot long. Well these guys are standing around
they got their chain saws, their malls, their axes, wedges,
    cant hooks, six-packs, a couple dogs, four five
kids, two pickups and a old Cat tractor covered
    with rust, these guys got pretty damn near anything
a man could need, four of them, wearing these greasy
    John Deere and Agway caps and old plaid shirts
half the buttons torn off. Day before yesterday is
    when I seen them about 7 A.M. I'm heading over
the city to that parking-lot job, yes ma'am is what
    I say all day just put it over there and no sir
you can't park that thing here withouten you got a

sticker – a hell of a way to make a living ain't it?
So next day, that's yesterday, I'm going by again
    and these guys are right there standing around
smoking talking looking at that goddamn block same
    as before only I seen now they got maybe a cord
of stove wood busted off of it, and then this morning
    damned if there ain't a woodpile near as big as a Grey-
hound bus when I go by must be a good twenty cord
    and these guys still standing around looking at what's
left of that block a big old bastard of a knotty
    chunk laying there on the ground sort of reminds me
of a big heart a hell of a big heart like a bull's heart
    or a elephant's only of course a different color. Chips
and bark everywhere sawdust the yard's all littered
    snow and ice mud and beer cans – why shit you know
how it looks you been working up firewood the same
    place three four days in a row. So this evening what
the hell I stop off at The Point myself for a couple
    what you might call compensating Friday afternoon
cold ones on the way home so of course it's near dark
    when I get to Five Chimneys. The block is gone.
The woodpile is humungous. Like it's a new hill
    growing right there on the landscape and this lady
wearing baggy pants a red sweatshirt setting on what's
    left of the porch steps smoking a Winston I seen
the red pack laying there on the step beside her
    and the guys are squatting on their gas cans leaning
against the pickups they got a case of Coors they're looking
    at each other with their caps tipped onto the back
of their heads like they think they done a hell of a good
    day's work setting around and talking and taking
a swipe at that goddamn block every once in a while –
    and you know what, I reckon they have. Ain't that
the life? How you figure those guys get so lucky?

➤ Crucifixion

You understand the colors on the hillside have faded,
    we have the gray and brown and lavender of late autumn,
the apple and pear trees have lost their leaves, the mist
    of November is often with us, especially in the afternoon
and toward evening, as it was today when I sat gazing
    up into the orchard for a long time they way I do now,
thinking of how I died last winter and was revived.
    And I tell you I saw there a cross with a man nailed
to it, silvery in the mist, and I said to him: "Are you
    the Christ?" And he must have heard me, for in his
agony, twisted as he was, he nodded his head affirmatively,
    up and down, once and twice. And a little way off
I saw another cross with another man nailed to it,
    twisting and nodding, and then another and another,
ranks and divisions of crosses straggling like exhausted
    legions upward among the misty trees, each cross
with a silvery, writhing, twisting, nodding, naked
    figure nailed to it, and some of them were women.
The hill was filled with crucifixion. Should I not be
    telling you this? Is it excessive? But I know something
about death now, I know how silent it is, silent even
    when the pain is shrieking and screaming. And tonight
is very silent and very dark. When I looked I saw
    nothing out there, only my own reflected head nodding
a little in the window glass. It was as if the Christ
    had nodded to me, all those writhing silvery images
on the hillside, and after a while I nodded back to him.

➤ Three Songs

1. CROSSING

Then at the very end
    when the time was almost remorselessly too late and the season
was turning
    she who had been my friend

crossed over.
    In one night and one morning
we were lovers forever
    and some say beyond all reason.

    2 . AFTERNOON
You said you were "never turned on
    by a man's body" meaning its appearance
meaning love is what brings you down
    with your lips to my cock in the afternoon
love being your desire and your arousal
    as loving is your proposal
and the lust comes two seconds later
                                whereupon I wondered
    could I match you in such forbearance
and by what standard
    should I judge myself this rough old godlet foundered
and gone weird and heady
    from the sight of a young body
here and open like this
    and causal
to his quick uprising and his desire to kiss
    in the press of time with only small endurance
all of your nakedness
    o my sexy lady

    3 . TRANSPOSITION
Blue eyes and auburn hair
are my delight when October skies
    are this azure and this clear,
    when the red and gold in the mapletrees

mix colors but stay separate, and when
the concords are clustering underneath
    the vine-leaves, purple, half hidden
    and half peeping out along the path

by the sunny stone seat, ripening late
in the ripening of my 67th year,
    and you are with me, my delight
    in blue eyes and auburn hair.

❯ *The Way of the Conventicle of the Trees*

Just yesterday afternoon I heard a man
Say he lived in a house with no windows
The door of which was locked on the outside.
This was at a party in New York, New York.
A deep Oriental type, I said to myself,
One of them indescribable Tebootans who
Live up on Quaker Heights and drink
Mulled kvass first thing every morning
With their vitamins. An asshole. And
Haven't I more years than he? Haven't
I spent them looking out the window
At the trees? Oh the various trees.
They have looked back at me with their
Homely American faces: the hemlocks
And white birches of one of my transient
Homes, the catalpas and honey locusts
Of another, the sweet gum and bay and
Coffee trees, the hop hornbeam and the
Spindle tree, the dogwood, the great
Horse chestnut, the overdressed pawpaw
Who is the gamine of that dominion.
Then, behind them, the forest, the sodality.
What pizzazz in their theorizing! How fat
The sentimentibilities of their hosannas!
I have looked at them out the window
So intently and persistently that always
My who-I-am has gone out among them
Where the fluttering ideas beckon. Yes,
We've been best friends these sixty-nine

Years, standing around this hot stove
Of a world, hawking, phewing, guffawing,
My dear ones, who will remember me
For a long, long time when I'm gone.

> ## Questions

Your voice comes to me, George, on the winter night
In the faint mazy stars, a murmur of hesitant light
In the air frozen solid, it seems, from here to Maine.
Lonely and late I made pancakes, awful pancakes,
And ate them with watery syrup and grease and with
Love of myself when young, with cognac in a glass,
And with cigarettes, the smoke coiling reflected
In the black window. What are you saying, George?
I strain to hear. Are you as smart and percipient
As you were, can you tell me what I almost know
In your words not mine as you used to, words
So French and accurate I thought Descartes
And Camus must live in you as well as Tolstoy
And Kropotkin, words of fierce loyalties and loves
For beautiful ideas and men and women? Tell me,
George, for Michael your boy's sake, where are you,
When will we see you, have your bones become dust,
Is your voice dust in your throat? Oh, let the thin
Dawn come now with its fishblood on the horizon,
Its icy fog. You are the lovingest memory in this
Rattling brain that shakes off its synapses like an old
Dog climbing out of a cold brook. George, George,
What in God's name must I do to get you back?

> ## Ray

How many guys are sitting at their kitchen tables
    right now, one-thirty in the morning, this same
time, eating a piece of pie? – that's what I
    wondered. A big piece of pie, because I'd just

finished reading Ray's last book. Not good pie,
    not like my mother or my wife could've
made, but an ordinary pie I'd just bought, being
    alone, at the Tops Market two hours ago. And how
many had water in their eyes? Because of Ray's
    book, and especially those last poems written
after he knew: the one about the doctor telling
    him, the one where he and Tess go down to
Reno to get married before it happens and shoot
    some craps on the dark baize tables, the one
called "After-Glow" about the little light in the
    sky after the sun sets. I can just hear him,
if he were still here and this were somebody
    else's book, saying, "Jesus," saying, "This
is the saddest son of a bitch of a book I've
    read in a long time," saying, "A real long time."
And the thing is, he knew we'd be saying this
    about his book, he could just hear us saying it,
and in some part of him he was glad! He
    really was. What crazies we writers are,
our heads full of language like buckets of minnows
    standing in the moonlight on a dock. Ray
was a good writer, a wonderful writer, and his
    poems are good, most of them, and they made me
cry, there at my kitchen table with my head down,
    me, a sixty-seven-year-old galoot, an old fool
because all old men are fools, they have to be,
    shoveling big jagged chunks of that ordinary pie
into my mouth, and the water falling from my eyes
    onto the pie, the plate, my hand, little speckles
shining in the light, brightening the colors, and I
    ate that goddamn pie, and it tasted good to me.

❯ None

You died. And because you were Greek they gave you
    a coin to carry under your tongue and then also
biscuits and honey. When you came to the riverbank

you saw a crazy-looking black bumboat on the water
with a figure standing in it, lanky and dressed
    darkly, holding a sweep. You were taken across,
and you gave your coin for the passage, and continued
    until you came to a three-headed dog, who snarled
and threatened you, even though you were not trying
    to escape. You gave him the biscuits smeared
with honey, and you passed onward to the field
    of asphodel and through the gate of Tartarus. Or

you died and you were Navajo. They had carried you
    out of the hogan earlier so you'd die in the sunshine.
Or if it happened inside suddenly, they stuffed up
    the smokehole and boarded the front entrance, and cut
an opening in the back, the north-facing, dark-facing
    side, to carry you out, and no one ever used
that hogan again. They took off your moccasins
    and put them on again wrong side to, the left one
on the right foot, the right on the left, so that your
    chindi would be confused and unable to return
along your tracks. They washed your hair in suds
    made from the yucca. Then they gave you
enough fried bread and water to last four days,
    and you set off on your journey. But actually

none of these things happened. You just died.

❯ *Woodsmoke at 70*

How it is never the same
but always changing. How
sometimes nevertheless
you recognize it. How you
see it from your window
plunging down, flattening
across the frozen lawn,
then rising in a wild
swirl and it's gone . . .

Notes

46. "Billie Holiday." One of her best-known songs was "Don't Explain."

48. "Existence Before Essence." A catch phrase of the Existentialist philosophy of mid-century, meaning that human beings, unlike all other things, create their own essences.

53. "Ekstase, Alptraum, Schlaf in einem Nest von Flammen." "Extase, cauchemar, sommeil dans un nid de flammes," Arthur Rimbaud, "Nuit de l'Enfer," *Une Saison en Enfer.*

669. "Life is an old casino in the park." Cf. Wallace Stevens, "Academic Discourse at Havana."

78. "Kennst du das land . . . " Goethe, "Mignon."

121. The sequence of poems titled *The Bloomingdale Papers* was published in 1975 but written in 1953–54.

166. "Indian runners." A breed of small domestic ducks.

169. "teakle rig." Block and tackle.

169. "bam-o-gilly." Vermontese for Balm of Gilead, a species of poplar.

182. Paragraphs 1–7 occur on the Campground Road from Waterville to Johnson, Vt., along the Lamoille River.

183. Kailas (pron. kilás), Tibetan range, paradise of Siva.

184. "Popple". Either the bigtooth aspen, *populus grandidentata,* or the quaking aspen, *populus tremuloides,* both common in Vermont.

185. "Morning Star." *Walden,* the last sentence.

185. Apollyon. *Pilgrim's Progress.* "Who will choose . . ."; Isaiah, 66.4. "Engrafted words . . ."; James, 1.21.

187. "*hic divisio* . . ." The "partition of Verdun," a.d. 843, a treaty establishing the division between what we now call Germany and France. "*ahi serva Italia.*" The beginning of Dante's bitter animadversion on the ills of 14th-century Italy, in the famous Sordello canto.

189. "In filthy Puerto Rico . . ." A story told to me by a Puerto Rican student.

190–91. Sections 15, 16. "La Commune de Paris et la Notion de l'État," Michel Bakounine, 1871.

196–97. Sections 26, 27, 28. Thanks to Nat Hentoff, who sent me to Ralph Gleason, who sent me to Milton Gabler. As Mr. Gabler said: "Not a bad parlay." The original recording was Commodore No. 1516B, now available on CD.

202. Inanna. Sumerian goddess. See translations of cuneiform texts by Stanley Kramer.

220. "A Little Old Funky Homeric Hymn for Herm." Adapted from the ancient *Homeric Hymn for Hermes*. See *Hermes, the Thief*, by Norman O. Brown, 1964.

227. "Almanach du Printemps Vivarois." The title is the same as that of an almanac in Occitan published at Aubeanas in the Ardèche, from which the proverb in ll. 37–38 is also taken. *Vivarais* is the name of the region in the old country of Langue d'Oc roughly coinciding with the modern Ardèche, *vivarois* being the adjectival form. The proverb can be translated: "On the fifth of April the cuckoo must sing, dead or alive."

247. *La*. French for A, the first tone of the scale, the tonic.

250. Norrland. The northern division of Sweden, inhabited chiefly by Laplanders.

250. "The Cowshed Blues." The epigraph is from Psalm 108. I would translate it: "Awake, my inspiration; awake, my psaltery and harp."

267. ". . . no fish, weedless, sunk deep in the earth. Waste. Barren . . . , etc." Cf. James Joyce, *Ulysses*, 1st American edition (1934), p. 60.

273. ". . . make it crackle, . . . " Roy Eldridge, *c.* 1938.

292. New Hartford. A suburb of Utica, N.Y.

295. "Griffiss." Griffiss Air Force Base, Rome, N.Y., an important base for nuclear-armed B-52s.

341. Pripet Marshes. A region in White Russia traditionally said to be inhabited by wild dogs.

351. "Thirty-Seventh and Indiana." An intersection formerly near the center of the black section of Chicago. "Southern More or Less Crosses the Dog." In Mississippi, an intersection between the Southern Ry. and the Yazoo and Mississippi Valley Ry., otherwise known as the "Yellow Dog," one of the few level crossings of two railways in the country and hence a topic of much folk mythologizing in earlier times. Cf. W. C. Handy, "The Yellow Dog Blues." Also "yellow dog contract."

352. Preacher. Ecclesiastes.

353. Mock orange. Syringa, sometimes called Jasmine by old-timers in

Vermont.

355. "Ovid, Old Buddy." After reading *The Mystery of Ovid's Exile,* by John C. Thibault, 1964.

356. "Professor Dilthey." German Empiricist philosopher, Wilhelm Dilthey (1833–1911), author of *Einleitung in die Geisteswissenschaften,* 1883.

357. "The World as Will and Representation." Arthur Schopenhauer, *Die Welt als Wille und Vorstellung,* 1859.

363. "I've Never Seen Such a Real Hard Time Before." Blues recorded by Ida Cox, *c.* 1939.

382. Zuk. Louis Zukofsky, the poet.

387–88. Mme. Defarge. See Charles Dickens, *A Tale of Two Cities.* Allen Tate. The poet; when he played his violin, which he did rather badly, his mouth twisted extraordinarily.

394. "Tanck's Song About Earl Hines." Both the quotations are spoken passages from different recordings by Hines.

398. "Tanck's Song About the Transportation Business." The quotation is from Studs Terkel, *American Dreams: Lost and Found,* Ballantine edition, 1981, p. 240. In the context "loaded" means rich.

415. George is George Dennison, fiction writer and critic, who lived in Temple, Maine.

415. Raymond Carver.

Index of Titles and First Lines

Titles in roman, first lines in italic.